Bahamas

"Uncovers rarely explored gems . . . in more than 50 Bahamian islands. It also offers standard travel information and is spiced with fun facts."
—*USA Today*

"Most visitors (to The Bahamas) come by cruise ship. The Hidden guide goes to these ports and beyond."
—*Chicago Sun-Times*

HIDDEN®
Bahamas

Richard Harris and Lynn Seldon

SECOND EDITION

Ulysses Press®

BERKELEY, CALIFORNIA

Published by:
ULYSSES PRESS
P.O. Box 3440
Berkeley, CA 94703-3440

ISSN 1524-5926
ISBN 1-56975-197-8

Printed in Canada by Transcontinental Printing

10 9 8 7 6 5 4 3 2

EDITORIAL DIRECTOR: Leslie Henriques
MANAGING EDITOR: Claire Chun
COPY EDITOR: Steven Schwartz
EDITORIAL ASSOCIATES: Lily Chou, Lynette Ubois,
    Aimee Benedict, Melissa Millar
TYPESETTER: Jennifer Brontsema
CARTOGRAPHY: XNR Productions, Madison, WI
COVER DESIGN: Sarah Levin, Leslie Henriques
INDEXER: Sayre Van Young
COVER PHOTOGRAPHY:
    FRONT: Jan Butchofsky-Houser (Hammocks on
    the beach on Paradise Island)
    CIRCLE: Pat Canova (Seahorse)
    BACK: Jan Butchofsky-Houser (Nassau constable)
ILLUSTRATOR: Doug McCarthy

Distributed in the United States by Publishers
Group West, in Canada by Raincoast Books,
and in Great Britain and Europe by World
Leisure Marketing

Write to us!

If in your travels you discover a spot that captures the spirit of The Bahamas, or if you live in the region and have a favorite place to share, or if you just feel like expressing your views, write to us and we'll pass your note along to the author.

We can't guarantee that the author will add your personal find to the next edition, but if the writer does use the suggestion, we'll acknowledge you in the credits and send you a free copy of the new edition.

ULYSSES PRESS
3286 Adeline Street, Suite 1
Berkeley, CA 94703
e-mail: readermail@ulyssespress.com

What's Hidden?

At different points throughout this book, you'll find special listings marked with a hidden symbol:

◄ HIDDEN

This means that you have come upon a place off the beaten tourist track, a spot that will carry you a step closer to the local people and natural environment of The Bahamas.

The goal of this guide is to lead you beyond the realm of everyday tourist facilities. While we include traditional sightseeing listings and popular attractions, we also offer alternative sights and adventure activities. Instead of filling this guide with reviews of standard hotels and chain restaurants, we concentrate on one-of-a-kind places and locally owned establishments.

Our authors seek out locales that are popular with residents but usually overlooked by visitors. Some are more hidden than others (and are marked accordingly), but all the listings in this book are intended to help you discover the true nature of The Bahamas and put you on the path of adventure.

Contents

Maps

OUTDOOR ADVENTURE SYMBOLS

The following symbols accompany national, state and regional park listings, as well as beach descriptions throughout the text.

🚶	Hiking	⛵	Windsurfing
🏊	Swimming	🚤	Boating
🤿	Snorkeling or Scuba Diving	🛥️	Boat Ramps
🏄	Surfing	🎣	Fishing
🎿	Waterskiing		

ONE

Islands in the Stream

Warmed by the Gulf Stream, the ancient coral archipelago now known as The Bahamas stretches 750 miles across the Atlantic Ocean. With one end just 40 miles due east of Palm Beach, Florida and the other 70 miles north of the shores of Haiti, the island chain is divided in half by the Tropic of Cancer. There are more than 700 islands and 2000 small cays, most of them clustered in 16 groups. The total dry land in The Bahamas is slightly less than the area of Connecticut.

The Bahamas is the only Caribbean nation that does not touch the Caribbean Sea, which lies on the far side of Haiti and Cuba. The islands' history of exploitation, slavery and piracy, their post-colonial, predominantly African American culture and their economic dependence on tourism, offshore banking and smuggling give them much in common with the islands of the Caribbean. In 1973, the same year it declared its independence from Great Britain, The Bahamas became a charter member of the Caribbean Community (CARICOM), a 16-nation organization striving to create a unified economic bloc.

The Bahamas is by far the wealthiest of the CARICOM nations. In fact, its citizens enjoy a higher standard of living than any other Western Hemisphere country except the United States and Canada. The reason, quite simply, is tourism. Proximity to the U.S. East Coast explains why 3,400,000 visitors head for The Bahamas each year—more than any other Caribbean destination. More than Cancún or Puerto Rico. More than the U.S. and British Virgin Islands, the Netherlands Antilles, Aruba, Antigua, Barbados, Guadeloupe and Jamaica combined. The ratio of visitors per year to Bahamian citizens is nearly 12 to 1. Tourist dollars account for an astonishing 70 percent of the Bahamian gross national product.

Tourism in The Bahamas has been guided to a large extent by international resort hotel developers and cruise ship lines. On the busier islands—New Providence, Paradise and Grand Bahama—visitors are channeled with cheerful efficiency into a few crowded, high-energy shopping and hotel zones. Only a few visitors break ranks with the cruise ship crowds and head off to explore the far sides of these islands, much less venture into the remote reaches of the Out Islands, a series of long, slender streaks of green and white, more beach than mainland, splashed across 700 miles of open ocean.

In the belief that the major islands have reached a saturation point when it comes to tourism, the government has turned its policy to encouraging Out Islands ecotourism. In The Bahamas, this means nature-loving sports such as scuba diving, snorkeling, birding, biking and sea kayaking, combined with stays at small family-run inns on secluded beaches. Most of all, it means exploring distant, infrequently visited parts of The Bahamas—places like Cat Island, with its low, thick jungle, historic ruins and hideaway bays fringed with gracefully curving strands of white sand; Inagua, with its astonishing flamingo flights; and San Salvador, the first New World shore Columbus set foot on.

Where to Go   Travelers who visit only the tourist meccas of Nassau, Cable Beach, Paradise Island and Freeport/Lucaya miss out on the simpler pleasures of the "real" Bahamas. If you are reading this book while lying by the pool at the Atlantis Paradise Island or one of the other world-famous luxury resorts of The Bahamas, we hope it will inspire you to dare an excursion to the Out Islands. Although many of the major Bahamian islands have similar physical attributes—great beaches, friendly villages, a lively watersports scene—each one has its own unique character.

To many visitors The Bahamas means only **Nassau** and **New Providence Island**, along with **Paradise Island** just across the bridge. In fact, if you are traveling almost anywhere in The Bahamas, chances are your route will involve a stopover in Nassau, since all regularly scheduled interisland plane flights and boat trips originate from the capital. This busy, historic port city is where you'll find more Bahamians than on all the rest of the islands combined. You'll also find the largest, most elaborate resorts and casinos and the widest choice of restaurants and nightclubs in The Bahamas.

Farther north and closer to the Florida coast, **Grand Bahama Island** is a more recent entry than New Providence in the tourism sweepstakes. With superior diving, cruise ship docks and several major resorts, the island now attracts a large share of visitors. The twin towns of Freeport in the island's center and Lucaya on the south shore offer hotels in various price ranges, casinos and duty-free international shopping. This cosmopolitan island also boasts several golf courses and formal public gardens, as well as two national parks preserving fragments of the lush natural forest that once covered the island.

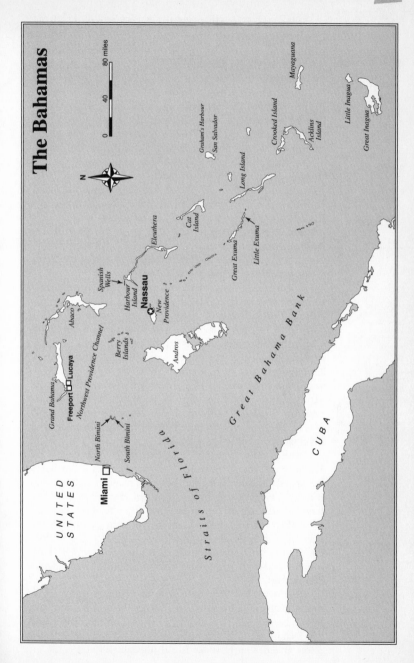

From spectacular sailing and plentiful fishing to luxurious accommodations and pretty New England–like towns, the **Abacos** offer the best of everything for sports enthusiasts and visitors who just want to relax in a tropical paradise. The Abacos stretch for more than 125 miles on the east of Grand Bahama, including the two major islands of Great Abaco and Little Abaco (which together are called the mainland) and a number of smaller cays. The main settlement, Marsh Harbour, is the third largest town in The Bahamas, and small resorts dot the island. The Abacos have more extensive tourist facilities than most other Out Islands.

The largest Bahamian island, **Andros** is also one of the least developed. It is actually a series of interlocking islands separated by creeks and bights and dotted with lakes and blue holes. Known as the "Bonefishing Capital of the World," Andros also has one of the longest barrier reefs on earth, making it an ideal, adventurous destination for scuba divers and snorkelers. The landscape features mangroves and pine and mahogany forests, with a few small towns that support limited facilities for divers. Colorful Androsian batik is produced here.

As a deep-sea fishing center, **Bimini** is world-renowned thanks to macho tales of Ernest Hemingway and legendary world-class fishing. Florida is just 50 miles away, and Bimini has such a yacht-club feel that it might as well be in the Sunshine State. Curiously, Bimini also attracts a growing number of New Age explorers seeking strange sites such as a blue hole that Ponce de Leon thought was the Fountain of Youth, an underwater "highway" that some believe to be a remnant of lost Atlantis, and giant sand mounds of unknown origin in the shapes of animals and fish. Bimini is easily reached by boat or seaplane from Miami. Though small, its limited tourist facilities are much more developed than many Out Islands.

Situated north of Bimini between New Providence and the Florida coast, the rarely visited **Berry Islands** have a tiny population and not much in the way of tourist facilities. Adventurous travelers find their way by boat to Great Harbour, the islands' largest settlement, just for the challenge of getting there. The cluster of 30 small islands boasts shallow coral reefs, a shipwreck and sea caves for divers, abundant marlin, sailfish and tuna for fishermen, and the nesting grounds of pelicans and terns for birdwatchers, as well as unspoiled beaches where human beings hardly ever set foot.

Eleuthera is probably the most attractive destination for first-time Out Island visitors. It offers the best of both worlds, with off-the-beaten-path Out Island experiences on the main island and **Spanish Wells**, alongside more developed and sophisticated resort facilities on **Harbour Island** (though still very much an

Out Island experience). All three islands offer stunning pink beaches and disarmingly friendly local residents. Harbour Island's historic Dunmore Town is a Bahamian classic. Fields of mangoes, melons and pineapples nestle among the lush, low forests and rolling hills of the narrow hundred-mile-long triptych of islands.

The **Exumas** get their share of tourists these days, with a wide range of lodging possibilities, superior sailing and some of the world's finest bonefishing. George Town, a great little Out Island village, provides the ideal mix of seclusion and activity. Stretching more than 90 miles to the north, the rest of the Exumas' 365 islands and cays offer sailing thrills, deserted shores and the protected Exuma Cays Land and Sea Park. The remote northern end of the chain is much closer to Nassau than to any town in the Exumas, and tour operators with high-speed boats have recently made this area a popular day trip from Nassau.

The **Southern Bahamas** are primarily made up of Cat Island, San Salvador, Long Island, Crooked Island, Acklins Island, Mayaguana and Inagua. **Cat Island** is a sleepy little farming island with lush hills and that is just starting to draw substantial numbers of visitors to its two small, secluded beach resorts. **San Salvador**, a superior dive destination with two major resorts, boasts historical significance as the official first landfall of Columbus in the new world. **Long Island** is a diving mecca, and most folks head for the famed Stella Maris Resort. **Acklins Island** is large, but has a small population and very limited tourist facilities. **Crooked Island**, near Acklins, has an even smaller population and fewer lodgings. **Mayaguana,** a sleepy island with limited facilities, separates The Bahamas from the neighboring Turks and Caicos. **Inagua**, the third largest island in the group, lies farther south than any other Bahamian island and draws birdwatchers to its large flamingo nesting grounds.

Mother Nature usually provides cooling trade winds, so temperatures in The Bahamas average between 70° and 80° Fahrenheit year-round. Though both the thermometer and the humidity are higher in the summer, it's still typically much more comfortable at that time of year than Florida beach destinations. During the winter, evenings can be surprisingly cool; you'll want to bring along a sweater, sweatshirt or light jacket. In January and February, the coolest months, temperatures run about 12° lower than in the height of summer.

▼▼▼▼▼▼▼▼▼▼
When to Go

SEASONS

Because of the large north-to-south extent of The Bahamas, it is generally cooler in the northern islands. The Gulf Stream provides perpetually warm waters throughout the area. The average rainfall in The Bahamas is a whopping 53 inches a year—

considerably more than drizzly Seattle or foggy London town. Fortunately for visitors, 80 percent of the rain comes during May to October, and then it usually comes in short bursts and squalls. Rarely does bad weather last longer than a day or two.

Hurricane season officially runs from June 1 to November 30. The most serious storms generally come between August and October. Hurricanes are statistically less frequent in The Bahamas than in the Caribbean, and the chances of one striking during your visit are very small. Hurricanes make landfall in The Bahamas, on the average, once every nine years, but when one does come, modern forecasting methods provide plenty of advance warning.

Prices are generally higher during the peak tourist season, from Christmas through April on most islands. (The exceptions are islands such as Bimini and the Abacos, where deep-sea fishing is the main attraction and the warm months, when big game fish are most abundant, are the busiest season.) The rest of the year, which is still quite pleasant with smaller crowds, offers lower prices—as much as 30 to 50 percent less. The late spring and fall shoulder seasons are among The Bahamas' best kept secrets.

CALENDAR OF EVENTS

The Bahamas boasts a year-round lineup of cultural activities and sporting events, as well as holiday celebrations. Specific dates vary; check with the Bahamas Ministry of Tourism for a current schedule. All events listed here take place annually unless otherwise noted.

JANUARY   **January 1**   The New Year's Day **Junkanoo Parade** in Nassau, one of the most colorful events in the islands, features hundreds of costumed locals celebrating with music from goatskin drums, cowbells and whistles; street marching, dancing and a lot of merry-making. Junkanoo is also celebrated in the Exumas—but earlier in December to make way for the **Staniel Cay New Year's Day Regatta.**

Mid-January   Golfers will enjoy watching top pros (and some not-so-top pros) in the Bahamas **Princess Resort & Casino Crystal Pro-Am Golf Tournament** on Grand Bahama. The **Sunshine Cup** on New Providence is a four-day invitational meet bringing together many top gymnasts. The **Quilt Show** in Nassau showcases hundreds of traditional Bahamian quilts and quiltmakers.

FEBRUARY   **Early February**   The **Ebony Fashion Fair** in Nassau highlights the most modern fashions in paradise, showcasing the latest collections of world-known designers. The **People of the Bahamas Annual Archives Exhibition** in Nassau offers visitors an opportunity to see an exhibition showcasing the diversity of ethnic make-up in the history of The Bahamas. The Exumas host the **Farmer's Cay Festival**, a rendezvous for yachts cruising the Exumas and a homecoming for the people of Farmer's Cay, with dinghy races, sailing competitions and parties.

Mid-February Food freaks can feast on local Bahamian fare and worldwide cooking in Nassau at the **Ministry of Health International Food Fair**. Nassau's **Heart Ball** raises funds that enable the Sir Victor Sassoon (Bahamas) Heart Foundation to underwrite heart surgery for needy Bahamian children.

Early March Nassau's **Red Cross Fair**, a charitable event held under the patronage of the Governor General of The Bahamas, features games, music and native and international foods.

MARCH

Mid-March Arts and crafts collectors will find plenty to purchase at the **Pineapple Art Festival** on Eleuthera. You won't get any bumps and bruises if you just watch the **Kalik 7-A-Side Rugby Tournament** in Nassau. The **International Dog Show and Obedience Trial** in Nassau attracts dog lovers (and dogs) from around the world. Nassau's **Alton Lowe Art Exhibition** is a one-man exhibition of one of The Bahamas' foremost painters.

Mid-April Amateur golfers compete in the **Lucaya International Best Ball Championship** on Grand Bahama. The Exumas host the **Family Island Regatta**.

APRIL

Mid-May The **Bimini Festival** has lots of local events, food and fun, including a popular fishing tournament. Cat Island is the scene of the annual **Rake 'n' Scrape Festival**, a local celebration with food and down-home island music.

MAY

Early June The month-long **Alton Lowe Spring Art Exhibition** in the Abacos highlights the work of the celebrated Bahamian painter. The **Eleuthera Pineapple Festival** features a junkanoo parade, crafts displays, dancing, pineapple recipe contests, tours of pineapple farms and a triathlon called the "Pineatholon."

JUNE

Early July Nassau's **Miss Commonwealth Beauty Pageant** has a bevy of Bahamian beauties vying for the coveted title of Miss Commonwealth Bahamas. The winner represents the islands in the Miss World Contest.

JULY

Mid-August **Fox Hill Celebration** in Nassau, which features ten days of music, dancing and feasting, begins with a junkanoo celebration on Emancipation Day and celebrates the end of slavery in The Bahamas.

AUGUST

Late August Grand Bahama hosts the **Ten-A-Side Rugby World Championship,** meaning Bahamas bumps and bruises for participants and excitement for spectators. The Abacos host the **Great Abaco Triathlon,** where top (and otherwise) triathletes swim, bike and run in a Bahamian paradise.

SEPTEMBER **Late September** The **Ladies Futures Pro-Am Golf Tournament** tees off in Nassau.

OCTOBER **Early October** Nassau hosts the **Great Bahamas Seafood Festival,** where visitors and locals celebrate the bounty of the sea with prize-winning spiny lobster tail and conch recipes. Eleuthera parties to the **Cupids Cay Festival,** a lively celebration featuring music, food and revelry.

October 12 **Discovery Day** is celebrated by a large, colorful parade commemorating the landing of Christopher Columbus on San Salvador.

Mid-October Grand Bahama's unique **McLeans Town Conch Cracking Contest** features contestants competing to see who can extract the largest number of conchs from their shells in a given period of time. Participants run, bike, then run some more at the **Grand Bahama Island Duathalon.** Nassau draws some of golf's best men and women duos in the **International Mixed Championship Golf Tournament.**

NOVEMBER **November 5** Nighttime parades on many islands include a traditionally British **Guy Fawkes Day** "hanging and burning." (Fawkes was a British citizen involved in London's famed Gunpowder Plot of 1605.)

Early November The **Grand Bahama Conchman Triathlon** brings some of the best swimmers, bikers and runners to The Bahamas.

Mid-November Top club pros and their members head to Nassau to shoot birdies (and attempt eagles) at the **Club Professionals Pro-Members Golf Tournament.**

DECEMBER **Early December** The week-long **Sun International Bahamas Open,** an international tennis event, draws some of the top-ranked players in the world. The **Paradise Island Invitational Golf Tournament** draws scores of professional and amateur golfers. See the locals all decked out in ornate costumes at the **Beaux Arts Masked Ball** in Nassau.

Mid-December Youngsters get a head start on the holiday Junkanoo celebrations with the **Junior Junkanoo Parade** in Nassau. Abaco's Green Turtle Cay welcomes visitors to a festival of art exhibits, concerts and international performing artists at the **New Plymouth Historical Cultural Weekend.**

December 26   Boxing Day is observed with an early-morning **Junkanoo Parade** on New Providence, Grand Bahama and most other major islands.

The **Bahamas Ministry of Tourism,** one of the most so-   ▼▼▼▼▼▼▼▼▼▼▼
phisticated and helpful tourist organizations around,   **Before You Go**
can provide invaluable trip-planning information, as
well as courteous assistance once you get to your island(s) of   **VISITORS**
choice. For a bevy of brochures, call them at 800-4 BAHAMAS.   **CENTERS**
The Ministry's international offices can answer specific questions
about almost anything. Bahamas Ministry of Tourism offices in
the United States and Canada include:

> 8600 West Bryn Mawr Avenue, Suite 820, Chicago, IL 60631; 312-693-1500, fax 312-693-1114

> 2050 Stemmons Freeway, World Trade Center, Suite 116, Dallas, TX 75258-1408; 214-742-1886, fax 214-741-4118

> 3450 Wilshire Boulevard, Suite 208, Los Angeles, CA 90010; 213-385-0033, fax 213-383-2966

> One Turnberry Place, 19495 Biscayne Boulevard, Suite 809, Aventura, FL 33180-2321; 305-932-0051, fax 305-682-8758

> 150 East 52nd Street, 28th Floor North, New York, NY 10022; 212-758-2777, fax 212-753-6531

> 121 Bloor Street East, Suite 1101, Toronto, ON M4W 3M5 Canada; 416-968-2999, fax 416-968-0724

For the Out Islands, a helpful organization that specializes in facilitating lodging arrangements is the **Bahamas Out Islands Promotion Board.** They offer a wide variety of publications, brochures and enthusiastic help to tourists interested in visiting the Out Islands. ~ 1100 Lee Wagener Boulevard, Suite 204, Fort Lauderdale, FL 33315; 954-359-8099, 800-OUT ISLANDS; www.bahama-out-islands.com.

Internet surfers will find the Ministry of Tourism's elaborate **Official Bahamas Travel Guide** web site at www.interknowledge.com/bahamas. Additional helpful information is available from **Bahamas Online** at www.bahamasnet.bs, from the **Bahamas National Trust** at flamingo.bahamas.net.bs/environment, and from the **Bahamas Ministry of Tourism's** web site, www.bahamas.com.

Take care not to pack too much; baggage restrictions are tighter   **PACKING**
on the turboprop commercial planes that fly to The Bahamas
than on the big jetliners, and excess or overweight baggage is
subject to being "bumped" from full flights. On the even smaller

planes that travel to the Out Islands, passengers may be restricted to one bag each plus a carry-on beach bag or day pack.

Life in The Bahamas is generally quite informal. The most important items to pack are a bathing suit, lightweight shorts, short-sleeve shirts and at least one pair of long pants or jeans. Bahamians tend to be religious and are conservative about exposed skin. Beachwear is inappropriate away from the water, and long pants are preferred in downtown Nassau.

Guesthouses are the lodging of choice for most Bahamians when they're traveling.

This is a semitropical environment, so lightweight wash-and-wear fabrics are your best bet. Most hotels provide laundry service. For footwear, low-cut hiking boots or athletic shoes will get you by just about anywhere. On the beach, sandals or flip-flops are perfect. Bring a sweater or jacket during the winter; evenings and rainy days can be chilly.

If plans call for staying at one of the more formal hotels, such as the Graycliff in Nassau, or if you are traveling to The Bahamas on a cruise ship, men may want to pack dress pants, jacket and tie to wear at dinner, and women may want to bring a dress or two. Otherwise, leave them home. Dress codes are uncommon even in New Providence and Paradise Island, and unheard-of elsewhere.

There are several other items to squeeze into the corners of your bag—sunscreen, sunglasses, a beach towel, mosquito repellent, a camera and, of course, your copy of *Hidden Bahamas*. You may also want to bring along a mask, fins and snorkel, though you'll find these items for sale or rent at most beach resorts.

LODGING

Accommodations in The Bahamas range from simply furnished guesthouses to huge resorts with every amenity imaginable. Whatever your lodging choice, there are a few guidelines to help save money. Try to visit during the off-season or shoulder season, avoiding the high-rate period from Christmas through April.

You can save money by choosing a hotel or room with a less desirable view. Oceanfront hotels are more expensive than their inland counterparts, and rooms with ocean views may cost more than others in the same hotel that overlook the swimming pool, a garden or the street. Another money-saving strategy is to rent a place with a kitchen, often called a housekeeping unit.

Throughout this book, hotel categories represent the lowest rate for a double room in high season. *Budget* hotels have rooms starting from $60 or less per night. *Moderate* facilities run between $60 and $150. *Deluxe* hotels offer rates from $150 to $225. *Ultra-deluxe* establishments? Well, if you need to ask. . . .

Bahamian **guesthouses** are an excellent budget choice when they are available; though they are becoming scarce on the more popular tourist islands, where budget hotels frequently offer a much lower rate for Out Islanders than for tourists. They range from a room at someone's home to a small local motel and are typically simple and clean, with bathrooms that are sometimes shared and usually no more than adequate. Many offer a small local bar and restaurant. Besides saving money, most guesthouses offer an ideal opportunity to get to know a Bahamian family.

For longer stays, rental **condominiums, villas** and **homes** are a wonderful choice. When kitchen facilities are included you save money, especially for families or groups traveling together. Such rentals can be arranged through **Caribbean Management** ~ 242-393-8618; **Grosham Property** ~ 242-322-7662; **Hideaways International** ~ 603-430-4433, 800-843-4433; **Ingraham's Real Estate** ~ 242-325-2222; **Jack Isaacs Real Estate Company** ~ 242-322-1069; **Rent-a-Home International** ~ 206-789-9377; **1st Choice Vacation Properties** ~ 208-578-0921; or **Vacation Home Rentals Worldwide** ~ 201-767-9393, 800-633-3284.

Home exchanges offer another possibility. **Intervac** ~ 800-756-HOME and **The Invented City** ~ 415-673-0347 both offer homes in The Bahamas that families may be willing to exchange with you for a stay in your home.

DINING

A few guidelines will help you chart a course through the numerous dining opportunities in The Bahamas. Each restaurant listed in this book is categorized by price range. Dinner entrées at *budget* restaurants usually cost $10 or less. The ambiance is typically informal and the crowd is often a local one. *Moderate* restaurant entrées range between $10 and $17 at dinner. *Deluxe* establishments tab their entrées above $17, featuring more sophisticated cuisines and surroundings. *Ultra-deluxe* restaurants generally price entrées above $25 and the service is comparable to the food.

Particularly in the Out Islands, most luxury resorts operate on the American Plan (AP—room rates include all meals) or the Modified American Plan (MAP—breakfast and dinner included). However, remote resorts that do not include meals often charge exorbitantly for their fare—$25 or so for breakfast and upward of $40 for dinner. Accommodations with a kitchen can be a big money-saver in these places.

The standard practice at tourist-oriented restaurants in The Bahamas is to automatically add a 15 percent tip, or "service charge," to the total bill. Fair enough, but because it is rarely identified except as "15%," visitors often assume that it is a tax and leave an additional tip on top of it. Food servers, of course, would never think of embarrassing them by calling attention to such extraordinary generosity.

The Bahamas boasts its own unique cuisine. Bahamian cooks take great pride in exposing visitors to local food and culinary traditions. Some of the best meals are found away from the resort areas, in small budget-priced establishments where locals eat. Unlike many tropical destinations, health risks from food and water in The Bahamas are minimal.

TRAVELING WITH CHILDREN

The Bahamas is an ideal vacation destination for family holidays in the sun. The pace is slow, and the atmosphere is casual. A few guidelines will help ensure that your trip to the islands brings out the joys, rather than the strains, of parenting and being a kid.

Use a travel agent to help with arrangements; they can reserve spacious bulkhead seats on airlines and determine which flights are least crowded. They can also seek out the best deals on inexpensive "housekeeping" accommodations, saving you money on room and board.

Trip planning with your kids stimulates the imagination—yours as well as theirs. Books about The Bahamas, airplane rides, beaches, the sea and marine life help prepare even a six-year-old for the adventure. This preparation makes the "getting there" part of the trip more exciting for children of all ages. Speaking of books, parents planning an excursion to the Out Islands with kids will find encouragement in *Bahamas—Out Island Odyssey* (Ashland, MA: 1995) by Nan Jeffrey, a travel writer who specializes in family adventure travel. The book recounts her experiences traveling to ten islands and cays with twin teenage sons and a 14-month-old infant.

"Getting there" often means two or three flights, sometimes on planes that carry four to ten passengers. Plan to bring everything you need on board the plane—diapers, food, toys, books and extra clothing for kids and parents alike. It's also helpful to carry a few new toys and books as treats to distract bored children, as well as a few snacks. Keep in mind, though, that your carry-on items may be limited in small planes.

Allow extra time to get places. Book reservations in advance and make sure that your accommodations have the extra crib, cot or bed that you require. It's smart to ask for a room at the end of the hall to cut down on noise. And when reserving your rental car, inquire to see if they provide car seats and if there is an added charge.

Besides the car seat you may need to bring along, also pack shorts and T-shirts, a cover-up for the sun, sun hat, bathing suits, sundresses and waterproof sandals or beach shoes. A baby carrier or foldable stroller with a sunshade helps on sightseeing sojourns; a shovel and pail are essential for sandcastle building.

Most important, remember to bring a good sunblock. The quickest way to ruin a family vacation is with a bad sunburn. Also bring indoor activities like books and games for ◆◆◆◆◆◆◆◆◆◆◆◆◆◆◆◆◆◆◆◆◆◆◆◆◆ evenings and the occasional rainy day.

All islands have stores that carry diapers, food and other essentials. Prices are much higher in The Bahamas. To economize, some people take along an extra suitcase filled with things like diapers and wipes, baby food, peanut butter and jelly.

Ninety-three percent of foreign visitors to The Bahamas are from the United States.

A first-aid kit is always a good idea. Check with your pediatrician for special medicines and dosages for colds and diarrhea. Physicians are plentiful on New Providence and Grand Bahama, with modern hospitals on each island. There are also more than 50 hospital facilities and government-operated clinics in the Out Islands.

The **Emergency Flight Service** provides air ambulance transportation to Princess Margaret Hospital in Nassau from anywhere in The Bahamas. ~ 911 or 322-2861.

Many hotels provide or have access to babysitters—either employees of the hotel or locals experienced with children. It's best to make arrangements in advance.

Some resorts and hotels have activity programs for kids during the summer and holiday seasons; some even offer them year round. Hotels often offer family plans, providing discounts for extra rooms or permitting children to share a room with their parents at no extra charge.

Premier Cruise Lines specializes in family-oriented cruises. ~ 407-783-5061, 800-473-3262. **Rascals in Paradise** organizes individualized family trips and three- to six-family all-inclusive group trips to smaller inns, mostly in the Out Islands, complete with a tour guide who babysits and supervises kids' activities. ~ 415-978-9800, 800-872-7225.

The incidence of sexual assault and other crimes of violence against women is much lower in Nassau and Freeport/Lucaya than in the U.S. Elsewhere in The Bahamas, they are unheard-of. Women can and do travel alone safely in The Bahamas.

WOMEN TRAVELING ALONE

In the morally conservative Bahamas, a myth persists that American women are promiscuous, so if a woman is alone in a bar, young local men may see it as an opportunity to try their luck. A sharp rebuff is enough to send unwelcome would-be seducers scurrying.

Solo travelers who would like to have some company on the road can find it through **Travel Companion**. Membership costs $159; a subscription to the organization's newsletter is $48 a year. ~ 516-454-0880.

**GAY &
LESBIAN
TRAVELERS**

"The Bahamas supports and in no way hinders gay and lesbian travel," according to an official statement released by Prime Minister Hubert Ingraham. "Our visitors represent all races and many ethnic groups; they practice one or other of virtually every religion known on the earth. Some are no doubt agnostic and others atheist; some are heterosexual, while others, I expect, may be homosexual. These visitors help to create a standard of living in The Bahamas envied by many and equalled by few countries of similar size in our region."

This declaration of tolerance was made in response to demonstrations organized by a religious group called the Save The Bahamas Campaign to protest the arrival of gay and lesbian cruise ships at Prince George Wharf. One such demonstration, on April 13, 1998, became a riot when about 300 demonstrators stormed police barricades after a lesbian cruise ship passenger defiantly kissed her partner on the cheek.

Since then, while gay groups continue to organize Bahamas cruises, the Save The Bahamas Campaign seems to have run low on energy. Homosexuality remains a hot topic in some circles, however, and it is not unusual to see vehement anti-gay sentiments expressed on newspaper editorial pages and radio talk shows. Conservative members of the leadership of the powerful Bahamas Christian Council have adopted an explicitly anti-gay stance. A few resorts such as Sandals have "opposite sex couples only" policies, and some hotels refuse to rent double-bed rooms to same-sex couples.

Still, homophobia has not reached the proportions in The Bahamas that it has in other Caribbean destinations such as Jamaica, where in 1999 officials reaffirmed a century-old law declaring homosexual activity a crime. The safest policy is to avoid public displays of affection while in Nassau, where the anti-gay groups focus their efforts. In the Out Islands, the locals maintain an attitude of casual acceptance toward all visitors' lifestyles.

For a list of travel agents that cater to the gay and lesbian traveler, contact the **International Gay and Lesbian Travel Association**. ~ 800-448-8550.

Several tour operators and travel agencies may have trips scheduled or can book individual trips specifically for gay and lesbian travelers: **Advance Travel** ~ 800-695-0880; **Atlantis Events** ~ 800-628-5268; **Kennedy Travel** ~ 212-242-3222, 800-988-1181; **Now Voyager** ~ 415-626-1169, 800-255-6951; **Skylink Women's Travel** ~ 310-452-0505, 800-225-5759; and **Yellowbrick Road** ~ 312-561-1800, 800-642-2488.

San Diego–based **Undersea Expeditions** specializes in gay and lesbian scuba diving trips, with several options to The Bahamas.

You don't have to be an experienced diver—or even certified yet—to enjoy these trips. ~ 858-270-2900, 800-669-0310.

SENIOR TRAVELERS

The Bahamas are a great place for senior citizens to visit. Many cultural activities, historic sights and even restaurants and hotels offer senior discounts that can cut a substantial chunk off vacation costs.

Along with your travel agent, good contacts for discount travel to The Bahamas include: the **American Association of Retired Persons** (AARP) ~ 800-424-3410, www.aarp.org; **Elderhostel** ~ 877-426-8056, www.elderhostel.org; **Grand Circle Travel** ~ 617-350-7500, 800-221-2610; and SAGA **International Holidays** ~ 800-343-0273.

Be extra careful about health matters. Consider carrying a medical record with you—including your medical history and current medical status as well as your doctor's name, phone number and address. Make sure your insurance covers you while you are away from home.

DISABLED TRAVELERS

Like many vacation destinations, The Bahamas have made progress in providing for the physically disabled traveler. More than 30 accommodation options have specific provisions for disabled guests, including lodging in the Abacos, Andros, Cat Island, Eleuthera, Grand Bahama, Great Inagua, Long Island, New Providence/Paradise Island and Spanish Wells. **The Bahamas Association for the Physically Disabled** can provide a list and contact information for accommodations possibilities that cater to the disabled. ~ 242-322-2393.

Other helpful organizations include: **Flying Wheels Travel** ~ 507-451-5005, 800-535-6790, www.flyingwheels.com; **Handicapped Travel Newsletter** ~ 903-677-1260; and the **Information Center for Individuals with Disabilities** ~ 212-620-2147. The So-

---

KEEP TO THE LEFT!

Driving on the left is a Bahamian peculiarity that requires American drivers to be constantly alert. It is harder to remember than in England because most cars in The Bahamas come from the United States and have the steering wheel on the left, meaning that the driver sits toward the side of the road rather than the center line. It's most confusing when turning left or right at intersections. If possible, use a "buddy system," asking a passenger to remind the driver to keep left after each turn.

ciety for the Advancement of Travel for the Handicapped offers information for travelers with disabilities. ~ 347 5th Avenue, #610, New York, NY 10016; 212-447-7284; www.sath.org. Travelin' Talk, a network of people and organizations, also provides assistance. ~ P.O. Box 1796, Wheat Ridge, CO 80034; 303-232-2979; www.travelintalk.net. Access-Able Travel Source has worldwide information online. ~ 303-232-2979; www.access-able.com.

Be sure to check in advance when making room reservations. A travel agent can be very useful with confirmation of specific facilities.

FOREIGN TRAVELERS   U.S. citizens become foreigners the minute they set foot on Bahamian soil. The Bahamas fancies itself the Switzerland of North America, a neutral nation that views all foreign nationals with equal courtesy, whether they come from another British Commonwealth country or from Ireland, China or Iraq.

Passports and Visas   Bahamian officials make it as easy as possible for tourists to enter their country. Citizens of the United States who are visiting The Bahamas for a period of eight months or less and citizens of Canada, the United Kingdom and its colonies who are visiting for three weeks or less must present proof of citizenship in the form of a current or recently expired passport or a birth certificate or voter registration card along with photo identification such as a driver's license. (U.K. citizens, however, will need a passport to reenter their own country.) Travelers with an air of vagabondism about them—a backpack, for instance—may be asked to show return or onward transportation tickets. Immigration officials also frequently ask where they will be staying and will not let them enter the country without an answer. That does not mean you need reservations; it *does* mean you should read this book's lodging listings in advance and identify a hotel to check out first upon arrival.

Most visitors to The Bahamas need not obtain a visa in advance. All international arrivals complete an immigration card. You sign the card and keep a copy to turn in when you leave the country. You pay a departure tax, $18 from Grand Bahama and $15 from anywhere else, when you leave The Bahamas. Nationals of the Dominican Republic, Haiti, Colombia, and most Asian countries must obtain a visa in advance from the nearest Bahamian Consulate.

Travelers coming to The Bahamas for an extended stay who would like to bring a pet along will want to contact the Ministry of Agriculture and Fisheries for information and an application well in advance. ~ 242-325-7502.

Customs Requirements   Though you don't fill out a customs declaration upon entering The Bahamas, you are subject to a customs inspection. Bahamian citizens do their big-ticket shopping in Florida and must pay an import duty on purchases exceeding $300. They may try to dodge this tax by asking other travelers—especially foreign tourists, who are rarely subjected to searches—to carry purchases for them. If you have any new or expensive items, be sure to bring the receipt.

It may seem a little like bringing coals to Newcastle in this land of Cuban cigars and duty-free booze, but every adult entering The Bahamas is allowed to bring in 50 cigars, 200 cigarettes or one pound of tobacco, as well as one quart of alcoholic beverage. Speaking of coals to Newcastle, it is highly illegal to bring marijuana into The Bahamas. True, most tourists' chances of being searched for a small quantity of pot are remote, but in the event that a customs inspector should happen to stumble across one's stash, the consequences are swift and severe, and tales of Bahamian prison conditions are horrific. Druggies can take comfort in the knowledge that such smuggling is unnecessary. People who make their living selling pot to tourists are about as common as conch fishermen. Caveat emptor. And remember, travelers boarding the plane to *leave* The Bahamas are subject to search by U.S. Customs agents whose main job is to apprehend drug smugglers.

When returning home, U.S. citizens can bring back up to $600 worth of goods duty-free, as long as they've been out of the country at least 48 hours and haven't used the exemption in the last 30 days. Travelers age 21 and older can bring back up to two liters of alcohol, as long as one liter was bottled in The Bahamas or another Caribbean Basin Initiative country. Every person regardless of age can bring back up to 100 non-Cuban cigars or 200 cigarettes.

If you're going to be close to your limits, you may want to mail some items home to yourself or to someone else, marking it as a gift, so it doesn't count as part of your exemption upon departure. The postal expense may or may not be less than the import duty. You can mail packages valued up to $200 to yourself and up to $100 to others (as an unsolicited gift), with a limit of one package per addressee each day. No alcohol, tobacco or perfume valued at more than $5 can be mailed.

Driving An international driver's license or a current driver's license from any country is valid for up to three months. Age restrictions are typically 25 for car rentals and 21 for motor scooter rentals. Road signs are in English and generally resemble those in the United States.

Motorists drive on the left. This quaintly British mannerism makes little sense on islands where most of the cars come from

Miami and have their steering wheels on the left side. It seems designed to constantly remind visitors that they are in a foreign country. Even visitors who choose not to drive may find themselves looking in the wrong direction when crossing the street, not to mention colliding with Bahamian pedestrians, who also keep left on sidewalks.

Currency   U.S. dollars are the de facto currency of The Bahamas. Official Bahamian money comes in the same denominations as U.S. money, as well as in $3 bills and 15-cent pieces. Its exchange rate is fixed at 1 to 1, making the two currencies interchangeable.

If you peek into the cash register drawer at any shop or restaurant, you'll see many more U.S. bills than Bahamian ones. There are two reasons for this. First, Bahamian money tends to leak out of the country as souvenirs; $3 bills, as well as square 15-cent coins, have all but vanished from circulation, and big, scallop-edged dimes are also becoming rare, though plastic-sealed displays containing all of them are sold at more than face value in curio shops. Second, so much of the money in circulation is tourist dollars that if the government required U.S. cash to be exchanged for local money, the expense of minting and printing sufficient amounts of Bahamian currency would skyrocket.

Bahamian pennies, nickels and quarters are the same size and color as their American counterparts and are so easily confused that you're bound to bring some home and likely get an odd look when a sharp-eyed supermarket clerk catches you trying to hand over a starfish penny or a pineapple nickel. Bahamian quarters are made to resemble U.S. quarters so closely that either one will work in most vending machines in both countries; the Bahamian ones will not work in casino slot machines, though, because of a law designed to prevent local residents from gambling.

Major credit cards are widely accepted for accommodations, dining and shopping. Some Out Islands stores and restaurants deal only in cash or limit credit card acceptance. Traveler's checks in U.S. dollars issued by all U.S. and some British financial institutions are also widely accepted. Foreign currencies other than U.S. dollars must be exchanged at a bank, of which there are hundreds in Nassau and few elsewhere. They are generally open from 9:30 a.m. to 3 p.m. Monday through Thursday and until 5 p.m. on Fridays. ATMs can be found at many banks, as well as at some hotels and casinos; you won't find them on the Out Islands.

Electricity and Electronics   Electric outlets deliver 110-volt, 60 cycle alternating current, just as in the United States. For appliances made for other electrical systems, you need a transformer or adapter. Travelers who use laptop computers for telecommunication should be aware that modem configurations, while the same as U.S. and Canadian systems, may differ from settings for European telephone systems. Souvenir videotapes are usually available in your choice of American or European format.

Weights and Measurements   The Bahamas uses the English system of weights and measures. English units and their metric equivalents are as follows: 1 inch = 2.5 centimeters; 1 foot (12 inches) = 0.3 meter; 1 yard (3 feet) = 0.9 meter; 1 mile (5280 feet) = 1.6 kilometers; 1 ounce = 28 grams; 1 pound (16 ounces) = 0.45 kilogram; 1 quart (liquid) = 0.9 liter.

International postage rates from The Bahamas are 45 cents per half-ounce to the United States and Canada and 50 cents to the United Kingdom. Bahamian stamps are varied and colorful, and more of them are sold as souvenirs than are ever licked and pasted on envelopes. Postal service is fast and reliable to and from New Providence and Grand Bahama, and Nassau's high-power banking industry means numerous international firms offer overnight courier service. When sending mail to or from the Out Islands, mark it air mail or it may go by the much slower mailboat. When contacting Out Island lodgings for reservations, it's best to use phone or fax.

MAIL

The government-run Bahamas Telecommunications Company (BATELCO) operates similarly to phone companies in the United States. Long-distance rates to the U.S. run about a dollar a minute. Telephone service is just like home on New Providence and Grand Bahama. In the Out Islands, phones can sometimes be hard to find, and guesthouses may have only a single phone for the whole establishment. When staying in a hotel beware of the added charges they tack on to calls made from your room.

PHONES

The area code for all islands in The Bahamas is 242.

The Bahamas area code is 242 throughout the islands. Listings in this book that do not include an area code are for The Bahamas. You do not have to dial a country code when calling to or from the United States. To make a calling card call to the United States, simply dial the local access 800-number for The Bahamas (AT&T's is 800-872-2881). You can dial direct from BATELCO public phones, including those on Prince George Wharf in Nassau; hotel switchboards often must dial the 800-number for you and call you back.

Beware those tourist telephones found in many hotel lobbies that let you phone home and charge it to your credit card. You may arrive home to discover that these charges amount to $8 a minute or more!

Strangely enough, there are no internet cafés or other public internet access in The Bahamas, so unless you're staying in one of those rare hotels where you can unplug the phone and plug in your computer, plan to let your e-mail pile up until after your vacation.

▼▼▼▼▼▼▼▼▼▼▼▼   The Bahamas are easy to reach by air or by sea. The first
Transportation   option is cheap, quick and easy from any of several
Florida airports. The second (unless you are fortunate
GETTING   enough to have your own boat) means taking a cruise ship:
TO THE   pricey, slow and utterly romantic. However you decide to go, be
ISLANDS   sure to consult a travel agent. They are professionals in the field,
possessing the latest information on rates and facilities, and their
service to you is usually free.

AIR   American Eagle, Bahamasair, Delta, Comair, Gulfstream
and USAir offer frequent daily passenger service on turboprop
commuter planes to Nassau and Freeport from various Florida
cities including Miami, Fort Lauderdale, West Palm Beach and
Orlando. Delta also flies to Nassau from Atlanta, Nashville,
Chicago, Cincinnati, Dallas, Los Angeles and New York, and
USAir offers service from Philadelphia, Raleigh/Durham and
Charlotte. Nassau's airport also has daily arrivals from Montreal
and Toronto on **AirCanada** and from London and Amsterdam
on **British Airways**. Other European airlines offer direct flights
from Paris, Frankfurt and Milan.

USAir Express and **PanAm Air Bridge** have regularly
scheduled service from Miami to the small Paradise Island Airport, which is actually closer to downtown Nassau than Nassau's Oakes Airport.

Scheduled flights from Florida to the Out Islands are on the
increase. Travelers can save a lot of time and often a little money
by flying direct instead of connecting through Nassau. From
Miami, there are direct flights to the Abacos, Andros, Eleuthera
and the Exumas on several carriers, including American Eagle,
Bahamasair and Gulfstream, which also flies in from Fort
Lauderdale and West Palm Beach. Smaller island destinations,
including Bimini, Long Island, Treasure Cay and Walker's Cay,
can be reached on passenger seaplanes operated by Pan Am Air
Bridge and Island Express. Some smaller air carriers may not be
listed on travel agents' computers nationwide, so if you en-
counter a problem in finding the flight you want, a phone call to
an airline's Miami customer service number may solve it.

Whichever carrier you choose, try to fly during the week;
weekend flights are often jammed by Bahamians traveling to
Florida to shop or from jobs to visit families in the islands. Fares
between Florida and The Bahamas, which are quite reasonable,

Won't You Let Me Take You on a Sea Cruise?

A large percentage of visitors arrive by cruise ship to spend a single day in Nassau and maybe another in Freeport/Lucaya. These vacationers experience the islands in romance-packed snapshot glimpses that seem almost beside the point; the cruise ship itself is the essence of the trip.

The 35 cruise ships that sail to Nassau on a regular basis are seagoing all-inclusive resorts, and like resort hotels on land, they vary in quality from the no-frills to the ultra-exclusive. **Royal Caribbean**, the reigning monarch of Bahamas cruise lines, runs *Sovereign of the Seas* between Miami and The Bahamas. The largest cruise ship ever built, it carries 2276 passengers and operates with a crew of 800. In addition to Nassau and Grand Bahama, four-day Royal Caribbean cruises put in at Cococay, a private 14-acre cay in the Berry Islands.

Cruise ship amenities—swimming pools, fine dining, showrooms, casinos—rival those of large land-based resort hotels, and the all-inclusive accommodations are priced competitively with resorts. Ticket prices vary widely depending on the time of year and on whether you take an inside (windowless) or outside (with portholes) cabin. Discounts and other little-known deals abound, so it's best to enlist the help of a travel agent who specializes in cruises; most of them emphasize this specialty in Yellow Pages listings.

Unless you're on your honeymoon, and maybe even then, the big drawback to cruise ship travel is that sailing schedules leave little time to explore ports of call beyond a few blocks of "cruise ship approved" galleries and shops. Shipboard luxury is the essence of most cruise experiences, and ports of call are almost incidental.

Travelers who want to combine a brief cruise with a longer stay in The Bahamas might consider **SeaEscape**, a company that offers one-day minicruises from Fort Lauderdale to Freeport and back. You can take the four-hour trip over and return the same day or make your return trip (by advance reservation) on a later date. The cost for deck passage is about the same as the plane fare from Florida to Grand Bahama and back. Cabins cost extra.

run the same every day of the week, and you do not save by purchasing your ticket in advance. Of course, advance purchase requirements and other restrictions are a big cost consideration if you are flying into either Florida or The Bahamas from a more distant city.

The small planes that fly between Florida and The Bahamas typically have tighter baggage restrictions than jetliners do. You can check one bag and carry one aboard; some flights allow you a second carry-on but require you to stow it in an auxiliary cargo hold and reclaim it when you get off the plane. You pay extra for overweight or excess baggage, as well as for cumbersome sporting equipment such as a bicycle or scuba gear.

For groups of four or five people traveling together, air charter services can provide convenient, flexible transportation at a reasonable per-person price, and take you to islands the airlines don't reach. And you get what amounts to a free guided tour in the bargain. Fort Lauderdale–based **Trans-Caribbean Air**, for instance, flies from either Fort Lauderdale or Opa Locka Airport to nine islands in The Bahamas including Long Island, Cat Island and San Salvador.

SEA The Bahamas' proximity to Miami, the world's largest cruise port, makes it the ideal destination for three- and four-day cruise excursions. Nassau has become the world's most popular cruise ship destination. Nassau's Prince George Wharf can accommodate up to 12 of the huge oceangoing hotels operated by **Royal Caribbean, Carnival, Disney, Holland America, Norwegian, Princess** and numerous other cruise lines. The ships tower high above the city's stately old stone churches and government houses for a few hours as up to 2400 passengers per ship shop their way along Bay Street; when they depart in late afternoon, downtown virtually shuts down. Hoping to inspire cruise ship passengers to stay for dinner, The Bahamian government now offers special tax incentives to cruise ships that remain docked at Prince George Wharf for at least 18 hours.

A second set of cruise ships sails each week for the port of Freeport/Lucaya on Grand Bahama, where the docks are several miles out of town and passengers ride a shuttle to the main shopping areas and casinos. Most cruises do not go to both Nassau and Freeport/Lucaya. Instead, the longer and more luxurious cruises often own private cays in the northern Bahamas where passengers can ride ashore on motor launches and have an unspoiled beach to themselves for the day.

GETTING BETWEEN ISLANDS

AIR **Bahamasair** has a monopoly on regularly scheduled passenger service within The Bahamas. This airline is not for the nervous. Oh, the planes are safe enough, but the reservation system may be in hopeless disarray. If you try to get a plane ticket on short notice, the computers are likely to show that all the flights are booked up. Don't panic. This does not mean that the planes are actually full. The ticket agent will probably suggest that you buy your ticket for the first open flight, usually a few days later, and then call early on the day you *really* want to travel to get on the standby list. You're all but assured of getting one of the seats vacated by passengers who did the same thing and went standby on earlier flights. In assigning standby seats, Bahamasair agents give preference to foreign visitors. Making up in optimism for what it may lack in efficiency, the airline claims to be revamping its reservation system.

Bahamasair offers a special airline pass that includes a Miami–Nassau round-trip plus travel to any three Out Islands except Grand Bahama. The cost, about $350, represents significant savings over buying separate tickets to the same destinations.

Charter service in small four- to six-seater planes costs more than flying Bahamasair—typically between $300 and $400 per planeload one-way between islands—and for groups of four or five the cost per person may work out about the same. Charters can be a time- and money-saver because they are the only way to fly from one Out Island to another without first returning to Nassau. Most of the inhabited Out Islands have at least one airport or airstrip or offer boat service to a neighboring island that offers flights. Some of the more remote Out Island destinations are served by seaplane.

BOAT Interisland boat traffic is fairly heavy, and adventurous travelers can often find boats leaving for the Out Islands from Nassau. Boat travel between the Out Islands is a bit harder to predict.

If you're flexible about time and destination, mailboats offer a fun way to travel between Nassau and the Out Islands. Operating on assigned routes under government charter, these small freighters ply the waters between the islands of The Bahamas and their home port at Potter's Cay in Nassau, carrying food, building supplies, people, livestock and practically anything else. They are particularly important to Out Islanders in general and especially to those living in the distant and secluded southern Bahamas.

Though the introduction of commercial air transportation in the 1950s and the relative convenience and cost of flights between the islands today has reduced the need and use of mailboats, the service is still very much alive and well. You can go practically anywhere in The Bahamas from Potter's Cay, if you're patient. You can also make your way back to New Providence by mailboat but, again, you'll have to practice patience.

Mailboat service has been a part of Bahamian life since the first boats were chartered in 1832; at that time, the boats were sail-powered and had no engines. Today, 22 mailboats provide vital links between Bahamian islands, with one or two trips a week between Nassau and most destinations. About half of the boats are government-subsidized. The schedule is often extremely flexible, and travelers should not expect to reach their destination at any particular time.

The trips can range from five hours between Nassau and Andros to 21 hours to Ragged Island. From the time they start loading pallets of beer and soft drinks, bags of cement, used cars, appliances and people aboard, you know you're in for a unique experience. The rhythms of mailboat travel are unique, with shared meals, constant conversation on deck and in the indoor passenger area, occasional sleep on limited bunks and potential bouts with seasickness and diesel fumes. Relatively few "visitors" (as international tourists are called in the Out Islands) ride the mailboats, so your fellow passengers will be curious about you and eager to tell you about the last visitor they encountered on a mailboat trip. By the time you reach your destination, you'll have met an assortment of Out Island locals, and before you've been there 24 hours, everybody else on the island will know who you are.

Mailboats run weekly to Andros, Cat Island, Eleuthera, The Exumas, Grand Bahama, Long Island, Ragged Island, and San Salvador, with others operating on a more sporadic schedule to Acklins Island, Bimini, Cat Cay, Crooked Island and Mayaguana. Mailboat passage costs about half as much as plane fare on Bahamasair. Plan to spend anywhere from $25 to $70 each way depending on the length of the trip.

Taking a mailboat is easy. First, stop in at the office of the **dockmaster**, located east of the Paradise Island Causeway on Potter's Cay Dock in Nassau, for the current schedule, which is subject to weather conditions. Then, an hour or two before the departure time listed on the schedule, find your boat by name among the vessels tied alongside the dock, get on board and toss your gear on an empty bunk if there is one. A crew member will collect your fare in cash once the boat is underway. ~ 393-1064.

CAR RENTALS

Renting a car in The Bahamas is as easy as anywhere, though a little more expensive. Expect to pay at least $75 a day. The freedom of renting a car makes it well worth the cost for at least a part of any stay, enabling you to explore out-of-town spots that are impractical to reach by taxi or bus. The renter must be at least 25 years of age and have a charge card with $400 to $500 available credit as a security deposit. Many national chains and local firms, mostly located at the airports compete for your business. The condition of the cars at the Nassau and Freeport airports is quite good. In the Out Islands, the availability and condition of rental cars vary greatly. Check the Grand Bahamas chapter in this book for special restrictions on the use of rental cars on that island.

Gasoline is sometimes called "petrol" in The Bahamas, though this and other Britishisms are fading quickly with the onslaught of American television. It is easily found around Nassau and Freeport. In the Out Islands, gas stations may only be found in a few towns.

MOTOR SCOOTERS

Many hotels and individual operators offer motor scooter, or moped rentals on New Providence and Grand Bahama. Though less prevalent on the Out Islands, they are sometimes available. The modern Japanese-brand scooters can carry two adults and have governors on the engines to limit speeds to around 45 mph. A driver's license is required to rent a scooter in Nassau or Freeport/Lucaya, though not necessarily in the Out Islands. Prices typically range from $25 to $35 a day. Either a credit card imprint or a cash deposit of around $100 is required. Larger Out-Island resorts also rent golf carts for road use at a somewhat higher fee.

BIKING

Although riding a bike is a hair-raising idea on the busy roads of Nassau and Freeport/Lucaya, it is an attractive option on the traffic-free Out Islands. Bicycle rentals are available at many resort hotels (though the cost of renting two bikes may be almost as much as a rental car), and some smaller inns and guesthouses provide them to guests for free.

TWO

The Land and Outdoor Adventures

GEOLOGY The territorial waters of The Bahamas cover more than 100,000 square miles, most of it under water so shallow and clear that air travelers can look down and see the ocean bottom between islands that rise just slightly above the surface. An early Spanish explorer dubbed the area Baja Mar—the Shallow Sea.

Today, the gigantic coral archipelago split by the deep Providence Channel is called the Bahama Banks. The Little Bahama Bank, in the north, surrounds Grand Bahama and the Abacos. The Great Bahama Bank, encompasses most of the other islands and cays, as small islands off the shore from major ones are called.

A Grand Canyon–sized underwater gorge called the Tongue of the Ocean, which cuts into the U-shaped Great Bahama Bank, is one of the deepest known ocean canyons, with sheer, coral-studded cliffs that drop nearly two miles to the ocean floor. It separates New Providence Island and the Exumas on the east rim from Andros on the west rim and runs southward for a hundred miles before reaching a dead-end far from any island, surrounded by the walls of the Great Bahama Bank.

If the present sea level were to rise just 120 feet, all the islands of The Bahamas except for a solitary hilltop on Cat Island would vanish beneath the sea. If sea level *fell* by 120 feet, dry land would fill ten times its present area, forming just two islands. During the last Ice Age, when more of the Earth's water was permanently frozen in glaciers and the polar ice caps, the Atlantic dropped 400 feet below its present level. Far enough south to escape year-round freezing, the Bahama Banks were mostly dry land, and much of what is now the shallow sea floor was covered with forest. In that and earlier Ice Ages, ocean storms blew soil and sand into huge dunes. When the sea level rose again, the top ridges of the dunes became long, narrow islands.

The formation of the Bahama Banks mystifies geologists. There is no evidence of any volcanic activity. Essentially gigantic coral reefs, the banks have been building up for 135 million years—almost since the Atlantic Ocean first came into being. The mystery is this: Coral grows best in warm waters 90 feet deep or less and cannot grow at all below 130 feet; yet drilling samples reveal that the petrified coral limestone of The Bahamas goes down at least 4000 feet. This means that the banks are sinking into the sea at exactly the same rate as they are building up.

Stranger yet, except for rare Ice Age interludes, the process has been continuing in the same delicate equilibrium, with exactly the same climate conditions and ocean currents, since dinosaurs walked the earth. Few other places show evidence of such perfect stability over such a long span of geological history.

All the main islands are honeycombed with underwater limestone caves, including Lucayan Cavern, the world's longest known underwater cave, beneath Grand Bahama island. Hundreds of "blue holes" extend straight down as deep as 600 feet. Most contain a surface layer of freshwater floating on saltwater depths. Unlike the limestone sinkholes found in Florida and the Yucatán, some blue holes in The Bahamas rise and fall with the tide, proving that they are connected to the ocean. According to local legend, these "ocean holes" may be sea monster lairs, and some people avoid going near them.

Flora and Fauna

FLORA

The vegetation of The Bahamas varies across a broad spectrum depending on distance from the tropics. The Pine Islands in the north, including Grand Bahama, the Abacos, Andros and undeveloped areas of New Providence, are covered with spindly monoculture forests of Caribbean Pine. Originally there were hammocks of subtropical tree species such as gumbo limbo, poisonwood and strangler fig, but most were destroyed by early inhabitants trying to reach scattered large hardwood trees that were used for furniture making and boatbuilding. Large areas were cleared 200 years ago to make short-lived cotton plantations.

In recent times, from the 1950s to the early '70s, the northern Pine Islands were clearcut by a U.S.-based forest products corporation for paper pulp, leaving only 12 pines standing per acre. The forests that cover the islands grew from the seeds of those few trees. The palmetto undergrowth is purposely burned off each year because it stimulates the pines, which are impervious to the fires, to produce more seed cones. The coastline of the Pine Islands is beautifully fringed with casuarinas, the tall, graceful evergreens sometimes called Australian pines. Originally planted to anchor the dunes, these imported ornamentals gradually exclude other coastal vegetation.

The major islands of the southern Bahamas are called the Coppice Islands. The forest, or coppice, is made up of low dense bush studded with a great variety of hardwood trees including lignum vitae, the national tree and the hardest wood known. The amazing variety of trees includes valuable hardwoods such as mahogany, horseflesh, mastic and sapodilla in an island version of tropical rain forests miniaturized by chronic shortages of precipitation. Farther south, the trees grow smaller until on the Inaguas, the southernmost island group in The Bahamas, only cacti, thorny bushes and isolated clumps of grass grow.

◆◆◆◆◆◆◆◆◆◆◆◆◆◆◆◆◆◆◆◆◆◆◆

The Ministry of Tourism takes an active part in the promotion and conservation of the country's ecological resources.

The islands of The Bahamas are host to more than 1370 species of plant life. The profusion of brightly colored flowers dazzles visitors. Interspersed among expanses of scrub, you'll find oases of hibiscus, bougainvillea, orchids, crepe myrtle, bright orange poinciana trees and yellow elder, the national flower.

Public gardens and botanical parks on New Providence and Grand Bahama present opportunities to get acquainted with the local flora. Then, too, Bahamians pride themselves on their home gardens. People from every walk of life plant them and love to show them off.

Bahamians, particularly Out Islanders, also consider themselves experts in the art of "bush medicine," using local plants and herbs to make teas and other preparations to cure everything from colds to high blood pressure. There are recipes for birth control, impotence, fertility and even abortion.

Thanks to environmental activists who lobbied for the islands' Ecotourism Policy and Strategy Act, many examples of Bahamian natural habitats are nationally protected. Conservation is not new to The Bahamas. The private nonprofit Bahamas National Trust (BNT), chartered in 1959, is responsible for the preservation of Bahamian places of historic interest and natural beauty. The BNT is internationally recognized for its achievements in the preservation of natural habitats.

FRUITS AND VEGETABLES   The Bahamas have poor soil and a relatively dry climate, making large-scale agriculture unfeasible. Small farmers in the central and southeastern islands use slash-and-burn farming methods to grow citrus fruits, tomatoes, sweet peppers, onions, avocados, cassava, corn, pigeon peas, watermelons, mangoes, guavas, bananas, coconuts and pears. Areas of bush are set afire and then left to lie fallow for a year as the mixture of ash and sparse soil settles into potholes in the coral limestone, where seeds are planted and allowed to grow with no irrigation and little tending. After a single year, the field is abandoned to return to its natural state. Only the extremely small scale of Out Island farming saves the islands' environment from wholesale destruction.

Most produce is either sold to the restaurants of resort hotels or sent on mailboats a bagful at a time for sale at the public food market on Potter's Cay Dock in Nassau. The only fruit that has ever been exported from The Bahamas in quantity is the pineapple; plantations on Eleuthera grew all the pineapples eaten in the United States before Hawaii became a U.S. territory in the 1890s. Although the Bahamian government has strived to make the islands agriculturally self-sufficient, 80 percent of the produce locals eat is imported from Florida.

Of the 13 land mammal species found in The Bahamas, the majority are various kinds of bats. Several of the larger islands also have wild populations of pigs, cats, donkeys and horses, descendants from the livestock of farms and plantations abandoned centuries ago. Raccoons are also common on Grand Bahama and other Pine Islands, though how they got there is puzzling; the prevailing theory holds that their ancestors must have floated from Florida on rafts of hurricane debris. The hutia, a small, rabbitlike Caribbean rodent, was hunted to the verge of extinction before the Bahamas National Trust reintroduced them on several cays off Exuma and Mayaguana; today they number in the tens of thousands.

FAUNA

Birders will be pleased with the possibilities on Abaco, Grand Bahama, Paradise Island and several other northern islands, where hundreds of migratory bird species arrive at various times of year to join about 40 year-round resident species. Farther south, tropical bird species include the reddish egret and the roseate spoonbill. Sometimes spotted are such unusual birds as the Bahamas wood star (a yellow and brown hummingbird), the grayish Bahamas swallow, the Bahamas parrot and the white-crowned pigeon, the national bird. The pink flamingo, which is represented on the national crest of The Bahamas, once lived in flocks throughout the islands, but the big, bright birds were hunted to the brink of extinction when a flamingo plume hat fad swept the 19th-century fashion world. Today, flamingos are found in the wild only on Inagua, where flocks totalling 60,000 birds are protected in a 276-square-mile national park.

Some 90 species of butterflies brighten the Bahamian countryside, along with the giant bat moth. Other bug life includes mosquitoes and no-see-ums, which are most bothersome between May and October, and several kinds of spiders. The only poisonous spider in The Bahamas is the black widow, known in the islands as the bottle spider. The centipede, which reaches eight inches long, can also inflict a painful bite.

Reptile life includes iguanas and both sea and freshwater turtles. All of them were considered good eating in earlier times. Today the green sea turtle and the New Providence iguana are protected as endangered species. Other reptile species include the curly-tailed lizard, which is unique to The Bahamas and is about as cute as a lizard can be. Snakes include the Bahamian boa constrictor and the smaller pygmy boa, docile snakes that inhabit the thick coppice in the interior of some islands. They eat rodents and lizards and avoid contact with humans. All lizards and snakes in the Bahamas are nonvenomous and harmless.

The most spectacular wildlife viewing in The Bahamas awaits underwater, along some 900 square miles of living coral reefs. The coral itself is made up of tiny polyps that close themselves within hard exoskeletons by day and open to catch microscopic plankton after dark. As older generations of coral polyps die, their exoskeletons leave rigid calcium formations that new generations cling to, so that the whole formation grows as years pass. The entire Bahama Banks and all the islands of The Bahamas are made up of coral formations as old as 135 million years. Diverse and intricate varieties of coral abound: star coral, fan coral, black coral, pillar coral, brain coral, gorgonians (soft coral), treelike elkhorn coral and stinging fire coral.

The coral formations provide shelter for many other marine species, ranging from tube sponges, Christmas tree worms, starfish, sea urchins and sea cucumbers to spotted dolphins and humpback and blue whales. Conch, spiny lobster, shrimp and many varieties of crabs also inhabit the reefs and shallows, along with moray eels, groupers and a profusion of other fish. Some of the most colorful fish species, such as parrot fish, triggerfish, squirrelfish and angel fish, are legal to catch and good to eat— and *are* commonly eaten in Jamaica and other parts of the Caribbean—but Bahamian fishermen throw them back because of their beauty.

Reef sharks, common in Bahamian waters, are normally not aggressive, and shark-watching scuba trips are conducted daily without incident. In fact, some divemasters feed sharks so they will come around at predictable times for dive groups to see. Hammerhead sharks, which occasionally put in an appearance, are considered more dangerous; fortunately, they tend to avoid areas where humans are diving. Sleeping sharks can be unpredictable if awakened suddenly, and divers should not go in the water with an open wound because sharks can smell traces of blood from a distance and may attack out of sheer excitement.

Other fish whose danger is often exaggerated include barracuda, which are not aggressive but will strike at shiny objects with their razor-sharp teeth, and moray eels, which are likely to bite a hand that feeds them. Statistically, the most dangerous fish in Bahamian waters is the stingray, which lies buried in the sand and, if stepped on, lashes its tail and can inflict an excruciatingly painful, though not fatal, wound with its poisonous stinger. However, the great majority of underwater injuries are caused by small stinging creatures such as jellyfish, fire coral, sea urchins and bristle worms.

National Parks
of The Bahamas

The Bahamas National Trust administers more than 240,000 acres in a dozen national parks and protected reserves. The trust also supports conservation education, research, policy planning, strategy development and historic preservation to protect the national heritage of The Bahamas. Membership of this non-governmental group has grown from 88 in the early 1960s to more than 3000 members today. ~ P.O. Box N 4105, Nassau, Bahamas; 393-1317.

Volunteers at **The Retreat**, the Bahamas National Trust Headquarters in Nassau, can assist with arrangements to visit the other national parks and protected areas. These include:

Grand Bahama: **Rand Nature Center**, a pine forest and coppice reserve with a resident flamingo flock; **Lucayan National Park**, a stand of ancient forest surrounding an underwater cave entrance and fronting on a secluded beach; **Peterson Cay National Park**, a small island surrounded by a spectacular reef, only accessible by boat.

The Abacos: **Bahama Parrot Preserve**, the forest habitat of the rare Bahama parrot; **Black Sound Cay**, a mangrove wildlife habitat; **Tilloo Cay National Protected Area,** a nesting area for tropical birds; **Pelican Cays Land and Sea Park**, an area of undersea caves and stunning coral reefs.

The Exumas: **Exuma Cays Land and Sea Park**, a thread of pristine cays protecting the first marine fishery reserve in the Caribbean region.

Conception Island: **Conception Island National Park**, a sanctuary for sea turtles and migratory birds, located midway between Cat Island and Long Island.

Great Inagua: **Inagua National Park**, the world's largest breeding colony of West Indian flamingos; **Union Creek Reserve**, a key nesting ground and research sight for green sea turtles.

▼▼▼▼▼▼▼▼▼▼▼▼▼▼

Outdoor Adventures

BOATING

The Bahamas, with their boundless expanses of open sea punctuated by islands with first-rate marinas, offer wonderful destinations for boat owners. Sailing yacht and sportfishing boat rentals, either bare-boat or crewed, can be arranged on any of the major islands.

Both major resorts and beachfront entrepreneurs rent all kinds of small-scale boats, from Sunfish, Sailfish and Hobie Cats to jet skis and Wave runners. Sea kayaks are growing in popularity as a means of exploring hard-to-reach bays and inlets.

BOATING EVENTS   Among the major regattas and other annual boating events held in The Bahamas throughout the year are these:

January 1   THE EXUMAS—Staniel Cay New Year's Day Cruising Regatta

January 1   NASSAU—New Year's Day Regatta

Early March   THE EXUMAS—George Town Cruising Regatta

Late March   NASSAU—Snipe Winter Championships

Mid-April   THE EXUMAS—Out Island Regatta (traditional Bahamian boats)

Mid-June   BIMINI—Phoenix Owners Rendezvous

Early July   THE ABACOS—Bahama Cup

Early July   THE ABACOS—Regatta Time in Abaco

Late July   THE EXUMAS—Black Point Regatta

Early August   ELEUTHERA—Governor's Harbour's Bay Festival

Early October   ELEUTHERA—North Eleuthera Regatta

FISHING

Sportfishing—trolling the deep waters of the Tongue of the Ocean or the Providence Channel with a huge fishing rod and reel in hopes of hooking a sailfish. Adventure writers Ernest Hemingway and Zane Grey put tiny Bimini on the map as a world-class sportfishing base, and its reputation has lost none of its luster in the years since. Great Abaco hosts major sportfishing tournaments, some of which offer seven-figure prizes. Deep-sea fishing charters are also available from Nassau, Freeport, and marinas on several Out Islands. Besides sailfish, anglers go after marlin, tuna, mahi mahi, sharks, barracuda, grouper, kingfish, wahoo and amberjack. Generally speaking, blue marlin, giant tuna and mahi mahi are best from May to July; king mackerel is best January to April, wahoo runs from November to April. White marlin can be caught in winter and spring, blue marlin during the summer months, and sailfish in summer and fall.

Until recently, the only people who had heard of bonefish were Out Island residents, who considered them barely edible trash fish. But now word has gotten out that these silver fish, weighing up to 15 pounds, can put up the kind of fight even the most jaded angler will never tire of telling about, and bonefishing has quickly become one of the most popular sports in The Bahamas. To begin with, they are so elusive that Bahamians nickname them "ghost fish." They live in deep water and come up to the shallows just offshore to feed in schools of 100 or more at unpredictable times and places. Anglers must stalk the wary fish, moving slowly and silently through waist-deep water. Bonefish are powerful and unbelievably fast swimmers, and experienced anglers claim that, pound for pound, their fighting ability is unrivaled. Bonefishing is done with a rod, reel and fly or jig, and in most places it is a catch-and-release sport. (If you try to eat one, you'll quickly find out why they got their name.) While all the major islands in The Bahamas have good bonefishing, Andros and Eleuthera are particularly known for it.

FISHING EVENTS   Among the major fishing competitions and events held in The Bahamas throughout the year are these:

Early February   BIMINI—Mid-Winter Wahoo Tournament

Mid-March   BIMINI—Bacardi Billfish Tournament

Late March   BIMINI—Hemingway Billfish Tournament

Early April   BERRY ISLANDS—Chub Cay Championship

Mid-April   THE ABACOS—Boat Harbour All Fish Tournament

Mid-April   THE ABACOS—North Abaco Championship, (part of the Bahamas Billfish Championships)

Early May   THE ABACOS—Green Turtle Club Fishing Tournament (for game fish, not turtles)

Mid-May   THE ABACOS—Treasure Cay Championship (part of the Bahamas Billfish Championships)

Early June   BIMINI—Luhrs Owners Rendezvous

Early June   THE ABACOS—Boat Harbour Championship (part of the Bahamas Billfish Championships)

Late June   ELEUTHERA—Harbour Island Championship (part of the Bahamas Billfish Championships)

Early July   THE EXUMAS—Staniel Cay Bonefish Tournament

Early August   BIMINI—Big Game Club Family Fishing Tournament and Bimini Native Fishing Tournament

Early September   BIMINI—Big Game Small B.O.A.T. Tournament

Mid-November   BIMINI—Wahoo Fishing Tournament

DIVING

Scuba diving is to The Bahamas as skiing is to Aspen. Blessed with generally ideal conditions, The Bahamas are a divers' and snorkelers' dream, and dive-trip operators are ubiquitous. From reefs to wrecks, there's a wide variety of places to explore underwater. Top dive destinations include the Abacos, Andros, the Berry Islands, Bimini, Eleuthera, Grand Bahama, Long Island, New Providence and San Salvador. Almost any island you choose will have at least one dive operator and some of the world's best scuba diving and snorkeling. While many people snorkel on their own offshore, scuba diving requires an organized trip with a divemaster who knows the waters and their hazards as well as the best places to go.

The Bahamas offer a variety of dive experiences. Among them are an impressive array of wrecks, from Civil War gunships and Prohibition-era rumrunners to boats and planes sunk intentionally for use as movie locations. And then there are the coral reefs, forestlike and teeming with colorful life. Wall dives such as the Clifton Wall, off the west tip of New Providence, offer a chance to glide down the side of a sheer cliff that drops more than a mile into the Tongue of the Ocean, an undersea Grand Canyon. There are spelunking dives in sea caves and blue holes, dives with friendly porpoises or dolphins, and dives to the purported ruins of ancient Atlantis. The biggest thrillers are the dives from New Providence, Grand Bahama and Long Island that let scuba enthusiasts swim among reef sharks, an experience offered nowhere in the world except The Bahamas. In a similar vein are the areas off New Providence and Great Exuma where stingrays cruise in large numbers.

If you don't already dive, this is a great place to try it or to get certified. Most dive operators offer complete certification courses as well as "resort courses"—one-day training sessions that qualify you to dive only with an instructor. Some scuba students opt to complete their classroom and pool instruction at home and then take their test dives in The Bahamas for full certification. Many dive operators offer full "dive packages," which include several scuba expeditions along with food and lodging. Most dive operations also offer snorkeling trips, and many resorts and beaches feature great snorkeling just offshore.

The epitome of organized snorkeling packages, **Jean-Michel Cousteau's Out Islands Snorkeling Adventures** have been offered in cooperative ventures with several Out Island resorts and inns for several years. The program has proven so successful that in 1999 the Bahamian government entered into a partnership agreement with Cousteau, sponsoring two-day, $99 programs at 25 resorts on nine islands. The programs include professional snorkeling instruction, two guided excursions, two slide presentations on Bahamian underwater ecosystems, a free T-shirt and free use of snorkeling gear and marine field guides at all participating resorts. For current program information, contact the Bahamas Out Island Promotion Board. ~ 954-359-8099, 800-688-4752.

OCEAN SAFETY

The waters of The Bahamas invite swimming, boating, scuba diving, fishing and many other recreational activities, luring water-

Legends
of Atlantis

Some visitors to The Bahamas—not to mention the promoters of the lavish Atlantis resort on Paradise Island—see a connection between the islands and the mythical lost continent of Atlantis, for which the Atlantic Ocean is named.

The Atlantis tale was first recorded in 380 B.C. by the ancient Greek philosopher Plato, perhaps based on an older myth or dimly remembered historical event. It became popular again during the Classical Revival of the 18th century. Some European explorers speculated that survivors of the earthquake and flood that destroyed Atlantis might have traveled just 650 miles by boat, hugging the coastline of Cuba most of the way, to become the Maya pyramid-builders of the Yucatán.

In the early 20th century, Rudolf Steiner, Swiss philosopher and founder of the Waldorf Schools, claimed visionary knowledge of Atlantis and believed a race of clairvoyant humans who had lived there was the source of all civilization. American psychic Edgar Cayce also described Atlantis, adding such details as when the continent sank: 9500 B.C. Twenty-nine years before the event, Cayce predicted the exact place (Bimini) and year (1968) when ruins of Atlantis would be discovered.

That year, a pilot for a scientific expedition reported what appeared to be a half-mile-long undersea "highway" of huge, square, evenly aligned stone blocks. Divers confirmed the phenomenon, now called the Bimini Road, and found other formations resembling ancient stone columns, archway keystones, sculptures and other artifacts in areas off Bimini that would have been dry land 11,000 years ago. Atlantis myths have spread so far that teachers in Bahamian public schools devote a good deal of classroom time to debunking them.

Strange. But true? If there were sunken cities, they would now be badly eroded and probably encased in an undersea layer of coral, sand and sediment. Those whose imaginations can admit the possibility of Atlantis point out that the vast coral banks did sink into the sea after the last Ice Age around 9500 B.C.—as some say Atlantis did.

In June 1998, archaeologists using side-scan sonar to survey an area 110 feet below the surface and 25 miles off the Bimini coast found what appear to be the remains of at least 15 buildings, a pyramid, an 18-foot spire and other seemingly manmade stonework. Today, the sheer number of strange stone artifacts is making it harder and harder for skeptics to scoff at the idea of a megalithic civilization in The Bahamas, and new archaeological expeditions to Bimini are being organized every year.

sports enthusiasts from all over the world to enjoy the beaches, the water and the coral reefs. Whether you're out for a short swim, a sail or a deep dive it is prudent to be aware of the risks the ocean presents. The western shore of most islands, commonly though inaccurately called the "Caribbean side" is calmer, with little wave action or undertow. The eastern shore, or "Atlantic side," may have strong waves and treacherous undertows. Enter the water on the "Atlantic side" with extreme caution. Many accidents can be avoided by approaching the ocean with respect for its power as well as appreciation for its beauty.

Because of the rich abundance of undersea life, most injuries result not from hazardous water conditions but from cuts, bites and stings. Around coral reefs, wear something to protect your feet against painful coral cuts. The popular "reef shoes" are ideal, and tennis shoes also work well. If you do sustain a coral cut, clean it with hydrogen peroxide, then apply an antiseptic or antibiotic ointment. This is also the proper treatment in the rare event of an octopus bite. If infection does appear, see a doctor immediately.

If you step on the sharp, painful spines of a sea urchin, soaking the affected area in very hot water for 15 to 90 minutes will draw the toxin out. Another remedy is to apply undiluted vinegar, ammonia or even urine. If these preliminary treatments don't work, consult a doctor.

A far more painful injury, and one that always calls for medical treatment, can be inflicted by the sharp, poisonous tail spine of a stingray. These creatures are not aggressive and prefer to bask peacefully on shallow, sandy sea floors. They will strike if a bather kneels or steps down on them directly, so it is better when walking in shallow water to shuffle your feet in a way that will send stingrays scooting off to safety.

THREE

History and Culture

COLUMBUS AND THE LUCAYANS Christopher Columbus wrote in his ship's log, "The shores are embellished with lofty palm trees, whose shade gives a delicious freshness to the air and the birds and flowers are uncommon and beautiful. I was so delighted with the scene, that I had almost come to the resolution of staying there for the remainder of my days; for believe me, Sire, these countries far surpass all the rest of the world in beauty and conveniency."

A national monument on the Bahamian island of San Salvador marks the spot where Columbus and his crew made their first landfall in the New World. (Some modern historians believe that the first landing actually took place on neighboring Cat Island, which is called San Salvador on some old maps.) They were met by a party of Lucayan Indians, of whom Columbus observed, "They should be good servants. . . . With fifty men they would all be kept in subjection and forced to do whatever may be wished."

About 40,000 Lucayans lived on the scattered islands of The Bahamas when Columbus arrived. They were a subgroup of the Arawak people, who inhabited Hispañola, Cuba, Jamaica and Puerto Rico. Until quite recently, archaeologists believed that the first Lucayans had fled to The Bahamas from the Lesser Antilles in the 10th century to escape their ancestral enemies, the Carib Indians, who were described by Spanish explorers as fierce warriors and, worse yet, cannibals. A series of newly discovered sites has convinced experts that the Lucayans inhabited The Bahamas much earlier than previously supposed, with major migrations from Cuba in the 4th century and from Hispañola in the 7th century. The Lucayans (the name meant "Island People" in the Arawak language) lived simply and peacefully in caves, where they left mysterious petroglyphs on the smoke-stained stone walls, and in small fishing villages of round thatch-roofed huts, until the day the *Nina*, the *Pinta* and the *Santa María* arrived. Within a mere 25 years the entire tribe would be wiped out.

Believing himself to be among the outer islands of Japan, Columbus island-hopped his way through the southern Bahamas for two weeks in October of 1492. Finding no gold, his initial enthusiasm quickly waned. He gave Spanish names to the major islands and then moved on to Hispañola, the big island to the south that today is divided between Haiti and the Dominican Republic. There, he established the first colonial city in the Western Hemisphere, with himself as governor. He also found mountains that contained meager deposits of gold ore. Taking advantage of the local Indians' gentle nature, he put them to work in the mines. When they all died within three years, Spanish eyes looked north toward The Bahamas and their inhabitants with renewed interest.

In 1495, soon after Columbus had relinquished his governorship and returned to Spain, the new governor sent a party of colonists to build a Spanish settlement on the southern end of Cat Island in The Bahamas. The town, called Columba, became the terminus for shipment of enslaved Lucayans bound for the mines. As many as five ships per day left Columba for Hispañola, their holds packed with Indian slaves.

On his fourth and last voyage to the New World, in 1504, Columbus found that six out of seven Indians in The Bahamas and the Caribbean were no longer alive. By 1520, the last Lucayans were gone. The handful of Spanish settlers in Columba had completely depopulated The Bahamas in a single generation. Pointed to the high death rate in the mines as proof that Indians were not durable enough to make good slaves, colonial leaders sought permission from the King of Spain to implement a different plan. By 1512, shiploads of slaves were being brought from Africa—first to replace the Indians in the mines of Hispañola and later to work in sugar cane fields throughout the Caribbean.

PIRATES' PARADISE   Following the demise of the Indian slave trade, Columba struggled along as a farming village. The biggest excitement of the decade was when explorer Juan Ponce de León stopped by on his way to the Florida coast in search of the fabled "fountain of youth." But the discovery of gold in Mexico in 1520 and Peru in 1531 promised the kind of opportunities that could never be found on Cat Island, and many residents moved on to the new colonies. As the first landfall of many Spanish ships riding the Gulf Stream across the Atlantic to the New World, Columba's remaining residents eked out small profits selling fresh water and firewood to passing ships. The population continued to dwindle, and by 1580, Columba had become a ghost town.

In colonizing the New World, Spain's century-long head start over its enemies, England and France, was secured by the Spanish Armada. The most powerful naval fleet of the time not only protected Spanish treasure galleons but also denied enemy ships access to Atlantic shipping routes. The Armada was defeated in a 1588 naval battle. It touched off a war between England and Spain that would rage throughout the Caribbean for the next 16 years, through the end of Queen Elizabeth I's reign.

Captain John Sayle sent ten tons of cut hardwood back to the Puritans to help raise money for Harvard College.

The British Parliament was reluctant to finance expeditions to America, so no permanent English-speaking colony was established there during Queen Elizabeth's lifetime. But British businessmen were more than willing to put up funding for "privateers," mercenary warships chartered by the government to rob the Spanish galleons that were engaged in the seemingly endless enterprise of transporting the treasure of the Aztecs and Incas to Europe. Officially sanctioned, corporate-sponsored pirates quickly found that The Bahamas afforded ideal hideouts—close to the main shipping lanes, yet scattered enough to be impossible for the Spaniards to patrol.

Lacking natural resources, The Bahamas continued to be a no-man's-land for many years after the war between England and Spain ended. Stripped of their royal authority and commercial backing, the English privateers based in the islands turned to freelance piracy against Spanish treasure galleons. Sir Walter Raleigh enlisted the aid of John Watts, a privateer based on the Bahamian island of San Salvador, to provide supplies for his Roanoake colony, the first English settlement in America, which failed under mysterious circumstances and is now remembered as the "lost colony."

In 1629, England's King Charles I made Sir Robert Heath governor of Carolina Colony and threw in the islands of The Bahamas as an afterthought. France soon laid claim to the same islands, and Spain had never relinquished its claim to them. But nobody actually settled in The Bahamas until the 1640s, when a group of clergymen in nearby Bermuda declared their congregation's independence from the Church of England and began organizing an expedition to find an island where they could establish a utopian colony.

The first group of 26 Bermudian pioneers set sale in 1647, calling themselves The Company of Adventurers for the Plantation of the Islands of Eleutheria (Greek for "freedom"). Their "Articles and Orders" created the first true democracy in the Western Hemisphere—on paper, at least, but by the time they reached their first landfall, on an island that may have been Great Abaco or New Providence, the band had split into two rival factions. The breakaway group stayed in the northern islands, while the Eleutherians' original leader, Captain John Sayle, led his group onward to the island now called Eleuthera, where they were shipwrecked and stranded. Those who stayed relied on a huge amount of provisions sent to them by New England Puritans in 1650.

The Eleutherian settlers of both factions led a Robinson Crusoe existence, surviving on wild fruit, and many left after a few years for better conditions in New England or back home in Bermuda. After a few years another group of 300 came to join them. Then Bermuda sent many of its most incorrigible slaves and all free blacks to the island, and some historians believe that the New England and Virginia colonies also exiled their troublesome slaves to The Bahamas. Captain Sayle himself finally gave up and returned to Bermuda in 1657. By 1670, the total population of The Bahamas was about 200, 60 percent of whom were black. Spanish warships burned the original Eleutherian villages to the ground in 1684, but by that time scattered settlements had appeared all along Eleuthera's coastline and neighboring cays.

The Eleutherians were the first people whom Bahamians call the Old Inhabitants—those who settled The Bahamas before the American Revolution. Sadly, none of them obtained legal title to their land. In 1670, King Charles II granted all of The Bahamas to a group of six British noblemen led by Anthony Lord Ashley, the Lord Proprietor of Carolina. The Proprietors, as the group came to be called, were attracted to New Providence Island because of its sheltered all-weather harbor. They established a commercial port on the site of present-day Nassau and named it Charles Town. Though none of the Proprietors ever lived in The Bahamas, they financed an expedition to bring 300 settlers from Bermuda.

The new seaport was inhabited not by idealistic farmers like the Eleutherians but by seafarers who had little use for laws and governments, so the absentee Proprietors lost control of the new colony almost immediately. Without legal authority, the local residents elected their own governor, sea captain John Wentworth, even though they knew that another governor, legally appointed by the Proprietors, was en route from England. When the official governor died at sea the proprietors had little choice but to confirm Wentworth's governorship. Ironically, when Wentworth began to take his responsibilities to the Proprietors seriously and enforce tax laws, the locals rebelled and he was removed from office. The new governor sent to replace him outraged the populace with his attempts to reform their "lewd, licentious" lifestyle and was shanghaied onto a ship bound for Jamaica, never to return. In 1685, the name of the port was changed to Nassau to honor of William, Prince of Orange-Nassau, the successor to the throne of England. But four years later, at nearly the same moment William was crowned king, Spanish gunships destroyed Nassau.

From the beginning, the most lucrative business in Nassau had been "wrecking"—salvaging the cargos of ships that broke up on the treacherous reefs of the Bahama Banks. The salvage business often bordered on piracy. Tales were recorded of islanders setting up false lighthouses and moving channel markers to lure ships onto the reefs. The wreckers often saved a ship's goods before attempting to rescue its passengers. Spain, which still claimed ownership of The Bahamas, took the position that the English colonists had no legal salvage rights to Spanish vessels. Declaring Nassau a pirate stronghold, Spanish authorities sent ships in 1689 to raid the town, burning every building to the ground, kidnapping the governor and carrying away about half the black population to slavery in the cane fields of the Caribbean. A month later, the ships returned to round up the rest of the blacks. The inhabitants who survived the raids scattered to homestead other islands.

At the end of the 17th century, the abandoned port of Nassau caught the interest of another group of seafaring entrepreneurs. Although piracy was illegal, for more than a hundred years Great Britain had been licensing privateers to attack enemy shipping in wartime. In 1688, Great Britain went to war against France, making French ships fair game for British "rovers," who patrolled the region in such profusion that, according to most estimates, the number of privateer ships in the Atlantic and the Caribbean exceeded the number of merchant ships sailing in the same regions. Although the tactics of the privateers were the same as those of pirates, patriotic motives made privateering an honorable—and profitable—profession. Two years after its first destruction, Nassau was rebuilt by a group of settlers from Jamaica who planned to make it a privateering capital.

By 1697, rovers were based out of Nassau in such numbers that the port, though still small, enjoyed one of the highest levels of prosperity in the American colonies. But these glory days lasted only a few years before the French and Spanish navies joined forces to destroy what they viewed as a pirates' haven. In 1703, they wiped out Nassau and most of its residents for the second time. News of the destruction was slow to reach the Proprietors, who appointed a new governor about three months after the town was destroyed. The governor arrived to find New Providence Island deserted and, after sleeping in the woods for several months, flagged down a ship to carry him back to Carolina. After that, the Proprietors abandoned their claim to The Bahamas.

Before the end of the year 1703, many of the privateers who had formerly based out of Nassau returned and proclaimed it a "Privateers' Republic" without laws or government. Surviving renewed Spanish naval attacks in 1704 and 1706, the port flourished until the end of the War of Spanish Succession in 1714, when England signed a peace treaty with Spain. News of the treaty was slow in reaching the New World, and even slower in getting to ships at sea. Privateer Henry Jennings thought he was just doing his job in 1715 when he attacked a Spanish salvage operation and made off with 5,350,000 pieces of eight. But when he sailed victoriously into port in Jamaica, he found that the British colonial government had branded him a pirate and issued arrest warrants for him and his crew. He quickly set sail for the twice-abandoned port of Nassau, where there was no government to answer to.

Other pirates who enjoy places in Bahamian legend include Anne Bonney and Mary Read, women who wore men's clothes—itself a felony in those days—and were reputed to be fiercer and bloodthirstier than their male counterparts.

In peacetime, many rovers found their ships, their crews and their own temperaments better suited to piracy than to mercantile trade. Some, like Jennings, turned their backs on England and took to raiding British tobacco ships from nearby Carolina, selling their booty to the Dutch. Under Jennings's leadership, The Bahamas was transformed from a "Privateers' Republic" to a "Pirates' Republic," a brawling, lawless town where bars and brothels were the main businesses.

At least 20 pirate ships, crewed by more than 1400 men, operated openly out of Nassau. The notorious pirate Edward "Blackbeard" Teach proclaimed himself magistrate of Nassau and enforced his own brand of law to maintain peace between the various pirate crews.

LOYALISTS AND SLAVES Responding to myriad complaints of piracy, the King of England in 1718 declared The Bahamas a Crown Colony independent of Carolina and appointed former privateer Woodes Rogers as Royal Governor of the islands to restore the rule of law. Arriving in Nassau with a fleet of four battleships bristling with cannons, Rogers offered amnesty for past crimes to all pirates who would surrender; those who would not, he announced, would be hanged and their ships sunk. After a brief, fierce battle, some 300 pirates gave up. Others slipped out of port in the night. They, along with those such as Blackbeard who were at sea when Rogers arrived, moved to other bases in the Caribbean. (Some moved only as far as Harbor Island, 60 miles away.)

About the same time, Great Britain and her allies again went to war against Spain, so Rogers' next order of business was to build Fort Nassau, the first of several fortifications designed to repel attacks from both pirates and Spanish warships. When the Spanish war fleet reached Nassau in 1720, loaded with so many soldiers that they outnumbered the island residents three to one, they were put to flight by Rogers' ragtag army of ex-pirates, who welcomed the chance to fight the Spanish once more.

His mission accomplished, Rogers fell ill and returned to England, where he found himself jobless, declared bankruptcy and went to debtor's prison. Bahamians petitioned the king to reappoint Rogers as their governor. He returned in 1729, opened the first House of Assembly in The Bahamas—one of the oldest standing legislatures in the New World—and presided over the colony until his death. The Assembly adopted the official motto coined by Rogers: "Expulsis Piratis, Restituta Commercia" ("Pirates Expelled, Commerce Restored.") The words still appear on the great seal of The Bahamas today.

The problem was, once piracy was laid to rest, The Bahamas had no economic base and few natural resources with which to create one. The soil was so meager that farming never rose above the subsistence level. The only products Bahamians exported to the mainland during the 18th century were salt, turtle shell, hardwoods and dye woods. The main industry, as always, was salvaging goods from shipwrecks.

Although a return of privateering in connection with a string of European conflicts including the War of Jenkins' Ear (1738), the War of the Austrian Succession (1748) and the Seven Years' War (1756) brought intermittent prosperity to the port, Bahamians found themselves back in desperate poverty each time Great Britain declared peace.

By 1772, the government was on the verge of collapse. The courts closed, the salaries of government officials went unpaid, and at last, the governor disbanded Nassau's 13-man militia because there was no money in the treasury to pay their salaries, which totaled £20 a month. The following year, The Bahamas declared bankruptcy. Then matters grew even worse as hostilities mounted between Great Britain and its colonies on the American mainland, and American merchant ships stopped coming to Nassau. All commerce in The Bahamas came to a standstill.

The American navy attacked Nassau in 1776 and easily seized the fort, harbor and town and kidnapped the governor. They were after the defunct militia's last 24 barrels of gunpowder. Nassau was "occupied" while American officers socialized with town officials and sailor crews caroused their way through the bars and brothels of Bay Street. Two weeks later they sailed away. Nobody died in battle on either side, though history records that ten American sailors died from tainted rum they had drunk in Nassau.

In 1778, another American warship sailed into Nassau Harbour, this time disguised as a merchant ship. Under cover of darkness, the Americans carried out their plan—to steal a British Navy ship that had put in at Nassau for repairs and capture Fort Nassau guarded only by two sentries. Another British warship came to the rescue, only to run aground, and the Americans sailed away with their prize.

Finally, in 1882, the American, French and Spanish navies assembled a multinational task force of 82 ships to invade Nassau, carrying 5000 men—outnumbering the entire population of The Bahamas by two to one. Again, the defenseless town was taken without bloodshed, and the islands were declared a Spanish colony. This time the conquerors made life miserable for their Bahamian enemies. Deliverance came in the form of a small band of Loyalists led by Colonel Andrew Deveaux, a former leader of South Carolina's militia. As the end of the Revolutionary War drew near, Deveaux gathered a small pro-British army of adventurers to strike a symbolic blow for the British Empire by capturing The Bahamas. By bluff and bravado rather than firepower, Deveaux captured Nassau and declared The Bahamas a haven for Loyalist expatriates from the newly constituted United States. Meanwhile, in Europe, Britain regained its legal claim to The Bahamas from Spain in the Treaty of Versailles by trading Florida for them.

After the war, wave after wave of Loyalists, who had opposed U.S. independence, fled the mainland to form pro-British settlements in The Bahamas. Many brought slaves with them. They built the colonial houses that dot the islands and gained reputations as some of the finest shipbuilders in the world. About 7000 people arrived in the islands in five years, tripling the Bahamian population.

The Loyalists, many of whom came from the Carolinas and other southern colonies, started large cotton plantations that transformed the economy and landscape of The Bahamas. By 1787, there were 128 cotton plantations large enough to keep ten or more slaves, and Bahamian planters were exporting nearly a million pounds of cotton to Great Britain each year. But in 1789, virtually all of the cotton crop failed when two tiny pests—the chenille worm, which eats cotton, and the red bug, which stains it—appeared in The Bahamas. The plague continued, and it soon became clear that cotton growing had depleted the islands' thin soil layer to the point where the plants could no longer survive. Within two decades after the first Loyalist planters arrived the last cotton plantations had been abandoned. While many Loyalists moved away from the islands, others stayed to become the colonial business and political elite of The

Bahamas. The slaves and their descendants would transform the demographics of The Bahamas. The Loyalists who remained made up a majority of the early political and business elite.

The failure of the cotton plantations left The Bahamas with a large surplus of slaves, and ambitious public works projects were dreamed up as ways to make them earn their keep. Most of the massive stone government buildings in downtown Nassau were erected between 1790 and 1813. A force of 600 slaves worked for 16 years to chop a roadway through the limestone ridge that separated the town from the rest of the island; the abolition of slavery left the project unfinished.

Not all blacks came to The Bahamas as slaves. By the end of the 18th century enough information had filtered back to Africa so that many people knew of the fate that awaited slaves in the New World. Shipboard revolts had grown so common that English slave ships could no longer get insurance. When captive Africans with no navigation knowledge seized a slave ship, the Gulf Stream carried them to The Bahamas, where many stayed rather than risk recapture or prosecution for mutiny.

In 1807, the slave trade was prohibited throughout the British Empire. This did not mean freedom for those born into slavery, but it did mean that when the British Navy caught a ship trying to smuggle slaves to the United States, the captive Africans were released and allowed to stay in The Bahamas as free citizens. Slaves were emancipated in The Bahamas in 1834, nearly three decades earlier than in the United States, inspiring a mass exodus of white Loyalists, and leaving a racial mix in the islands substantially the same as it is today. Black members were voted into the House of Assembly from the first election after emancipation, but voting districts were manipulated to assure that they would remain a small minority in the legislature. The racial balance of the legislature was in inverse proportion to the islands' population makeup and would stay that way for more than a century.

SMUGGLERS' HAVEN   The Bahamas' rollercoaster economy got another big boost during the Civil War. Great Britain favored the Confederacy because the huge British textile industry depended on Southern cotton. Nassau thus became a pro-South port despite the fact that most of its population was recently freed slaves who might naturally have favored Northern goals. The Union imposed a total embargo on Confederate ports throughout the war, and only small, fast boats had a chance of slipping past the naval blockade.

Smuggling became a respectable profession in The Bahamas beginning with the U.S. Civil War. Blockade runners would cover the distance of 560 miles from Charleston to Nassau with full loads of cotton, transfer them to big British oceangoing vessels, and return to Charleston with supplies from England. The risks they faced were enormous, but so were the rewards. A quantity of quinine bought for $10 in Nassau could be sold for $400 in Charleston; the same $400 would buy cotton that could be sold to the British in Nassau for $4000. The huge cash flow and the riskiness of Confederate banks marked the beginning of the off-shore banking industry in Nassau.

The smuggling industry brought with it a constant flow of prosperous "business travelers" in need of food and lodging. The elegant Royal Victoria Hotel, the first large luxury hotel in Nassau, was built by the British government in 1861 to accommodate them, and Graycliff, a private mansion originally built by a retired pirate in 1720, was converted into a small luxury hotel. These two lodgings marked the beginning of the tourist trade in The Bahamas. Even after the U.S. Civil War ended and The Bahamas slipped back into the economic doldrums, wealthy American and British visitors came to the islands on cruise ships during the winter for the same sun and sea that continues to attract tourists today. Railroad and hotel tycoon Henry Flagler, who later established Palm Beach and Miami, bought the Royal Victoria from the government in 1898 and began a publicity effort in the United States to promote The Bahamas as a tourist destination.

Prohibition in the United States brought another economic boom to The Bahamas beginning in 1919 as large shipping operations were established to smuggle liquor to the mainland. Great Britain and its colonies, including The Bahamas, did not support Prohibition because it hurt sales of Scotch whisky, an important British export. The colonial government expanded Prince George Wharf, where the cruise ships now dock in Nassau, into one of the largest port facilities in the Caribbean region to accommodate the huge flow of liquor. The banking business boomed, and Nassau's first casino opened its doors. The grandiose new Colony Hotel, the first luxury beach resort in the islands, overflowed with party-minded tourists lured by the prospect of cheap, legal liquor. No doubt it was around this time that some local entrepreneur invented that great Bahamian tourist tradition, the "booze cruise."

By the time Prohibition was repealed in 1933 and the smuggling boom ended abruptly, The Bahamas had gained recognition as a high-class tourist destination. The image was enhanced in 1939 when the Duke of Windsor—formerly King Edward VIII of England—was appointed governor of the islands. Three years before, the duke had become a popular and notorious figure in the world press by abdicating the British throne to marry American divorcée Wallis Warfield Simpson. The British government thought that sending the former king to a remote island in the Atlantic would put him, and his controversial wife, out of the public eye and quiet the embarrassment to the royal family. Charles and Wallis were happy to remove themselves from Europe on the verge of World War II.

Another wealthy 1930s immigrant who benefited Bahamian tourism was Canadian-born gold tycoon Sir Harry Oakes, one of the British Commonwealth's richest citizens. Immediately upon moving to Nassau he became both a politician and a public philanthropist, sharing his wealth by building two golf courses and Nassau's first airport, keeping an eye toward tourism. In 1943, when Sir Harry was murdered in his bed, the Duke of Windsor declared that he would personally lead the investigation. A day later, Sir Harry's son-in-law was charged with the crime. Newspapers worldwide followed his month-long trial, one of the most famous events in Bahamian history. In the end, the son-in-law was acquitted, and the killer remains unknown.

World War II brought Bahamians out in full patriotic force to support Britain, as had World War I. The 300-man Bahamas Battalion, which fought in Egypt and Italy, was one of the first racially integrated combat units. On the home front, The Bahamas had strategic importance because the Providence Channel and Tongue of the Ocean, great undersea canyons that form a mile-deep labyrinth surrounded by the Bahama Banks, offered an ideal hideout for German submarines close to the United States coastline.

The U.S. Army undertook to build a large airbase, which would become Nassau International Airport after the war. The project provided plenty of jobs, putting an end to Depression-era unemployment in Nassau, but riots and looting, killing ten people, soon rocked Bay Street because the U.S. defense contractors only paid Bahamians a small fraction of what their American co-workers were earning. In the end, the governor settled the matter by ordering the minimum wage raised from four shillings a day to five shillings and a free lunch.

TOURISM EXPLODES   Nassau was already a vacation spot when Florida's Gold Coast was still a mangrove swamp. International visitors had supported one or more large luxury hotels continuously since 1844. Queen Victoria, Howard Hughes, Sir Winston Churchill, Ernest Hemingway, Zane Grey and Ian Fleming had sojourned at its elegant resort hotels. But this stately style of tourism did little to prepare the people of The Bahamas for Fidel Castro's revolution.

Until 1959, Cuba virtually monopolized big-scale tourism in the Caribbean with its glitzy casinos and tropical beach resorts just an overnight ferry cruise from Key West. The Cuban Revolution and subsequent U.S. embargo forced sunseekers to choose other beaches, and Nassau's were the easiest to reach. Sir Stafford Sands, chairman of the Bahamas Development Board, in 1960 announced his goal to boost tourism statistics from the existing level of 32,000 visitors a year to one million a year during the next decade. The U.S. air base on New Providence Island was converted into an international airport to accommodate commercial airliners. A $20 million causeway was built across the harbor to provide access to the beautiful beaches of Hog Island (which was quickly renamed Paradise Island) and the first air-conditioned resort hotels and casinos were built. Nassau's harbor was dredged so that instead of anchoring at sea and carrying passengers to shore in small boats, up to six cruise ships at a time could dock at the huge downtown wharf that had been built by rumrunners in the 1920s—just a block from the Bay Street shopping district.

Along with tourism development, Sir Stafford Sands promoted banking into The Bahamas' second-largest industry. U.S. and other foreign businessmen were drawn to Nassau banks by the anonymity, the protection from U.S. court seizures and the freedom from income and estate taxes they offered. Within a few years, branches of 400 international banks—U.S., Canadian, European, even Soviet and Chinese—were operating in Nassau. Bank franchise fees became the government's main source of revenue. The banks not only provided employment but also, far more importantly, created an almost limitless supply of loan financing for local businesses.

As Nassau tourism skyrocketed, Wallace Groves, a one-time ringleader of the Bay Street Boys, an exclusive ring of white Bahamians who controlled business and politics throughout the islands, initiated an ambitious plan to develop a tourist infrastructure similar to Nassau's on the island of Grand Bahama. The Hawksbill Creek Agreement authorized Groves' timber company to clear-cut the forests of Grand Bahama and also gave him control over the water supply, public utilities, land development and business licensing on the western third of the island. In exchange, Groves agreed to build a deep-water cruise ship port. Groves also built an international airport, an international duty-free shopping district and four golf courses, all in the name of the Grand Bahama Port Authority, a private corporation controlled by Groves and his associates. Tourist response to the promotion of Grand Bahama was lukewarm at first, but when the island's first casino opened in 1963 business boomed. The powers granted by the Hawksbill Creek Agreement were so vast that Grand Bahama has become virtually independent from the rest of The

People
to
People

As a visitor to The Bahamas, it's easy to find yourself isolated in one of the islands' compact, self-contained tourist zones, where the only genuine Bahamians you're likely to meet are food servers and retail clerks. If you want to experience the real world as local residents know it, the Bahamas Ministry of Tourism has pioneered a unique program just for you.

More than 1000 volunteers from all walks of life—from preachers and lawyers to farmers and lobster fishermen—participate in the People-to-People program on New Providence, Grand Bahama, Eleuthera, Great Abaco, Great Exuma, Bimini and San Salvador. Given two weeks' advance notice (it can be done at the last minute, though the agency does not recommend it), the tourist office on any of these islands will arrange a visit with a volunteer host.

The agency plays matchmaker between visitors and volunteers based on age, interests, hobbies, occupation or religious affiliation. Volunteers plan the activities they want to share. They pick you up at a prearranged place and time and may bring you home for dinner or invite you to join a family gathering, attend a church service or spend some time at their workplace.

Besides individually arranged activities, the program includes People-to-People Tea Parties, traditionally attended by the Governor General's wife, at Nassau's Government House on the last Friday of each month from January to August. There, guests mingle with locals amid arts-and-crafts displays and entertainment.

Participation in the program is free. No lodging is offered. For a People-to-People application form, write Bahamian Ministry of Tourism, P.O. Box N-3701, Nassau, The Bahamas, or call 326-5371.

Bahamas, with its own quasi-government and its own set of rules, often creating political friction between Grand Bahama and the capital.

Sir Stafford Sands' goal of a million international visitors to The Bahamas annually was realized in 1968, two years ahead of schedule. The figure would rise to two million a year by 1980 and three million by 1986, peaking in the early 1990s at 3,400,000 a year—more than 100 times the 1950s level!

But with prosperity came social discontent as Bahamians watched the small white ruling class grow obscenely rich by exploiting the islands and their people. The time was ripe for the political change that would sweep British colonialism into oblivion.

BAHAMIAN INDEPENDENCE   The Bahamas did not have political parties distinct from Great Britain's Labor and Conservative parties before 1953. The colony was run by a parliament dominated by British appointees and the Bay Street Boys. In 1953, a coalition of black politicians banded together to form the opposition Progressive Liberal Party (PLP), forcing the Bay Street Boys to formalize their political machine as the United Bahamian Party (UBP) as they faced their first partisan elections.

The UBP held onto its power easily for more than a decade, largely because of constitutional provisions that only males who owned real estate could vote. In 1961, a suffragette movement led by Dr. Doris Johnson triumphed and won women the right to vote. Then in 1967, flamboyantly charismatic PLP leader Lynden Pindling, seen by many as the George Washington of The Bahamas, succeeded in eliminating the property ownership qualification, giving many black Bahamians the right to vote for the first time. And vote they did: the same year, Lynden Pindling was elected Premier of The Bahamas. Doris Johnson subsequently became President of the Senate.

Bahamian independence, a notion that seemed to inspire more enthusiasm in the British government with its teetering postcolonial economy than among the people of the islands, became a reality as a result of a narrow victory in a September 1972 public referendum. The Bahamas legally became its own nation on July 10, 1973, which is celebrated as Bahamian Independence Day. Pindling continued as premier, a position he would hold for 20 more years. The Bahamas continues to have a symbolic link to Great Britain as a member of the British Commonwealth, a worldwide alliance of former English colonies that pledge their allegiance to Queen Elizabeth II.

With a long tradition of smuggling, it was perhaps inevitable that The Bahamas would be affected by the explosive growth in the international drug trade. The islands provided a long, safe 750-mile corridor from the Caribbean to a point within small-boat range of the shores of Florida—all without a single customs inspection. Bahamian banks provided handy money-laundering facilities beyond the reach of the U.S. Internal Revenue Service.

Scandal rocked the Pindling administration in 1984 with the discovery that Columbian cocaine traffickers had corrupted the Bahamian government at the highest levels. Two ministers resigned, though no involvement on Pindling's part was ever proven. In the wake of the scandal, the United States Drug Enforcement Administration (DEA) moved into The Bahamas in force. U.S. Air Force jets were allowed to monitor small aircraft movements in Bahamian airspace, and in 1987 the government agreed to let the U.S. Navy impose a blockade around the islands of Bimini and search all arriving and departing boats.

Thanks primarily to tourism, Bahamians enjoy the lowest unemployment rates and the highest standard of living of any Western Hemisphere country except the United States and Canada.

Today, the DEA shares its Nassau headquarters with the Bahamian police academy and plays a major role in cadet training. Prospective builders or purchasers of marinas and airstrips must first obtain DEA clearance. The extent of Bahamian government cooperation with U.S. drug enforcement authorities is perhaps the most hotly contested political issue in The Bahamas.

In 1992, Lynden Pindling suffered a trouncing defeat at the hands of conservative Hubert Alexander Ingraham and his Free National Movement (FNM) party, which had been formed 20 years earlier by a coalition of black and white opponents of the independence movement, and had absorbed the Bay Street Boys' United Bahamian Party. The FNM leadership favors policies that promote increased international trade, industrialization and real estate development; many charge that it has also passed punitive restrictions to hamper economic development on other islands where voters opposed the FNM in the 1992 elections. But Ingraham had larger problems on his hands. After 24 years of FNM rule, The Bahamas had a national debt exceeding one billion dollars. To make matters worse, the day after Ingraham was inaugurated, Hurricane Andrew struck, causing such devastation that for several years the populated parts of the islands took on the look of a vast construction site.

The FNM has implemented aggressive policy of tourism development. With a 1993 law called the Hotels Encouragement Act, the government began allowing materials and equipment for hotel construction to be imported duty-free and provides financing through special banking provisions. Since then, more than $200 million worth of new hotel construction and upgrading has been completed. Many resorts that were formerly government-owned have been sold to international corporations, and the Grand Bahama Port Authority, the corporation through which the late Wallace Grove wielded governmentlike powers under the Hawksbill Creek Agreement, has entered into partnership with a Hong Kong financial corporation to create the world's largest container shipment port and new resort development in Freeport/ Lucaya. Most significantly, hotels can qualify for aid under the new policies with as few as five guest rooms, as the Bahamian government undertakes its first serious attempt to develop low-impact, nature- and adventure-oriented ecotourism in the Out Islands.

Spokespersons for the Bahamian tourist industry express growing unease over the possibility that the islands' booming economy may collapse if and when the United States normalizes relations with Cuba, which dominated Caribbean cruise ship and resort tourism until Castro's 1959 revolution. Their strategy to protect Bahamian tourism in this event is twofold: first, to develop major resorts, such as Atlantis, which Cuban resort hotels cannot compete with, and second, to stimulate ecotourism, displaying The Bahamas' natural wonders to maximum advantage. The Ministry of Tourism has created a separate division devoted exclusively to environment-oriented, sustainable tourism. Hotel operators are encouraged to participate in solar energy seminars and "green management" workshops. Noting that environmental tourism is growing 30 percent a year—more than six times the rate for conventional tourism—Ministry of Tourism representatives point out that birdwatching has overtaken golf as a tourist draw.

Culture

PEOPLE

About 295,000 people live in The Bahamas today. Close to 60 percent make their homes on New Providence, mostly in greater Nassau. Another 25 percent live on Grand Bahama, the island with the fastest growing population thanks to industrial development. The other roughly 40,000 people are scattered among the Out Islands, where the biggest settlements are on Great Abaco, Andros, Eleuthera and Exuma.

It is often said that 85 percent of Bahamians are of African descent, the legacy of the many slaves freed in The Bahamas in the early 19th century. The exact racial demographics of the islands today are unknown because, since independence, census surveys and other government forms do not ask about race. At any rate, the population is overwhelmingly black—"no matter what colour their skin might be," as Bahamians say with a twinkle in their eye.

Turning their backs on centuries of exploitation under British rule, today's residents reject all racial discrimination and simply separate the world into "Bahamians" and "Visitors." Interracial marriages, a common practice for generations on some Out Islands, are widely accepted. Black and white aside, the main ethnic minorities are Greek and Chinese. Haitian refugees flock to The Bahamas illegally in large numbers to escape the Caribbean's poorest country in favor of the richest. Widely despised and exploited, they now form a sizeable new underclass. Human rights activists report that more than 90 percent of the inmates in The Bahamas' notoriously brutal prison system are Haitian.

If Bahamians do not talk about race, they make up for it by discussing religion ceaselessly. Churches, more than any other institution, bind the island society together. It is not unusual to find church news headlined on the front pages of Nassau and Freeport newspapers and world events buried on page 12. Two-thirds of Bahamians attend Baptist churches. Anglican and Catholic churches are found throughout the islands, along with growing numbers of evangelical and Mormon missions. Nassau also has small congregations of most other faiths, including Judaism and Bahaism, and Paradise Island has a Hindu ashram known locally as "Club Meditation." Obeah, a folk religion with African roots, is one of the few topics Bahamians avoid discussing with visitors. Obeah rituals were illegal under British rule, and since independence attempts to decriminalize it have failed because of powerful Baptist Church opposition.

School attendance is compulsory through age 16, and the education level in The Bahamas is admirable. The College of The Bahamas only offers degrees related to hotel and restaurant management, attracting students from all over the Caribbean. Bahamians who wish to major in academic or technical subjects attend other regional schools such as the University of the West Indies or schools in the United States. The Bahamas host program, sponsored by the Ministry of Tourism, trains taxi drivers, tour guides and others involved in the tourism industry.

CUISINE

Seafood reigns supreme in The Bahamas. Almost all other food is imported from abroad and priced accordingly. A cheeseburger often costs more than lobster tail.

The country's leading export is spiny lobsters, known locally as "crawfish" although they are not the same species as the freshwater crustacean that goes by that name in some parts of the United States. More than three million pounds of lobster tails are shipped from the islands each year. Fishermen are only allowed to take lobsters that measure at least 8.75 inches long, and those of marginal size are sold to local restaurants instead of exporters. Throughout the August-to-March lobster season, lobster tails are abundant and cost about the same as shrimp. They are broiled and served whole, sliced into bite-size pieces and "steamed" (stewed), or "minced" (shredded, cooked with tomatoes, onions and peppers, and served in the shell).

The mainstay of the local diet is the queen conch (pronounced "conk"), a large mollusk found in enormous numbers in the shallows of the Bahama Banks. Unlike lobster, conch cannot be exported because the local price is far below the price that could be obtained on the world market. The government fears that exports would push the local price sky-high and attract corporate fishing operations, putting local conch fishermen out of business. So much conch is eaten in The Bahamas that disposing of the shells (the ones that aren't sold to tourists) has become one of the islands' biggest environmental problems. Served at virtually all restaurants and innumerable roadside stands, conch dishes are generally the cheapest items on the menu—and the tastiest.

Conch is prepared in enough different ways to fill a cookbook. It may be chopped, marinated in lime juice and spices and served raw in a salad, or the conch fillet may be "scorched" (tenderized with a mallet), grilled and served whole with the creature's single inedible leg left intact to use as a handle when eating it. "Steamed" conch is ground or finely chopped and stewed with vegetables and spices. Conch chowder is similar but contains more liquid and is served in a bowl instead of on a plate. "Cracked" conch is sliced into strips and deep-fried, as are conch fritters, smaller fried tidbits served on toothpicks as appetizers to be dipped in spicy pepper sauce. Conch is also used in place of meat in a wide range of international dishes; you're likely to run across curried conch, conch chow mein, linguini with conch sauce, conch submarine sandwiches and conch pizza. Probably because of the distinctly Freudian appearance of the shell opening, Bahamians believe that conch is an aphrodisiac. Skeptical? There's only one way to find out. . . .

Of the myriad scalefish that inhabit the Bahama Banks, only a few species are favored for eating. By far the most popular, grouper is usually sliced into strips and batter fried to make "grouper fingers." Snapper, grunt and jack appear on menus generically as "fish" and are most often served in raw fish salads or steamed like conch. Shark meat is used in curries and other spicy sauces. Game fish such as barracuda and swordfish may appear as daily specials in finer restaurants.

For a change of pace from seafood, restaurants may offer a few chicken, lamb, goat or pork selections. Whatever the entrée, it is accompanied by "peas 'n rice." The peas are pigeon peas, which look much like blackeyed peas but taste different. Peas 'n rice, flavored with salt pork, tends to be greasy; diet-conscious diners may opt for yellow "spicy rice," flavored with a mild curry powder. At local eateries, meals usually come with pan-fried bread called johnnycakes. The typical breakfast consists of tuna and grits, corned beef and grits, or just plain grits. The traditional dessert is guava duff (usually just called "duff"), a jelly-roll of bread pudding and minced guava, smothered in rum and butter sauce and served warm.

Chief among other Bahamian favorites that may defy conventional mainland tastes is *souse*, a tangy stew made from spare chicken, pork, lamb or goat parts. Sheep souse, whose basic ingredient is chopped sheep tongue, is considered a special delicacy. Another local favorite likely to gross out visitors is spiced pig's head. Wild boar meat is common on some Out Islands where hunters stalk the giant boars through the coppice. Genetic throwbacks from domestic pigs brought to Bahamian plantations more than 200 years ago, the huge boars are the most dangerous land dwellers on the islands, and every order of boar meat seems to come with a heroic tale of how the monster was hunted down.

Locals spice up just about everything in a fiery yellow pepper sauce made from several varieties of Bahamian chilis including bird peppers, bonnet peppers and lady finger peppers. It is universally assumed that tourists do not like hot peppers, and if you ask for hot sauce in a restaurant you will usually receive a bottle of Tabasco diluted with vinegar. For the genuine item you must request "pepper sauce."

The Bahamian national beverage, Kalik beer, is brewed on New Providence and served chilled. Rum is distilled on New Providence and Grand Bahama from sugar cane imported from other Caribbean islands. It is often flavored with pineapple, coconut, banana, mango or lemon to make a potent dessert liqueur. Locals like to drink gin and coconut water, though among tourists this strange concoction cannot rival sweet, fruity boat drinks like the Bahama Mama.

English is the official language of The Bahamas, and most locals **LANGUAGE** are fluent in two different versions. Bahamian Standard English (BSE), or Queen's English, is taught in schools and used to conduct government and banking business and communicate with U.S. and Canadian tourists. Bahamian dialect, which locals of all races use in everyday conversation, is intentionally incomprehensible to outsiders. Accents and slang words differ between islands. In some Out Island towns with a strong Loyalist heritage, the local dialect sounds almost Shakespearean.

Even today, many residents of the more remote Out Islands speak only the local dialect, and particularly if you travel by mailboat you may have conversations in which you can't understand a word. That's okay. Out Islanders are friendly and curious about visitors and will do their best to hurdle the dialect barrier, even if it means repeating the same incomprehensible sentence two dozen times. Simply talk in your own version of English and allow tone of voice and gestures to carry the communication.

MUSIC

The musical art form of goombay combines Africa's tribal heritage and the American Indian and British colonial influences of the New World. Goombay is the Bantu word for "rhythm" and the name given to the particular type of African drum used in the music.

The goatskin goombay drum is the centerpiece of the gentle rolling rhythm of this type of Bahamian music. The melody in goombay is typically produced by either a piano, a guitar or a saxophone and often accompanied by the beat of bongos, maracas and rhythm sticks (called "click sticks").

Many Bahamians believe the term "junkanoo" was derived from John Canoe, an African freedom fighter.

The musical form of junkanoo is derived from the traditions of goombay. Until the 1940s, the name junkanoo was reserved for the festival and parade that celebrates Boxing Day, the day after Christmas. The goombay music and dancing that were the core of this procession strayed from its traditional style into a louder, more rapid and cacophonous musical sound that assumed the name junkanoo.

During World War II, Bahamian musicians colored the sounds of junkanoo even more by adding a piano, electric bass and guitar to many ensembles. From there, junkanoo evolved into what is today the most predominant musical form in The Bahamas. On any given night on New Providence or Grand Bahama, you can probably hear goombay or junkanoo at one of the resorts or local nightclubs. In the Out Islands, ask if there's local music anywhere.

The Bahamas host a year-round assortment of musical events, including these:

February　Music lovers enjoy the **Nassau Music Society Presents** recitals featuring international classical stars.

March　Nassau's **Bahamas Concert Orchestra** presents an opportunity to hear classical music performed by talented local musicians.

May　The Queen Elizabeth Sports Center near Nassau is the site of the **Caribbean Muzik Festival**, three days of music featuring more than 30 of the region's hottest goombay, soca, reggae, swing, roots, calypso and junkanoo performers.

June　The **Goombay Summer Festival** in Nassau kicks off in June and continues through four months of Bahamian musical events. Nassau's **Bahamas Heritage Music Festival** brings the sounds of Bahamian musicians to the capital.

July   Grand Bahama Island boasts its own **Jazz Festival,** with new and veteran jazz musicians from around the world.

August   The **Coca Cola Bash** on Grand Bahama Island highlights Bahamian goombay and rake-'n'-scrape music.

September   Paradise Island and Cable Beach host the two-month **Bahamas Jazz and Blues Festival,** drawing international jazz and blues artists as well as big crowds.

November   Residents of the Abacos kick off the holiday season with a **Christmas Concert under the Stars,** and Nassau features **A Night of Christmas Music.**

December   The **Renaissance Singers Concert,** with classical, modern and ethnic Christmas music, is held at Nassau's Government House ballroom. Paradise Island hosts its own **Christmas Music Evening,** with choirs, chorales and the Royal Bahamas Police Force Band.

FOUR

New Providence

Pirates of the Caribbean picked Nassau as their base of operations, as did Civil War blockade runners, Prohibition-era rumrunners and modern-day drug traffickers, not to mention the international clients who deposit their cash untouchably in Nassau's hundreds of "offshore" banks. That's the shady side of this unique little city's character. On the sunny side, it's a city where people value their churches and love to talk about them, where the police wear spotless white uniforms and don't carry guns, and where the locals display a wide-open friendliness to strangers that some visitors from the U.S. find disturbing. James Bond slept here, they say, as did Rhett Butler, Queen Victoria, Howard Hughes and the Beatles.

With a past so steeped in romance and adventure, is it any wonder that Nassau has emerged as the most popular honeymoon destination for the Atlantic seaboard? It's a city whose sole occupation and purpose is to feed the fantasies of millions of vacationers who crowd its cruise ship docks, casinos and picture-perfect beaches.

You wouldn't think there could be much hidden on a tiny island like this, but the fact is, Nassau tourism has been carefully designed to focus tourist crowds into a few areas and steer visitors gently away from local neighborhoods and lifeways, which local residents humbly believe to be of no interest to Americans or Europeans.

When in Nassau, savor the tourist zones; they're incomparable. But sometime during your stay, make a point of searching for ways to break away from the resorts and fancy shops. Rent a scooter or hop on one of the myriad minibuses that seem to serve every cove and cul-de-sac, and search out the "real" New Providence Island. You'll find it in forgotten fishing villages on the far side of the island, and in the old neighborhoods collectively known as "Over-the-Hill," in nature reserves and on green winding lanes through opulent suburbs, and as close as the conch stands, fruit vendors, street musicians and goombay dance clubs hidden in the back streets of historic Old Nassau.

Old Nassau, the capital's downtown historic district, covers an area ten blocks long and four blocks wide along Bay Street and the waterfront. Its character is shaped by Georgian Revival government buildings constructed of massive limestone blocks and painted in tropical pastel hues. Many of them have been withstanding hurricanes and invasions since the 18th century. Others, like the huge old British Colonial Hotel, which forms the west end of the historic district, evoke the faded elegance of the English empire's waning years.

Old Nassau

Prince George Wharf is the city's most noticeable landmark because the cruise ships that dock there loom high above the two-story buildings that make up downtown Nassau. The dock was built during the Prohibition era in order to handle the unprecedented numbers of boats engaged in smuggling liquor into the United States. When Prohibition was repealed in 1933, the dock stood nearly abandoned until the 1960s when the government dredged a deep channel into the harbor to accommodate cruise ships.

SIGHTS

Woodes Rogers Walk leads west along the waterfront from the cruise ship wharf to the British Colonial Hotel. Along the way, a brightly painted warehouse building houses the **Junkanoo Expo**, a museum dedicated to the colorful costumes and masks of the Junkanoo celebrations that have been a Nassau tradition for more than a century. Junkanoo festivals—part parade, part dance performance, part athletic contest—are held in the early morning hours of Boxing Day (December 26) and New Year's Day each year; competing teams called rushing crews, with names like Roots, One Family and the Valley Boys, start preparing for the celebration in the summer months and devote incredible time and energy to developing dance routines and making costumes. Admission. ~ Woodes Rogers Walk; 356-2731.

The natural route for a first stroll in Nassau is up Woodes Rogers Walk and the parallel Bay Street, the main downtown street, a block to the south, looping back to Rawson Square and the wharf. Alleyways and indoor malls fill the space between Woodes Rogers Walk and Bay Street with small shops.

The most authentically Bahamian part of this cruise ship–oriented commercial zone is the **Straw Market**, a cornucopia of color and atmosphere. The little lanes are packed with vendors' stalls offering a wide variety of arts and crafts, especially handbags, hats and gift items woven from "straw"—actually fiber from palm fronds. Straw work is the most widespread handicraft in The Bahamas, though because of increased demand since the tourist boom, many straw market vendors now sell goods imported from Asian and Latin American countries. Besides straw products, shoppers will find clothing, jewelry, leather and curios in the market. Bargaining is accepted and expected.

A block north of the Straw Market, at George and Bay streets, the **Vendue House** served as a slave market before the Emancipation Act of 1834. Renamed after the leader of a slave revolt on Exuma, the 18th-century building now houses the **Pompey Museum of Slavery & Emancipation**, containing historical displays on slavery in The Bahamas and paintings by well-known Bahamian artist Amos Ferguson. Admission. ~ West Bay and George streets; 326-2566.

Downtown Nassau's latest "museum," the commercial attraction **Pirates of Nassau** seems designed for cruise-ship day visitors with more money than time. The stiff admission fee is justified by the nearly six million dollars it cost to create the exhibits, which include a historically accurate reconstruction of the Nassau waterfront circa 1716 complete with a three-quarter-size replica of a French pirate ship. Visitors descend below deck level for a look at the mate's cabin and the lower deck where pirate sailors lived, then confront an attack by Blackbeard and his crew. All exhibits were made by motion picture set designers from Vancouver, B.C., with human figures by Swiss craftsmen. Although they have no moving parts, sound and lighting are used to maximum dramatic effect. Admission. ~ George and King streets; 356-3759.

A two-block detour up Market Street from the Straw Market will bring you to **Balcony House,** the oldest wooden house in Nassau, built by ships' carpenters in the late 1700s. It now houses a local history museum, including slaves kitchens and a staircase from a ship among the exhibits. Admission. ~ Market Street; 326-2566.

Beyond Balcony House, **Gregory's Arch** spans Market Street at the entrance of a tunnel through the rock ridge that separates downtown Nassau from the rest of the island. Built in 1852, the tunnel leads to Grant's Town, one of the earliest settlements of freed slaves and their descendants.

A block south of the arch, a larger-than-life statue of Christopher Columbus poises on the stairway leading up to **Government House,** where it has stood since 1830. It is particularly striking at night, when the statue and stairs are illuminated with colored lights. A formal changing of the guard ceremony takes place every other Saturday in front of this building.

Directly south of Prince George Wharf is **Rawson Square**, the town square of downtown Nassau, where the Ministry of Tourism Reception Services Office offers free maps and information as well as free guided walking tours of Old Nassau. Rawson Square's main feature is the **Churchill Building**, where several

New Providence Island

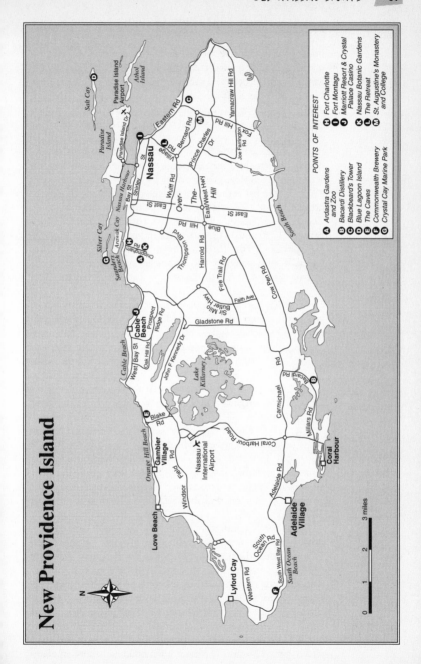

government officials have offices. In the center of the square stands a bronze **statue of Sir Milo Butler**, the former neighborhood grocer who became the first governor of The Bahamas after the islands gained independence in 1973. Previously, the **Sands Fountain** occupied the spot where Butler's statue is now. Named after Sir Stafford Sands, who promoted The Bahamas' 1960s tourism boom, the fountain pool and its dolphin statues were moved to the north side of the square to make room for Sir Milo's statue.

Bay Street separates Rawson Square from **Parliament Square**, directly across the street. A statue of a young Queen Victoria seated on her throne presides over the square, as she has since 1905. Behind her is the Senate Building, and flanking the square are the House of Assembly and a government office building. The three big pink buildings were constructed of local limestone between 1790 and 1813, during the influx of Loyalists from the U.S. mainland. The elegant Georgian architecture, with massive Greek Revival columns and pediments, was patterned on the colonial capitol of North Carolina. ~ Parliament Square; 322-7500.

Walking south on Parliament Street from Parliament Square, you pass the **Supreme Court Building** and come to another public square flanked by government buildings, with a stone cenotaph in the center inscribed with the names of Bahamians who lost their lives in the two world wars; a plaque has been added to honor four Bahamian Defence Force crewmen killed when their patrol cruiser was sunk by Cuban fighter planes in 1980.

> Nassau has many throwbacks to British times, including bewigged judges and the changing of the guard ceremony every other Saturday.

On the south side of the square, the octagonal **Nassau Public Library and Museum** was originally the island's jail. Today, the cellblocks hold bookshelves, historical exhibits and a seashell display. On the third floor of the library is an open-air public verandah that commands a good view of the government complex and Prince George Wharf. ~ Bank Lane; 322-4907.

Immediately uphill from the library, the **Royal Victoria Gardens** were originally the landscaped grounds of the Royal Victoria Hotel, the first luxury hotel in The Bahamas. The hotel was originally built by the government in 1859 under a contract with shipping tycoon Samuel Cunard to provide steamship passenger service to the islands. Such illustrious visitors as Queen Victoria, Prince Albert and Winston Churchill stayed there. It was bought by Florida railroad and hotel developer Henry Flagler in 1898 and continued to operate until 1971, when it was completely gutted by fire. The main hotel building is now an aban-

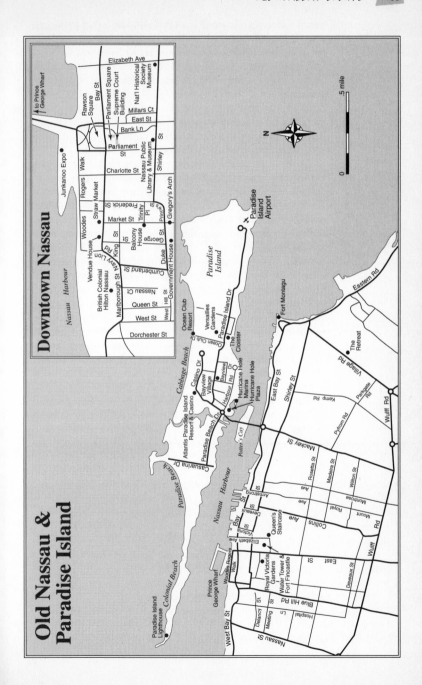

Old Nassau &
Paradise Island

Downtown Nassau

doned ruin across the street from the southeast corner of the gardens. Other buildings of the old hotel complex now house Ministry of Health facilities and other government offices.

Three blocks south of the gardens on Shirley Street at the corner of Elizabeth Avenue, the **National Historical Society Museum** provides a historic overview of The Bahamas. Exhibits of drawings, photographs, documents and memorabilia trace the history of the islands from before Columbus' landing to the present day, including the islands' largest collection of Lucayan Indian artifacts. Admission. ~ Shirley Street; 322-4231.

HIDDEN ►

From the museum, take a right on Elizabeth Avenue to reach the **Queen's Staircase**, probably the most bizarre sightseeing attraction in town. Town developers in the early 19th century, when The Bahamas had a surplus of slave labor, conceived the idea of providing access to new residential areas by carving a level road through the limestone ridge that lies between downtown Nassau and the rest of the island. Six hundred slaves labored for 16 years to hack a 90-foot-deep cut through the ridge, but the project remained unfinished when slavery was abolished, making completion impossible. Instead, a long stairway was built up the dead-end of the cut, making for a steeper climb than simply walking over the hill on another road. Later, in the 1920s, a tourism promoter noticed that there were the same number of steps as years in Queen Victoria's reign—69—and gave the staircase its name. Beautified with palm trees and a recirculating waterfall, the sheer-walled manmade box canyon makes a shady oasis on hot days.

Fort Fincastle, at the top of the Queen's Staircase, was built in 1793. The small fort was built in the shape of a ship's prow

---

✔ **CHECK THESE OUT**

- Stroll through a bit of Bahamian history with a **walking tour** of Old Nassau. *page 59*
- Feast on lobster, grilled snapper or a side order of johnnycakes at the **Bahamian Kitchen**, a local eatery where you'll probably be the only tourist. *page 70*
- Live like a star when you stay at Chris Blackwell's **Compass Point Beach Club**, where some of the guests are popular Caribbean recording artists. *page 80*
- Dive to new depths at **Shark Buoy**, where your companions are likely to be nurse sharks, reef sharks or maybe a hammerhead or two. *page 92*

by a colonial governor who was a former naval officer. Its cannons were never fired in battle. Sight down the barrel of one of the cannons at the cruise ships docked below and pretend you're a pirate. ~ Elizabeth Avenue.

Next to the fort stands the 126-foot **Water Tower**. Ride the cramped little elevator to the top—the highest point on New Providence Island—for a view that takes in the entire island and the sea beyond in every direction. Admission. ~ Elizabeth Avenue; 322-2442.

Just off West Bay Street a mile west of the downtown Nassau historic district stands a much larger fortification, **Fort Charlotte**. It was built in the 1780s by Lord Dunmore, for whom Harbour Island's Dunmore Town is named; the fort itself was named for King George III's concubine. A moat with a drawbridge surrounds it, and underground passages lead to old dungeon cells. Like Fort Fincastle, Fort Charlotte was never used in battle. ~ Chippingham Road; 322-7500.

Just south of Fort Charlotte, **Ardastra Gardens and Zoo** is a five-acre paradise with paths that lead among native trees and plants identified by small signs. The zoo, the largest in The Bahamas, has native iguanas and parrots as well as exotic species from the Caribbean, Central America and South America. The park's claim to fame is its flock of trained pink flamingos, who march on parade in response to voice commands. Flamingo shows take place Monday through Saturday at 11 a.m., 2 p.m. and 4 p.m. Admission. ~ Chippingham Road; 323-5806; www.ardastra.com.

Nassau Botanic Gardens, a lush 16-acre park in the quarry that provided limestone blocks for the government buildings downtown, contains more than 600 different species of tropical flora and has staff guides to show you around. The terraces on the east side afford fine views of the entire park. Admission. ~ Chippingham Road, near Fort Charlotte; 323-5975.

North of Fort Charlotte, a causeway crosses the water to two manmade islands. **Arawak Cay** is the site of public utility projects, including the port where fresh water is brought to Nassau.

Beyond Arawak, Silver Cay boasts Nassau's **Crystal Cay Marine Park**. Much of The Bahamas' beauty lies hidden beneath the ocean surface. Local entrepreneurs make it easy for visitors who are not scuba-certified to see what divers see in a variety of ways, none more ambitious than this marine park. There are ten aquarium tanks, including a shark tank, a turtle tank and a stingray pool, as well as a beach, tropical gardens and a reef trail for snorkeling. The highlight of the park, the **Underwater Observation Tower** lets visitors descend 20 feet below the surface to view marine life and a living reef through huge windows. Admission. ~ North Arawak Cay and West Bay Street; 328-1036.

LODGING   Downtown Nassau lodging, though not cheap, tends to cost less than accommodations in the Cable Beach and Paradise Island resort areas. One of the city's major landmarks, the big Mediterranean-style **British Colonial Hilton Nassau** was built in 1922 on the site of the original Fort Nassau, and reigned as The Bahamas' premier resort hotel for over 40 years. It had deteriorated badly before 1999, when the Hilton chain took it over, repainted it from its traditional tropical pink to bright yellow, added a grand new entranceway and completely renovated the lobby and 291 rooms.The British Colonial's too-urban guests-only beach can't compare with Cable Beach or Paradise Island, but the elegant lobby and the antique charm of its private landscaped grounds take guests back to the era of rumrunners and British nobility. With complete meeting and convention facilities and business services, as well as a location within walking distance of most of the island's offshore banks, the hotel's new incarnation seems intended more for business visitors than for the resort trade. ~ 1 Bay Street; 322-3301, 800-774-1500, fax 322-2286; www.hilton.com/hotels/NASHITW. DELUXE.

The most elegant accommodation in Old Nassau, **Graycliff** is more than 250 years old. The Georgian colonial mansion was built by 18th-century pirate John Howard, who accepted amnesty and retired in 1726 after his ship, the *Gray Wolf*, was sunk by the British Navy. It has been operated as a guesthouse off and on since the 1860s; Sir Winston Churchill and the Beatles slept here. The poolside cottage and 12 guest rooms are furnished with period antiques. ~ West Hill Street; 322-2796, 800-423-4095, fax 326-6110; www.graycliff.com. ULTRA-DELUXE.

The neighborhood south and west of the British Colonial Hotel is where you'll find small hotels and restaurants that cater to predominantly European travelers. One of the most charming, the Greek-owned **El Greco Hotel** has 26 guest rooms, decorated in Spanish style and made to seem more spacious than they are by mirrors, odd angles and archways. The most desirable rooms are those that open onto the second-floor balcony over the entrance, with views of the public beach a block away. There's also a small swimming pool. ~ West Bay Street; 325-1121, fax 325-1124; www.bahamasnet.com/elgrecohotel. MODERATE.

The **Towne Hotel**, right in the heart of the historic district, has 46 guest rooms decorated with strange lavender-painted Danish modern furniture and equipped with erratic old TVs and even less reliable air conditioners. The hotel has a small swimming pool and a big third-floor rooftop sundeck, and the price is right. ~ George Street; 322-8452, fax 322-8152. BUDGET TO MODERATE.

The Truth About Offshore Banking

At last count, there were 410 banks in The Bahamas—most of them located in downtown Nassau. They include multinational financial institutions based in the United States, Canada, England and even Russia, as well as local Bahamian banks. These banks cater less to local checking account holders than to companies and wealthy individuals who, for various reasons, want to keep their money outside the United States.

Money in Bahamian banks is beyond the reach of judgment creditors in lawsuits brought in the United States, and U.S. courts lack the power to subpoena records of offshore bank accounts. A bank account in The Bahamas can also help avoid U.S. federal taxes on some international business transactions. A special trust arrangement through a Bahamian bank can be used to conceal the ownership of funds, giving rise to the islands' claim to be a "little Switzerland."

The secrecy and unreachability of offshore banking has its limitations, though. In the 1990s, the government of The Bahamas has passed a series of sweeping changes in banking laws, primarily to help the U.S. Drug Enforcement Administration and Internal Revenue Service fight money laundering operations. Today, funds in a Bahamian bank are effectively protected from civil lawsuits but not from U.S. federal law enforcement agents.

Recent banking policy in The Bahamas has been aimed at providing greater stability through government oversight. Still, an offshore bank account is not without risk. Since it does not have Federal Deposit Insurance protection, the account would be lost entirely in the event of a bank failure.

HIDDEN ▶ One of the most affordable lodgings in the downtown area is the **Mignon Guest House**, a simple eight-room hotel concealed behind a narrow, inconspicuous side-street entrance in the heart of Old Nassau. Rooms are air-conditioned, though otherwise featureless. It's often full, so call ahead. ~ Market Street; 322-4771. BUDGET.

East of the Paradise Island Causeway, the **Nassau Harbour Club** has 50 guest rooms with stark white walls that set off the colorfully jungle-patterned bedspreads and drapes. Rooms overlook the club's marina, and there are a swimming pool and a small private beach. The lounges here are favorite "yachtie" party spots. ~ East Bay Street; 393-0771, fax 393-5393. MODERATE.

The lowest-priced rooms in Nassau—$50 a night—are at the **Harbour Moon Hotel**, a workingman's lodging near the docks. Its 54 dinghy pink rooms have seen better days, and you get your choice of street noise toward the front of the building or cranes loading and offloading boats (louder, but only in the daytime) toward the rear. On the positive side, rooms have TVs, air conditioning, and shared balconies with views of Bay Street and the harbor, and the location is convenient to the mailboat dock. ~ West Bay and Deveaux streets; 323-8120, fax 328-0374.

On the eastern end of Nassau, **Orchard Garden Apartment Hotel** has 12 pink cottages as well as 10 small apartments in a newer building. There's a pool, and a beach and supermarket are nearby. The furnishings are simple, and the owners are knowledgeable and helpful. ~ Village Road; 323-1297. MODERATE.

Families traveling together may want to consider **Villas on Coral Island**. Though the location can be quite busy during the day, it is peaceful in the evening. There are 22 villas and they all offer ocean views, two beds, kitchens and small private pools. It's a relatively short walk or taxi ride to either downtown Nassau or

◆◆

BRING HOME A NEW "DO"

One of the great Bahamian souvenir enterprises is hairbraiding. A few years ago, freelance hairbraiders began to outnumber craftspeople in the Straw Market, so the government banned them from the market and set up a **Hairbraider's Centre**, between the cruise ship docks and Rawson Square, where they could practice their craft on tourists. A braid hairdo is guaranteed to impress, or at least amaze, the folks back home, and it doesn't last as long as a tattoo. The cost varies with the number of braids, typically $5 for 20. If you get your hair braided, be sure to use sunscreen on the exposed parts of your scalp.

Cable Beach, and the hotel offers free shuttles. ~ Silver Cay, P.O. Box 7797; 328-1036, 800-328-8814, fax 323-3202. DELUXE.

To rent a house for an extended stay on New Providence or Paradise Island, contact the **Bahamas Real Estate Association**. ~ Shirley Street, P.O. Box 8860; 325-4942. MODERATE TO ULTRA-DELUXE.

DINING

For an elegant dining experience, head to **Graycliff**. This historic inn offers some of the finest Continental cuisine on this side of the Atlantic. Most menu items feature at least one Bahamian ingredient, and the house specialty is fresh-caught spiny lobster tails. The 175,000-bottle wine selection is by far the largest in The Bahamas, and the cigar selection, featuring the finest Cuban cigars as well as cigars handmade on the premises, presents American tobacco connoisseurs with irresistible temptations. Not only the finest restaurant in The Bahamas, Graycliff is also the most expensive. Jackets required. ~ West Hill Street; 322-2796. ULTRA-DELUXE.

Near the Government House, **Buena Vista** offers some of the city's most innovative cuisine. Garden patio tables at this colonial mansion are some of the most sought-after seats in town after dark. The fare is seafood, and novel dishes such as fresh smoked mahimahi and curried grouper topped with coconut share the menu with standard favorites such as Bahamian spiny lobster tail. Many of the huge portions are suitable for sharing. Jackets recommended. ~ Meeting and Delancy streets; 322-2811. DELUXE.

Also overlooking the harbor, the **Poop Deck** offers great views and local-style cooking. Grouper fingers with peas 'n rice are a good bet, and the chef prepares lunch or dinner specials daily. The best views are from second-floor deck. ~ Nassau Yacht Haven Marina, East Bay Street; 393-8175. MODERATE.

Situated at the end of Sugar Reef Dock, the headquarters for a number of small dive and fishing charter operations, the open-air **Sugar Reef** flaunts its tropical style with huge, fruity boat drinks and a palm-thatched roof. The cuisine—conch, shark and lobster dishes prepared with a touch of nouveau flair—lives up to the ambience. Offering perhaps the best nighttime view of the harbor and the Paradise Island hotel zone on the far side, this is one of the most romantic restaurants in town. ~ East Bay Street at Deveaux Street; 356-3065. MODERATE.

◄ *HIDDEN*

Situated in a 125-year-old mansion one block south of East Bay Street, **Gaylords** features authentic East Indian cuisine including Tandoori, Punjabi, Nepalese and Mughali dishes. It's part of a world-famous British Commonwealth chain that also has locations in London, Bombay and New Delhi. ~ Dowdeswell Street; 356-3004. DELUXE.

HIDDEN ▶   Located just off East Bay Street behind the Royal Bank of Canada, **Ro-Lay's TakeAway Restaurant** sells conch burgers and other fast-food fare to go, catering to a mostly local crowd. Featuring some of of the most affordable food in Nassau, it's the ideal place to pick up a picnic lunch. ~ Victoria Avenue; 328-5857. BUDGET.

HIDDEN ▶   For local food at local prices, there's no better place in the historic district than the simple, clean and friendly **Bahamian Kitchen**. The little storefront café features local lobster, steamed fish, grilled snapper and side orders like johnnycake and peas 'n rice. And you may not see another tourist here. ~ Trinity Place and Market Street; 325-0702. BUDGET.

Skans is another classic local hangout. Situated next to the Straw Market, this informal restaurant serves up hearty full Bahamian meals as well as American-style fast food. One of the oldest eateries on West Bay Street, it has recently been upgraded in an effort to trade its traditional workers-and-vendors clientele for cruise ship passengers and the international café crowd. ~ Bay Street; 325-5536. MODERATE.

HIDDEN ▶   For the most authentic food in town, dine like the locals—standing up—at the **Conch Vendors' Village**, off West Bay Street at the causeway to Arawak and Coral cays near Fort Charlotte and Ardastra Gardens. For many years, friendly seafood sellers have been preparing conch salad and cracked conch at dozens of ramshackle open-air stands, selling mainly to the lunch-break crowd who eat in their cars in the nearby casuarina-shaded parking area. Increasing numbers of tourists have discovered the conch vendors in the last couple of years, and the row of stands has grown to fill all sides of the Arawak and West Bay Street intersection. Some stands have expanded into full-fledged restaurants. Prices have risen, too, though they are still competitive with the lowest-priced local restaurants and cafeterias downtown—about $6 for a good, filling meal. What makes the conch vendors' village special is that you can stroll among dozens of stands as you select the daily special that sounds most tantalizing. ~ Western Esplanade; no phone. BUDGET.

SHOPPING   Virtually all the stores along Woodes Rogers Walk and West Bay Street are primed for the tidal waves of daytrippers that gush from cruise ships at Prince George Wharf. The main shopping area is about the size of a major shopping mall in any U.S. city, and at least as self-explanatory. Visitors whose idea of a great vacation involves lots of shopping will find that in The Bahamas this is the place to do it.

"Duty-free" is the appeal used to encourage visitors to buy. This means the store sells one or more of the ten categories of products—perfume, watches, jewelry, china, crystal, sweaters, linens, photographic equipment, leather goods and liquor—that the Bahamian government has exempted from import tariffs since 1992. When you buy perfume that was brought from France duty-free in Nassau, where there is no sales tax, and then take it back to the United States under your $600-a-person U.S. Customs exemption, you're avoiding all French, Bahamian and U.S. taxes and so, theoretically, getting a bargain on French perfume. In reality, the "duty-free" policy was designed to help retailers compete with U.S. prices. Savings are minuscule, often less than the discount you could get where Bahamians do *their* shopping— in downtown Miami. Still, visitors from many parts of the United States, Canada and Europe find that the retailers in Nassau offer some sleek, chic and sensuous items that might be hard to find back home.

The **Straw Market**, a traditional arts-and-crafts market with narrow, lively aisles between the indoor vendors' stands, bursts with all the local color vacationers imagine in a Caribbean port of call. Bags, baskets and hats woven from palm fiber and bright handprinted fabrics fill stall after stall. The high-volume business that the cruise ships bring has inspired many vendors to supplement their stock with imports from other countries. "Price negotiation" is expected. ~ Bay Street and Straw Market Plaza; no phone.

Bahamian arts and crafts are also available, without any price haggling, at several downtown shops. **Island Tings** features a full range of locally made items, from trinkets to unique works of folk art, including one of the best fabric selections in town. ~ Bay and East streets; 326-1024.

The Green Lizard carries batik and handprinted sarongs, handwoven hammocks and Haitian metal sculpture, as well as a selection of souvenir foodstuffs that runs the gamut from pepper sauce and dried pigeon peas to guava jam and canned conch chowder. ~ Prince George Arcade, 356-5103; and West Bay Street, 356-3439.

You'll find the full range of Bahamian folk art, from Junkanoo dolls and driftwood-and-seashell mobiles to paintings and handprinted fabrics, as well as straw work of a quality rarely found in the Straw Market, at **The Plait Lady**. ~ Bay Street and Victoria Avenue; 356-5584.

You'll feel like you've stepped into a little bit of Great Britain at **Marlborough Antiques**, a wonderful shop full of old books, silverware, maps, paintings and photographs, many of them imported from England. The store also carries an exceptional selection of lustrous pink queen conch pearls, a Bahamian treasure that was exported around the world in the 19th century but is now sold only in the Bahamas. ~ Queen and Marlborough streets; 328-0502.

Music-lovers sing the praises of **Cody's Music and Video Center**, with by far the best collection of island music in The Bahamas. Cody Carter, the friendly and knowledgeable owner, appreciates visitors' interest in Bahamian and Caribbean music. ~ East Bay and Armstrong streets; 325-8834.

The Island Shop, located across Bay Street from the Straw Market, has a large curio shop on the ground floor selling everything from postcards and swimwear to imported perfumes and paintings by local artists. The second-floor book shop has a whole room of books on The Bahamas, as well as a good selection of imported U.S., Canadian and British books and magazines at premium prices. ~ Bay and Fredericks streets; 322-4183.

You'll smell the tobacco aroma of the **Pipe of Peace** before you reach it. The store deals primarily in Cuban cigars (savor them in Nassau; it's illegal to bring them into the United States) and has a wide selection of other fine cigars and pipe tobaccos. ~ Bay Street, near Charlotte Street; 325-2022.

> Much of the island's drinking water is imported by barge from Andros, where there is much less demand on the underground aquifiers.

NIGHTLIFE   Downtown Nassau is all but deserted after 6 p.m. Most nightlife is found in the casinos and nightclubs of Paradise Island and Cable Beach megaresorts, with a few notable exceptions. The **Silk Cotton Club**, located a block up the hill from the Straw Market, features live jazz by local legend Henry Moss, who owns the club, as well as various guest artists Wednesday through Saturday evenings. Cover. ~ Market Street; 356-0955.

If dining and dancing fits your plans, head for the **Drop Off Pub**, where you'll find live bands and disco music and big-screen TVs showing European sporting events. Music, drinks and meals are served until 6:00 a.m. ~ Bay Street across from Planet Hollywood; 322-3444.

Club Waterloo, located half a mile east of the Paradise Island Causeways, is Nassau's largest nightclub. It has five indoor and outdoor bars including a sports bar and a big, packed dance floor where you can groove to live island music far into the night. ~ East Bay Street; 393-7324.

BEACHES   **BLUE LAGOON ISLAND** 🏃 ⛱ 🛥 This tiny island just three miles offshore is reached by boats operated by Calypso Getaway, departing from a dock under the Paradise Island Causeway. Excursions last about six hours. Depending on the crowds, you'll probably be able to find your own deserted beach (or at least a section of one); there are seven from which to choose. Dolphin encounters are also available (call 363-1653), as are diving and snorkeling with stingrays. Admission. ~ Calypso Getaway, Paradise Island Bridge; 363-3577.

▼▼▼▼▼▼▼▼▼▼

Cable Beach

Cable Beach was a remote stretch of coastline beyond the western outskirts of Nassau in 1892, when the first undersea telephone cable linking The Bahamas to the United States mainland was completed here, giving the beach its name. What was then a beach as beautiful and isolated as many Out Island beaches are today is now a booming resort area.

Cable Beach is about three miles west of downtown Nassau. Buses run back and forth so frequently that you will rarely have to wait more than a few minutes for one.

SIGHTS

Cable Beach is a self-contained megaresort with a half dozen big high-rise hotels and several chic shopping malls. Aside from the broad, beautiful beach itself, the only tourist sight is the **Crystal Palace Casino**, until recently the largest casino in The Bahamas. The beach scene is generally lively, with swarms of hairbraiders and souvenir vendors winding their way among the basking tourists. ~ West Bay Street.

LODGING

The **Marriott Resort**, Cable Beach's garish centerpiece, is a self-contained resort that's like a Las Vegas pleasure palace—with an ocean beach. It's a huge place, with 867 rooms and suites in five separate high-rise towers. Facilities include a showroom, a golf course, tennis courts, lush gardens and a giant swimming pool with a 100-foot waterslide. The guest accommodations are modern and roomy, with cheerfully utilitarian furnishings that faintly echo the opulence of the vast maze of public areas. Most rooms have ocean views and spacious balconies. If the architecture of this hotel, with its curvilinear spaces, brass fittings and porthole windows, seems vaguely reminiscent of a cruise ship, it may be because the resort, which originally included the neighboring Radisson, was designed and built by Carnival Cruise Line. ~ West Bay Street, P.O. Box N-8306; 327-6200, 800-331-6358, fax 327-6459; www.marriotthotels.com/NASB5. ULTRA-DELUXE.

The **Radisson Cable Beach Resort** was originally part of the same resort as the Marriott next door, which explains why the Crystal Palace Casino is equally accessible from both hotels. Since the split, the Radisson has undergone extensive renovations inside and out and now looks quite different from its neighbor. The grounds now feature seven acres of freshwater pools, waterfalls and jacuzzis nestled amid lush tropical landscaping and rock formations. The 700 rooms and suites are light and spacious, with sleek, modern decor. Balconies overlook the sea. Guests can choose an all-inclusive plan that provides all meals, drinks, activities and sports, including free golf, as well as round-trip airport transportation, and costs about twice as much as the European plan option. The hotel is designed for the family trade, with supervised care for kids 3 to 12 at its extravagant play area, Camp Junkanoo. ~ West Bay Street, P.O. Box 4914; 327-6000, 800-333-3333, fax 327-6987; www.radisson.com. ULTRA-DELUXE.

In a more traditional vein, **Nassau Beach Hotel** was the original Cable Beach resort hotel, built in the 1940s. A total renovation in 1992 took care to preserve old-time Bahamian touches such as ceiling fans and wicker furniture in the 410 guest rooms and the tropical landscaping outside. ~ West Bay Street, P.O. Box 7756; 327-7711, 888-627-7282, fax 327-8829; www.nassaubeachhotel.com. DELUXE.

Today, Nassau is the world's busiest cruise ship port and can dock up to six of the huge floating hotels at one time.

Sandals Royal Bahamian Resort & Spa, located on the quieter end of Cable Beach, is one of the showpieces of the Jamaica-based Sandals resort chain. It operates on an all-inclusive plan, with all meals and sports activities included in the room rate. It features a wide range of water sports, a complete spa, five restaurants and a full schedule of organized social and entertainment activities. In addition, it has a small, away-from-it-all beach club across the bay on the eastern tip of Blackbeard's Cay. The 172 guest rooms and suites are exceptionally luxurious, with traditional English furnishings and huge bathrooms. Many rooms have ocean views. ~ West Bay Street; 327-6400, 800-726-3257, fax 327-6961; www.sandals.com. ULTRA-DELUXE.

Another excellent all-inclusive option is **Breezes Bahamas,** part of the SuperClubs group of resorts. Practically everything is included at this 391-room resort, including all kinds of water sports. The feel is casual, and guests can choose between buffet dining and a fine Italian restaurant. Rooms are spacious, though not as elegant as those at Sandals. ~ West Bay Street; 327-5356, fax-327-5155. ULTRA-DELUXE.

HIDDEN ▶

The locally owned **Casuarinas of Cable Beach** offers a smaller, more homelike feel in the heart of Cable Beach. The 70 rooms are located in several buildings amid stands of the graceful evergreen casuarinas, or Australian pines, that are the hotel's namesake. The less expensive rooms are across the street from the beach, while the pricier ones are right on the water. ~ West Bay Street, P.O. Box 4016; 327-7921, fax 327-8152. DELUXE.

A couple of miles west of Cable Beach, **Orange Hill Beach Inn** is as affordable as it is attractive. The British-born innkeeper, a long-time Bahamas resident, welcomes scuba divers and honeymooners for surprisingly inexpensive packages. Originally a private mansion dating back to the 1920s, it has 32 rooms and apartments that vary widely in size and price. Some have kitchenettes.

There are three acres of landscaped grounds, and a quiet beach ideal for snorkeling is down the hill. ~ West Bay Street, P.O. Box 8583; 327-7157, fax 327-5186; www.orangehill.com. MODERATE.

DINING

The Marriott has no less than nine restaurants, ranging from the **Black Angus Grille**, a pricey steak and seafood house, to **Goombay Mama**, a Pizza Hut franchise that also serves Bahamian specialties. The best bet for big appetites is the **Seaside Buffet**, near the casino, serving an all-you-can-eat array of soups, salads, seafood, pasta and desserts until two in the morning. ~ West Bay Street, 327-6200 for all restaurants, extension 6861 for reservations. MODERATE TO DELUXE.

There are six more restaurants in the Radisson Cable Beach Resort. Standouts include the indoor-outdoor **Bimini Market Grill**, which has elaborate breakfast and lunch buffets as well as a full menu of grilled meat, poultry and seafood specialties for dinner; **The Forge**, where guests can order steaks or seafood raw and cook for themselves on a tabletop grill; and **Islands**, serving Caribbean specialties in a colorful, festive atmosphere. ~ West Bay Street; 327-6000 for all restaurants. MODERATE TO DELUXE.

The **Round House Restaurant** at Casuarinas of Cable Beach is a favorite among visitors and locals alike. Bahamian cooking is the specialty, with seafood and chicken entrées in assorted savory sauces. Top off your meal with a tempting slice of guava duff. ~ West Bay Street; 327-8153. MODERATE.

◄ HIDDEN

Tucked away in a shopping mall across West Bay Street from Sandals Royal Bahamian Resort, **Capriccio Ristorante** is a small, locally owned Italian restaurant with Old World marble and wrought-iron decor and just ten tables. Soft Mediterranean music sets the mood for delicious pasta dishes such as homemade lasagna and *salmone alla bisanzio*, seasoned with fresh herbs grown on the premises. ~ Cable Beach Shopping Center; 327-8547. MODERATE.

SHOPPING

The hub of shopping action in Cable Beach is the **Radisson Shopping Mall**, contained within the Radisson Cable Beach Resort. Most of the shops here are the kind you want to whisper in—purveyors of fine apparel, goldwork and objets d'art. Shopping downtown is somehow more fun.

NIGHTLIFE

The **Palace Theater** at the Crystal Palace Casino presents Las Vegas–style stage shows nightly except Monday. A fixed-price dinner is served before the show, but those in the know dine elsewhere first and take in a later performance of the glitz-fest. This 800-seat showroom can get a bit stuffy when crowded with cruise-ship passengers. Call early for reservations. Cover. ~ West Bay Street, Cable Beach; 327-6200.

The Forte Nassau Beach Hotel has three lively bistros that feature live music and late-night hours: the young, hip **Rock and Roll Café** ~ 327-7711, the mellow, moody **Banana Boat Bar** ~ 327-7711 and the island ambience of **Café Johnny Canoe** ~ 327-3373. All charge cover.

BEACHES   **CABLE BEACH** Named for the nearby telecommunications cable terminals that connected New Providence Island to Jupiter, Florida on the U.S. mainland in 1892, Cable Beach is long, lively and lined with several of the largest resort hotels in The Bahamas. ~ Located just to the west of Nassau proper.

BLACKBEARD'S CAY This private island across the bay from Cable Beach must be the most-often-renamed cay in The Bahamas. Originally known as North Cay, with changes of ownership it became Balmoral Island and, more recently, Discovery Island. In its most recent incarnation, it has been transformed into a beach club with a bar, dive shop, and broad beach on the bay side as well as new manmade beach with exceptional snorkeling on the ocean side. The interior of the 17-acre property has tall hardwood trees and walking trails ideal for birdwatching. Motorized water sports are prohibited around the cay. Laid-back and secluded-feeling for most of the week, the Cay gets packed with cruise ship party groups of as many as 300 people on Tuesday and Saturday. ~ Half-day and all-day trips to Blackbeard's Cay can be arranged through major hotels or, at a reduced rate, directly from United Shipping, Woodes Rogers Walk; 323-5519; fax 323-8779.

SAUNDERS BEACH On weekends, many Nassau locals head for this stretch of beach located on West Bay Street, midway between downtown and Cable Beach. Close to Fort Charlotte and just west of the causeway to Coral Island, it is sheltered by the island from rough seas. Within walking distance of downtown, it is usually quiet on weekdays—except during lunch hour, when local workers may be found picnicking on cracked conch from the cluster of vendors' stalls nearby. ~ West Bay Street.

▼▼▼▼▼▼▼▼▼▼▼▼
Greater New Providence Island

Most of the commercial and resort development on New Providence lies along the north shore. Except for Nassau, Cable Beach, Paradise Island and a few other pockets of development, the rest of the island is surprisingly quiet. Inland, residential neighborhoods fill the eastern half of the island, while most of the western half is scrub forest surrounding several shallow, swampy lakes. The mostly beachless south shore is taken up by a military base of the Royal Bahamian Defence Force (functionally similar to the U.S. Coast Guard) and a ragged shoreline, more easily accessible by boat than by road, with several secluded, mosquito-infested coastal ponds and inlets that only birdwatching and bonefishing enthusiasts are likely to love.

WEST OF NASSAU As you follow West Bay Street beyond crowded Cable Beach, traffic dwindles and the coast road becomes one of the island's most scenic drives. The Bahamian government urges cab drivers to bring arriving visitors into town from the airport by this beautifully landscaped route, reserving the shorter, faster but less idyllic cross-island route for departures. From Rock Point on, the road clings to the shore and offers beautiful sea views. **The Caves**, a pair of large natural caverns in a limestone shelf at the ocean's edge, mark the east end of Orange Hill Beach.

SIGHTS

◀ *HIDDEN*

About ten miles out of Nassau, after skirting **Orange Hill Beach** for a long stretch, the road nears the northwest corner of the island at the small residential community of **Love Beach**. The road veers south there, away from the seashore, and soon passes the entrance to **Lyford Cay**, one of the island's longest-established old money enclaves. All tourists get to see is the front gate.

Just past Lyford Cay, the road starts changing names whimsically. West Bay Road becomes Western Road, then Southwest Bay Road as it rounds the southwest corner of the island and runs past the **Commonwealth Brewery**, makers of Kalik beer, the unofficial national beverage, on its way to the South Ocean Beach & Golf Resort. Free tours of the brewery are available by appointment. ~ Clifton Pier; 362-4789.

The population of New Providence is almost twice the population of the rest of the Bahamian islands combined.

Beyond South Ocean Beach & Golf Resort, the main route's name changes to Adelaide Road as it enters the little oceanfront town of **Adelaide Village**. The community dates back to 1831, when the governor established it as a home for Africans liberated from a captured Portuguese slave ship. Though electricity, television and indoor plumbing have come to Adelaide in recent years, you'll still find the slow rhythms of a traditional fishing village life here. **Adelaide Beach**, which runs both directions from the village, has a faraway feel with hardly a hint of tourism.

◀ *HIDDEN*

Once again, the road changes names to Carmichael Road. About five miles out of Adelaide Village, Bacardi Road turns off to the right and leads to the **Bacardi Distillery**. Originally based in Cuba, it was relocated to The Bahamas after the Cuban Revolution in 1959, even though the sugar cane from which rum is made does not grow here. The company must import their sugar cane from other islands around the Caribbean. To learn more, take the free tour of the huge liquor factory. ~ Bacardi Road; 362-1412.

Carmichael Road eventually meets Blue Hill Road. If you turn right, you will soon come to **South Beach**, the most remote beach on the island. A left turn leads you back into Nassau. The drive will take you through **Over-the-Hill**, on the south side of Old Nassau, separated from the Bay Street area by the steep ridge topped by Fort Fincastle and the water tower. Old, historic and poor, this neighborhood grew up out of the villages of Grant's Town and Bain's Town, which were established in the 1820s to provide housing for the blacks that were set free when the British Navy intercepted slave smugglers. A decade later, when Great Britain abolished slavery in The Bahamas, thousands of people left the plantations where they had worked and moved into Over-the-Hill.

Although it has spent much of its history as a slum, locals are fiercely loyal to the old neighborhood. As most Bahamians' standard of living has climbed in recent years, old 19th-century houses have been preserved and sometimes renovated. Old-fashioned corner grocery stores still sell their wares. Folks on their front porches look up from their contests of warri, a board game imported from Africa, at the spectacle of tourists on this side of town. Within minutes, you'll crest the hill and find yourself practically in front of the British Colonial Hotel in downtown Nassau.

EAST OF NASSAU   As you follow Bay Street east past Potter's Cay and the Causeway to Paradise Island, it soon leaves the city and changes its name to Eastern Road. Nassau's third fort, **Fort Montagu**, sits east of town. Built in 1741, the fort was believed to be strategically important because the channel between New Providence and Paradise islands was so narrow that ships could not sail through without coming into range of the fort's cannons. But each time Nassau was actually attacked—by American rebels in 1776, Spaniards in 1782 and British loyalists in 1783—the invaders captured the fort at night without a single shot being fired. Today, there's less to see here than at Fort Fincastle or Fort Charlotte.

HIDDEN ►   Village Road, on the right at the Shirley Street intersection a short distance past the fort, takes you south to **The Retreat**, the headquarters of the Bahamas National Trust, which maintains the islands' national park system. The 11-acre tropical garden was originally part of a lavish estate whose owners, Arthur and Margaret Langlois, indulged in a rare hobby. They collected palm trees from all over the world. Half-hour guided walking tours, conducted Tuesday through Thursday at 11:45 a.m., as

James Bond
in
The Bahamas

One of the biggest boosts in the history of Bahamas tourism came in 1965, when the motion picture *Thunderball* was filmed here and shamelessly touted Nassau at every opportunity. This second James Bond film, which involved a search for a stolen nuclear warhead, inspired the modern action-flick genre and established Sean Connery, then an obscure Shakespearean actor, as an international masculine archetype.

British spy novelist Ian Fleming, who had created James Bond in the 1950s, was partial to The Bahamas as one of the last bastions of the British Empire. Fleming migrated to Nassau to write during the winter. The island of Inagua inspired the setting for one of his early Bond novels, *Doctor No*, which would later be made into the first James Bond movie.

Thunderball not only revealed to the world the beauty of The Bahamas' reefs and undersea coral forests, but also left behind a series of movie set "wrecks" that have become popular scuba diving sites.

Sean Connery returned for one last performance in the James Bond role in the 1983 extravaganza *Never Say Never Again*, which used a story-line all but indistinguishable from that of *Thunderball*, as an excuse to return to classic Bond haunts, including Nassau. The film company sank two more wrecks, Connery apparently dined and usually had his picture taken in just about every hole-in-the-wall eatery in town, earning himself a lasting place in the mythology of The Bahamas.

Today, *Thunderball* and *Never Say Never Again* are available for rent in most video stores. The footage of scuba chases along the coral reefs of New Providence is as eye-popping as ever.

well as by advance appointment, introduce you to 176 species of palms and show you a 19th-century cottage; you can also stroll through the gardens on your own. Admission. ~ Village Road; 393-1317.

Eastern Road continues along Montagu Bay, where many yachts drop anchor. About five miles beyond The Retreat, a few swashbuckling tourists make it out to **Blackbeard's Tower**, now closed to the public. Some tour guides claim Edward "Blackbeard" Teach, the most notorious of Nassau's pirate leaders of the early 1700s, used this overgrown ruin as a lookout point. Historians tell us that while Blackbeard may well have aimed his spyglass from this small hilltop, the tower itself was not built until long after the pirate had been hanged.

HIDDEN ►

You can return to Nassau by following Fox Hill Road inland through Fox Hill, another old village settled by freed slaves in the early 1800s. Before looping back toward Eastern Road and the coast, Fox Hill Road passes the stately **St. Augustine's Monastery and College**, built by Benedictine monks under the direction of Father Jerome Hawkes in 1947. After finishing the monastery, Father Jerome left to become a hermit on Cat Island, where he is buried. The monks offer fascinating tours and rare glimpses into the monastic life. ~ Fox Hill Road; 324-1511.

LODGING

Chris Blackwell, the Jamaican reggae promoter who "discovered" Bob Marley, joined forces with the Miami-based Island Outposts to create the rainbow-colored **Compass Point Beach Club** on a little cove about three miles west of Cable Beach, and a world apart. The 18 brightly painted bungalows overlook the water next to Blackwell's Compass Point recording studio. All units are airy, with lots of windows and feature Bahamian decor. Half of them come with kitchenettes. Banana trees planted around each hut provide privacy and a junglelike ambience. Gambier Village, the residential district around Compass Point, dates back to the year 1807, when it was one of the first Bahamian villages settled by Africans liberated by the British Navy from illegal slave ships. ~ West Bay Street, Gambier Village; 327-4500, fax 327-3299. DELUXE.

HIDDEN ►

Even more secluded is the **South Ocean Golf & Beach Resort**. Located on the island's south shore, 45 minutes from the airport and considerably farther from Old Nassau, this sprawling self-contained resort has 250 rooms, half of them inland and the other half on the beach. The waterfront rooms are decorated in early plantation style with period reproduction furnishings. The resort offers a wide array of water sports and is close to some of the island's best scuba diving sites. ~ Southwest Bay Road, P.O. Box 8191; 362-4391, 800-992-2015, fax 362-4810. DELUXE.

The Restaurant at Compass Point serves Bahamian/Caribbean cuisine as colorful as the resort itself. Meat and seafood entrées come smothered in sauces made from fresh fruits and vegetables. The dessert menu is formidable. ~ West Bay Street, Gambier Village; 327-4500. DELUXE.

Nearby, **Traveller's Rest** is a good choice for casual native cuisine. Set at the edge of the beach amid tropical trees, the restaurant serves fresh-caught conch, lobster and grouper. Owner Joan Hanna says she treats every visitor like a celebrity—and she's had experience. She has served her homestyle seafood to the likes of Sean Connery and Bahamian native Sidney Poitier. ~ West Bay Street, Gambier Village; 327-7633. MODERATE.

Except for a few little local shops in Adelaide, most shopping possibilities are along the roadside, where vendors appear at whim in permanent stalls to display straw folk art, T-shirts and sunglasses. In unfavorable weather, there may be nothing for sale but queen conch shells—one of the most authentic Bahamian souvenirs, and the most affordable. Selling them to tourists is a creative solution to what the Bahamian government says is one of the country's most serious environmental problems: getting rid of the shells from the more than two million pounds of conch that Bahamians consume each year.

Not much happens after dark on this end of the island. **Compass Point** sometimes presents live jams or scheduled concerts by well-known and as-yet-unknown island musicians who are recording there. ~ West Bay Street, Gambier Village; 327-7309.

Farther out, the only option is the **Flamingo Room** at the South Ocean Golf & Beach Resort. Find out why guests here tend to go to bed early. ~ Southwest Bay Road; 362-4391.

ORANGE HILL BEACH 🧍 🏊 🐟 Located seven miles west of Nassau, past Cable Beach and adjacent to Gambier Village, this mile-long beach is used mainly by guests at Compass Point and rarely visited by vacationers from the huge resort hotels just down the road. ~ It's located just past the turn for the airport.

LOVE BEACH 🧍 🏊 🐟 Just east of Northwest Point, Love Beach is under an approach path for Nassau International Airport. It is a good bathing beach, used mainly by guests at the small Compass Point resort and people who live in the Love Beach residential area. ~ It runs alongside West Bay Street nine miles west of Nassau.

ADELAIDE BEACH 🧍 🏊 🐟 Running both directions from Adelaide Village on the south shore of New Providence Island, this quiet little beach rarely sees international visitors. It's long and secluded enough that you're sure to find a quiet area all to yourself. ~ Take the Adelaide Village turnoff from Southwest Bay Road on the south shore; the beach adjoins the village.

HIDDEN ►   **SOUTH BEACH** 🏃 🏊 ⛵ This long, slender strand directly across the island from the center of downtown Nassau is probably the most "local" beach on the island. You'll probably be the only out-of-towner there. On weekdays, you may not find anybody else on this beach at all. ~ To get there, head south on Blue Hill Road or East Street, as hundreds of Over-the-Hill residents do most weekends.

▼▼▼▼▼▼▼▼▼▼▼
Paradise Island

Unlike Nassau, four-mile-long Hog Island saw few inhabitants or visitors before 1960, when supermarket tycoon Huntington Hartford bought up most of the real estate on the island. There was no bridge to the island then, and guests at the first small resorts had to travel back and forth by water taxi. Hartford changed the name to Paradise Island and persuaded the Bahamas Development Board to support his resort development scheme by building a $20 million causeway across Nassau Harbor. Paradise Island experienced a resort boom in the early- and mid-1980s that was never matched in The Bahamas or the Caribbean—until 1999, when the huge expansion of the Atlantis resort dwarfed all other resort developments in the islands. As part of the Atlantis expansion, a second causeway was built; today, one multi-lane bridge runs to the island and the other returns to Nassau. Though the island now seems packed with high-rise hotels and resort facilities, tourists tend to gather in a few places—the casino, the central part of Paradise Beach, and the golf course, leaving other parts of the island pristine.

Most of Paradise Island can be explored on foot, and many visitors are surprised to find quiet, forested areas and secluded beaches within easy walking distance of the major resort hotels. Once you cross the bridge, the lay of the land is easy to follow. Boating facilities are on the bridge side of the island. The beaches lie straight across the island on the north shore.

A partly manmade boat channel splits the island in half, and the only way across it is Paradise Beach Drive, which turns off the roundabout near the Paradise Island end of the causeway.

SIGHTS

HIDDEN ►

Motorists pay $2 to cross the lofty arch of the Paradise Island Causeway; if you walk, it's free. Before starting the long trek over the causeway, detour beneath it to **Potter's Cay**, where fishermen pull their boats up behind rows of small stands where they sell their catch, ranging from lobster to whole barracuda—and, of course, conch. Even if you lack the facilities to cook your own seafood meals, the market offers a colorful spectacle and a chance to watch the surprisingly hard work involved in prying conchs out of their shells and tenderizing them with a hammer. There is also an indoor fruit and vegetable market where small farmers and gardeners sell their wares. Chefs from many Nassau and Paradise Island restaurants buy fresh seafood and vegetables here daily. Mailboats dock at Potter's Cay and provide once- or twice-weekly passenger service to most of the main Out Islands. ~ Potter's Cay Dockmaster; 393-1064.

> Paradise Island was originally called Hog Island, thanks to hundreds of porcine residents raised on a farm for consumption in Nassau.

The must-see attraction on Paradise Island is **Atlantis**, probably the world's largest and most elaborate beach resort. For non-guests, a "Discover Atlantis" ticket is required to sightsee your way around the hotel (except for the casino and shopping areas, which are free to the public). At $25 per adult, it's one of the priciest visitor attractions in The Bahamas—and worth it. With straight faces, the resort's publicists present it as the fulfillment of clairvoyant Edgar Cayce's prediction that the legendary lost continent of Atlantis would rise from the sea again near the end of the 20th century. Grand-scale architecture, blending ancient Greek and Mayan motifs with archaic-looking Neptunian designs, fills the hotel's multiple lobbies and labyrinthine common areas. Million-dollar sculptures in oxidized bronze and blown glass are everywhere. Outside, walkways wind among stingray and sea turtle ponds and through manmade sea caves with windows onto coral-studded pools dancing with angelfish, parrot fish, moray eels, sawfish, lionfish, 300-pound groupers and more than 150 other species of reef denizens, and culminate in a glass-roofed underwater tunnel where five species of sharks glide oh so close to your face. Together, the fish tanks comprise the world's largest aquarium, with over 100,000 specimens on exhibit, nearly all of which were captured in nearby Bahamian waters. Behind the scenes, Atlantis employs a staff of 60 oceanic biologists, scuba divers and food preparation specialists to care for the marine life and maintains the world's largest fish hospital; the water within the aquarium tanks—over six million gallons of it—is circulated from the open ocean four times a day. Although only guests are allowed to use the hotel's swimming pools and water park, visitors can stroll through and marvel at the spectacular complex, where the high point is the Mayan Temple, a pyramid containing several water slides including one that starts with a near-vertical drop and hurls bathers at 45 mph into a plexiglass tube that shoots them through a tank of live sharks. Atlantis's ultimate showpiece is The Dig, an imaginary undersea archaeological site developed with careful attention to the myths of Atlantis passed down by visionaries from Plato to Rudolf Steiner and Edgar Cayce. Tour guides lead visitors through The Dig, recounting the (fictitious) story of how the Atlantis ruins were discovered and what scientists have been able to deduce from the hieroglyphs, murals and toppled statues, strange technological artifacts and relics of everyday life found there. Admission. ~ Casino Drive; 363-3000, 800-285-2684.

The **Versailles Gardens**, near the center of the island, were a centerpiece of Atlantic and Pacific Tea Company (A&P) heir Huntington Hartford's Paradise Island splurge. The 35-acre terraced grounds feature lush vegetation, reflecting pools, fountains, waterfalls, a graceful stone gazebo, and statues of people Hartford admired, such as Hercules, Napoleon Boneparte, Dr. David Livingstone and Franklin D. Roosevelt. The public gardens are open at all times.

Across the road from the gardens, in front of the Ocean Club resort, stands **The Cloister**, a maze of Gothic columns and archways originally built by Augustinian monks in the 14th century at Lourdes, France. William Randolph Hearst bought the cloister and ordered it transported stone-by-stone to the United States, planning to install it at his California estate. Unfortunately, the contractors who disassembled it kept no plans to show how the stones fit back together, so Hearst left the pieces in a Florida warehouse for years and finally sold them to Hartford, who re-assembled them on Paradise Island with more concern for aesthetics than authenticity. ~ Ocean Club Drive; 363-3000.

Returning from the Ocean Club, take a detour on **Bayview Drive**, which runs behind the Bayview Village condominium complex and takes you past the largest and most magnificent mansion in The Bahamas. Local people claim that nobody in the islands knows who owns it. Sightseers can't go in; peer at it through the front gates.

On the west side of the island, past the older and more affordable hotel zone along Paradise Beach, a narrow spit of land stretches south for nearly a mile to the picturesque red-and-white-striped **Paradise Island Lighthouse** at the very tip. The lighthouse towers over Colonial Beach, the most remote on the island.

LODGING   The **Ocean Club Golf & Tennis Resort** offers a taste of the paradise that Huntington Hartford envisioned for the island. Small by Paradise Island standards, this luxury resort built around what was originally Hartford's private Georgian Revival mansion has 71 guest rooms, suites and villas furnished in period decor. In addition to the Versailles Gardens and The Cloisters, the most idyllic spots on the island, the hotel grounds boast the finest tennis complex in The Bahamas as well as the beautiful Paradise Island Golf Club, surrounded by the sea on three sides.

The resort fronts on what is referred to as Hartford Beach, actually the quiet end of Cabbage Beach. ~ Ocean Club Drive, P.O. Box 4777; 363-3000, 800-321-3000, fax 363-2424. ULTRA-DELUXE.

Originally founded by hotel and casino mogul Donald Trump and subsequently owned by entertainer Merv Griffin's resort conglomerate, **Atlantis** was taken over by international casino magnate Sol Kerzner's Sun International. Between them, the three owners have invested more than $800 million developing this lavish resort hotel and casino. It's by far the largest structure in The Bahamas and the first thing you see when you approach Nassau by sea. The vast complex offers more than 2300 rooms with a wide range of rates depending on size, decor and location, starting from $240 a night in peak season ($180 a night off-season) and going all the way up to $25,000 a night for the Bridge Suite, which is said to be the world's most expensive hotel suite. Besides the magnificent swimming pools, aquariums, water slides and beach, described above under Sightseeing, facilities include a complete health spa, a water sports center, the largest casino in the Caribbean, two theaters, 18 restaurants and 12 bars, as well as tennis courts and a golf course minutes away by shuttle. Free shuttle service is provided around Paradise Island and into Old Nassau. ~ Casino Drive, P.O. Box 4777; 363-3000, 800-285-2684, fax 363-3957; www.sunint.com/atlantis. ULTRA-DELUXE.

Paradise Island's **Club Med**, one of the French chain's three resorts in The Bahamas (the others are on Eleuthera and San Salvador), features 300 rooms in beachside bungalow buildings along Casuarina Beach on the harbor side of the island. As with other Club Meds around the world, rates here are all-inclusive. Activities such as snorkeling, sailing, windsurfing and tennis are free to guests, as are meals, including beer and wine; you only pay for cocktails. The rooms are as simple as can be, with white furnishings and walls. Walkways meander amid 21 acres of verdant, tropically landscaped grounds. ~ Casuarina Drive, P.O. Box 7137; 363-2640, 800-258-2633 (800-CLUB MED), fax 365-3496. DELUXE.

The **Paradise Island Fun Club** is another all-inclusive option. The hotel, with its 250 modern one- and two-bedroom suites, is situated on a private beach on the harbor side of the island east of Potter's Cay. It is the island's most family-oriented hotel, with play areas and organized games as well as free snorkeling excursions and sunset cruises. Meals, included in the rate, are huge all-you-can-eat buffets. ~ Harbour Road, P.O. Box 6249; 363-2561, 800-952-2426, fax 363-1803. MODERATE.

Away from the beach, several housekeeping accommodations present economical options for families or groups traveling together. Set amidst a pretty tropical garden, **Bay View Village** offers a home-away-from-home feel with their 43 apartment units of varying sizes that sleep one to six people and have kitchens. It's a short walk to the beach or the Paradise Island Causeway. ~ Harbour Road, P.O. Box 6308; 363-2336, 800-757-1357, fax 363-2370; www.bayviewvillage.com. MODERATE TO DELUXE.

Another inland apartment option, a little more timeworn than Bay View Village, is **Club Land'or**, a timeshare complex that rents one-bedroom condominiums when they aren't being used by owners or timeshare exchangers. ~ Paradise Beach Drive, P.O. Box 6429; 363-2400, 800-423-8859, fax 363-3403; www.clublandor. com. MODERATE.

There are also several standard inland hotels for budget travelers content to stay within walking distance of paradise. The **Comfort Suites Paradise Island,** just across the street from Atlantis, has 150 modern guest rooms with a respectable motor inn ambience as well as small kitchens that enable guests to save money and savor fresh seafood and produce from the public market on nearby Potter's Cay; guests also enjoy signing privileges at the dozen different Atlantis restaurants. ~ 1 Paradise Island Drive, P.O. Box 6202; 363-3680, 800-228-5150, fax 228-5150. MODERATE.

On Paradise Beach, a 100-room Bahamian-style inn called **Paradise/Paradise Beach Resort**, owned by the Atlantis complex and operated with fun-loving budget-conscious travelers in mind, stands amid a forest of casuarina trees. Half of the spartan rooms have beach views, and the others look out on the woods. The laid-back beach features free snorkeling and windsurfing and a small open-air restaurant. There's a free shuttle to the Atlantis Paradise Island Casino, as well as free bicycles for guests' use. ~ Casuarina Drive, P.O. Box 6259; 363-3000, 800-321-3000, fax 363-2540. MODERATE.

HIDDEN ►

The most unusual Paradise Island accommodations are at the **Sivananda Ashram Yoga Retreat**, in a secluded location at the far end of Casuarina Beach. A sign at the entrance says it all, "Club Meditation." The only such ashram in the Caribbean, the retreat features lodging in private huts, shared dormitory rooms or your own tent. Special workshops on yoga, meditation and fasting are offered. No smoking or drinking is allowed on the premises. The daily rate includes accommodations, meals and classes. ~ P.O. Box 7550; 363-2902, 800-783-9642 fax 363-3783. BUDGET.

DINING

There's no such thing as an inexpensive eatery on Paradise Island. Resort operators are keenly aware that their restaurants can separate you from your cash just as fast as the casino can. Those whose goal is to see Paradise Island as cheaply as possible should bring their own lunch—or skip a few meals first. Among the many restaurants in the **Atlantis** complex are two widely separated, equally large and luscious buffets where you can eat all-you-can-eat for slightly under $20. The resort has no less than 16 other restaurants, though you can wander around for a while looking for one. Standouts include **The Café at the Great Hall of Waters**, serving exceptional presentations of fish, poultry and beef dishes in a casually elegant setting surrounded by aquarium tanks, and **Five Twins**, featuring Asian nouveau dishes and a fabulous sushi and sake bar. ~ Casino Drive; 363-3000. DELUXE TO ULTRA-DELUXE.

Café Martinique, in spite of its deceptively simple-sounding name, is the top of the line at the Atlantis resort. James Bond dined here in the 1965 action film *Thunderball*, as the hotel reminds guests at every opportunity. The menu, more Continental than Double-Oh-Seven, actually has the aplomb to offer a $20 appetizer of escargot bourguignon with a straight face in a country where the staple protein is queen conch—the world's biggest, toughest snail. Chateaubriand is perhaps the ultimate self-indulgence here, since beef, which must be imported, is quite rare in The Bahamas. ~ Casino Drive; 363-3000. ULTRA-DELUXE.

SHOPPING

A grand-scale luxury shopping complex was planned as part of the Atlantis expansion, but fierce opposition from other Paradise Island hotels and West Bay Street merchants put a stop to it. There are a number of exclusive shops within the **Atlantis** complex, as well as a slightly less prestigious enclave of duty-free perfume, jewelry and T-shirt shops in **Hurricane Hole Plaza** near the east causeway. Across the street from the plaza is the new **BahamaCraft Market** (322-3740), a clean, spacious arts and crafts market operated by the Bahamian government where Out Islanders bring their straw work, wood carving, blown glass and other handicrafts for sale to visitors. More inviting than the Nassau Straw Market, it is probably the best place in The Bahamas for one-stop folk art shopping.

NIGHTLIFE

Paradise Island is the liveliest place in the Nassau area after dark. The center of attention is the **Paradise Island Casino** in the Atlantis complex. The vast casino—the largest in the Caribbean—never stops. The BahaMen, Nassau's top club band for many years, are now the casino's permanent lounge act, and you can hear them practically for free by finding a video poker machine close to the elevated stage and gambling away a roll or two of quarters very slowly and thoughtfully while waitresses bring you free drinks. Adjoining the casino, the Cabaret Theatre presents Las Vegas–style shows nightly except Sunday. Also in the resort,

Joker's Wild presents stand-up comedy acts. Cover. ~ Casino Drive; 363-3000.

BEACHES　　**CABBAGE BEACH (HARTFORD BEACH)** 🏃 ⛵ 🚤 ⛵ ⛴ The open-ocean beaches on the north side of Paradise Island are the most beautiful in the Nassau area, and this is the most popular. History does not record how Cabbage Beach got its name, but ever since developers started building world-class resorts along it, they have been trying to rename it to something more dignified—like Hartford Beach. The Ocean Club, which was built by Huntington Hartford, not only changed the name of its end of the beach but transferred the name Cabbage Beach to a small strip of sand along the back nine of its golf course, all to no avail. Local maps, which are produced across the bridge in Nassau, call the beach by what locals know as its right name. Cabbage or Hartford, it is one of the best-known beaches in the world. Both the resorts and private entrepreneurs offer every type of water sport imaginable, and you can't walk down the beach without someone offering to rent you a wave runner, sailboard, sea kayak or snorkel and fins. Most of the activity focuses around the stretch of beach in front of the huge Atlantis complex, which accommodates more guests than all other hotels on the island combined. You don't have to walk far to find a quieter stretch of beach. ~ It's easy to find: just stroll through the Atlantis lobby, past the swimming pool area, and you're there.

SNORKELER'S COVE BEACH 🏃 ⛵ 🚤 East of Cabbage (Hartford) Beach, this stunning beach is deserted and as romantic as your wildest fantasies—about half the time. It's a favorite destination for "booze cruises," which descend on the beach several times a day with little warning and disgorge 40 or 50 passengers for an hour-long picnic in paradise, then leave nothing but footprints in the sand. The expensive all-you-can-drink boat trip takes longer than walking. ~ To get there, walk north from Hartford Beach around a rocky point. (You can't reach this beach by road without trespassing on the private Paradise Island Golf Club grounds.)

▼▼▼▼▼▼▼▼▼▼▼▼▼▼
Outdoor Adventures

BOATING

Boaters heading to Nassau generally come in between Chub Cay and New Providence. Nassau Harbour, between Paradise Island and New Providence, has many marinas, including the famed Hurricane Hole, a small, sheltered bay on Paradise Island that has been protecting ships for centuries.

For visitors who lack boats of their own, Nassau operators offer a variety of sea excursions. Among them are **Booze & Cruise** ~ 393-3722; **Calypso Cruises** ~ 363-3577; **Majestic Tours** ~ 322-

2606; **Nassau Cruises** ~ 363-3577; **Topsail Yacht Charters** ~ 393-0820; and, on Paradise Island, **Flying Cloud** ~ 363-2208.

The **Seaworld Explorer** semi-submarine takes you on a 90-minute journey among intricate coral formations teeming with colorful tropical fish. Although the boat, originally designed for sightseeing on Australia's Great Barrier Reef, does not actually submerge, passengers sit in air-conditioned comfort at picture windows five feet below the water line and get fantastic views of the undersea world. ~ 356-2548.

The northernmost cays of the Exumas are actually closer to Nassau than to the island of Great Exuma. **The Fantastic Exuma Powerboat Adventure** takes visitors on an all-day trip to the iguana preserve on Allen Cay for nature walks, snorkeling, and a grouper barbecue. ~ 327-5385. **Island World Adventures** runs high-speed 45-foot powerboats to Saddleback Cay for a day of sunbathing and birdwatching. ~ 363-3577.

FISHING

Nassau is a big lure to anglers, thanks largely to the close proximity of the Tongue of the Ocean, a 10,200-foot-deep underwater box canyon that corrals bonito, tuna, marlin and amberjack. To arrange a charter or headboat trip out to the deep water, contact the **Charter Boat Association** ~ 363-2335; **Brown's Charters** ~ 324-1215; **Chubasco Charters** ~ 322-8148; or **Nassau Yacht Haven** ~ 393-8173.

GOLF

The **Cable Beach Golf Course**, co-operated by the Radisson Hotel and Arnold Palmer Golf Management, is open to the public. The back nine features challenging water hazards. ~ West Bay Street; 327-6000.

Farther out on the western tip of the island, the **South Ocean Golf Course** boasts one of the most beautiful seascape settings in the islands. ~ South Ocean Beach & Golf Resort; 362-4391.

The Dick Wilson–designed **Paradise Island Golf Club** is a popular daytime diversion for many Paradise Island and New Providence visitors. The 14th hole is one of the prettiest golf holes in The Bahamas, running along the Atlantic Ocean and the beach. ~ Paradise Island Drive; 393-3625.

TENNIS

Paradise Island is popular with tennis players. Several of the resorts have tennis courts, which allow nonguests to play for a fee, including **Atlantis Paradise Island Resort & Casino** ~ 363-3000 and **Pirate's Cove Holiday Inn** ~ 326-2101. Serious players can often be found at the **Ocean Club** and it's nine well-maintained courts, which also allows nonguests to pay and play. ~ 363-3000.

RIDING STABLES

Happy Trails Stables arranges trail rides in the New Providence countryside. It's a pretty way to see another aspect of the island, where you'll find quiet woods and an even quieter beach. No experience is required, though children must be at least eight years old. ~ Coral Harbour; 362-1820.

**BIKING/
KAYAKING**

Perhaps the most unique tour experience on New Providence Island is offered by **Peddle & Paddle Ecoventures**, which guides visitors on trips to rarely visited parts of the island by mountain bike and sea kayak (full-day trips include both experiences; half-day trips feature one or the other). Each "ecoventure" is custom-designed for the participants' interests and may include reef snorkeling, birdwatching, and exploring the island's forests or freshwater lakes and creeks. ~ 362-2772.

BIRDING

Nature lovers find Paradise Island—and especially the Paradise Island Golf Club—home to abundant waterfowl and wading birds. During a morning walk, observant birdwatchers may see great blue herons, snowy egrets, tricolored herons, little blue herons, green herons, great egrets, yellow-crowned night herons, black-crowned night herons, olivaceous cormorants, Bahama pintails, ruddy ducks, common moorhens and Caribbean coots. Up in the sky, you will surely see ospreys and belted kingfishers.

During the fall and winter seasons, when migratory songbirds travel to The Bahamas, many warblers are active in the wooded areas on Paradise Island. It is not uncommon to see American redstarts, black-and-white warblers, black-throated blue warblers, Cape May warblers and palm warblers busily feeding in the wooded areas on the island. Two other birds easily seen are the smooth-billed ani (a large black bird with a parrot-like beak) and the endemic Bahama woodstar (a hummingbird), who visits flowering plants all over the island.

Anyone wishing to walk on the Paradise Island Golf Club to view the bird life should first check in at the office, since it's first and foremost a golf course. The **Bahamas National Trust** has a very active ornithology group that organizes monthly walks to different areas on the island, and their office can also recommend guides for serious birdwatchers. ~ Bahamas National Trust, Village Road; 393-1317.

DIVING

NASSAU Nassau's most famous dive site is **Thunderball Reef**, the location for the speargun scene in the 1965 action movie *Thunderball*. This small, shallow reef typically sparkles with fish in the daylight hours and also makes for a great dive at night, when the lobster come out.

Other popular sites include the **Alcora Wreck**, a captured drug smuggling boat that was sunk on government orders to serve as a dive site, and the LCT **Wreck**, a World War II landing craft used as an island freighter after the war, which sank in shallow water.

Conveniently based at the Yacht Haven Marina, **Bahama Divers** offers a wide variety of scuba diving and snorkeling trips to nearby and offshore reefs on the north side of the island. Free transfers from your hotel are included. ~ East Bay Street; 393-5644, 800-398-3483.

Another busy East Bay Street dive shop, **Divers Haven**, is probably the city's largest store. They also feature free transfers from hotels and daily snorkeling trips right from their shop. ~ East Bay Street; 393-0869.

Located at the British Colonial in downtown Nassau, **Sun Divers** is another north shore dive operation. Owner/operators Lambert Albury and Steve Sweeting run morning and afternoon trips from the British Colonial dock. They also have snorkeling outings to Athol Island and elsewhere. They have excellent packages that include lodging at the British Colonial. ~ 1 Bay Street; 325-8927, 800-258-2786.

Snorkeling right off the beach works well almost everywhere—especially **Snorkelers Cove Beach** off Paradise Island and **Love Beach** off New Providence. For organized snorkeling trips, contact **Island Fantasy** ~ 393-3621; **Robinson Crusoe Shipwreck Cruises** ~ 322-2606; **Sea Island Adventure** ~ 325-3910; or **Topsail Yacht Charters** ~ 393-0820.

For nondivers, **Hartley's Undersea Walk** offers a unique ex- ◄ HIDDEN
perience. Hartley's boat, the *Pied Piper*, takes participants out to a dive site, where they "walk" along the coral reef. You are attached to the boat (and air) by a helmet and tube. Non-swimmers are welcome and feel remarkably comfortable and safe. ~ East Bay Street; 393-8234.

NEW PROVIDENCE ISLAND   The **Bond Wrecks**, which are ideal for divers of all levels, are a popular destination. The 100-foot freighter, sunk as a set for the film *Never Say Never Again*, sits

---

LIVE AND LET DIVE

Scuba operators sometimes offer packages that include lodging in private accommodations close to major dive sites. On New Providence, staying on the south shore, close to the Clifton Wall and the Bond Wrecks, saves divers a long van shuttle or boat trip from Nassau on the opposite end of the island. **Dive Dive Dive** has six villas on the south shore for rent to its customers. ~ 362-1401, 800-368-3483.

Sunskiff Divers, too, has a three-bedroom canal house for rent on the south shore. Rates range from moderate to deluxe. ~ 362-1979, 800-331-5884.

in just 50 feet of water and is packed with fish and photo possibilities. Nearby, the fake "jet fighter" used in *Thunderball*, actually just a bunch of connected pipes, has developed over the decades into a mature, thriving artificial reef.

The **Clifton Wall** offers truly vertical diving on an undersea cliff teeming with an amazing variety of coral. Groupers, angelfish and trumpetfish dance along the edge of the dropoff that plunges into the vast undersea canyon, the Tongue of the Ocean.

Perhaps the ultimate Nassau dive site, **Shark Buoy** is a U.S. Navy sonar buoy floating on the Tongue of the Ocean, in water nearly two miles deep. It attracts big sharks, as well as divers who like adrenaline rushes. Dive operators chum the water to attract the nurse sharks, reef sharks and occasional hammerheads. Many shark dives throughout the world place divers with their backs against a reef or oil drum, but this dive occurs in open water.

Though there is some shore snorkeling to be found on the southern side of the island, your best bet is to take one of the frequent boats or snorkel excursions out to **20,000 Leagues**, one of the better snorkeling sites in The Bahamas. The shallow reef is alive with many tropical fish, large groupers and delicate coral formations.

HIDDEN ►   **Stuart Cove's Dive South Ocean** is a New Providence outpost for serious dive enthusiasts of every skill level, located close to top dive sites including Clifton Wall, the Bond Wrecks, the Runway and Shark Buoy. ~ Lyford Cay; 362-4171, 800-879-9832.

PARADISE ISLAND   Scuba divers find little along the Paradise Island coastline to rival the great dive sites of neighboring New Providence Island. However, two intriguing possibilities are **Trinity Caves**, a series of caverns with spectacular coral growth along the Paradise Island coastline, and the **Mahoney Wreck**, fragments of a sunken steel freighter.

▼▼▼▼▼▼▼▼▼▼▼
Transportation

AIR

It's easier to fly directly to Nassau and New Providence than any other destination in The Bahamas. **Nassau International Airport**, by far the largest and busiest airport in The Bahamas, serves as a hub for the rest of the islands. Regularly scheduled turboprop commuter planes as well as charter flights arrive from Miami, Fort Lauderdale, West Palm Beach and Orlando on a frequent schedule, and from New York, Montreal and Toronto. It's about a half-hour's flight from Miami to Nassau and about two and a half hours from New York to Nassau.

Carriers include Air Canada, American Airlines, Bahamasair, Comair, Delta Air Lines, Gulfstream International and Trinity Air Bahamas. The airport is about half an hour from Nassau in the western part of the island's interior, and there is no bus service or other budget alternative to the long taxi ride between the airport and town.

The much smaller **Paradise Island Airport** has daily USAirways service from Miami, Fort Lauderdale and West Palm Beach. Pan Am Air Bridge flies to Paradise Island from Miami and Fort Lauderdale in seaplanes.

The inexpensive **Paradise Island Ferry** runs from Prince George Wharf to the island every 30 minutes from 9:30 a.m. to 6 p.m. Water taxis also shuttle back and forth to Paradise Island, charging higher fares.

BOAT

There are many independent taxi operators, and it's easy to get a cab from the airport and from the entrance of any of the large resorts. Elsewhere, if there are none around, you can call 323-5111 for a pickup. Prices are controlled by the government, and although the taxis are metered, fixed-price zone fares apply to major tourist destinations. For example, from the airport it costs $12 to go to Cable Beach, $18 to downtown Nassau, and $22 to Paradise Island.

TAXIS

More than 40 small companies with names ranging from the whimsical (the Moonrock Transportation Company) to the mildly reassuring (the Competent Bus Service) operate virtually identical Japanese minibuses on standardized routes that run to all parts of New Providence Island, except Nassau International Airport. The fare is 75 cents, exact change required; it is customary to pay when you get off the bus, not when you board. All buses run until 7 p.m. Buses do not cross the causeway to Paradise Island, but once you walk or taxi to the other side you can get around the small island on the Atlantis Casino's free shuttle, which stops at the major hotels.

BUSES

Car rentals are available from offices across from Nassau International Airport. They include **Avis** (326-6300, 800-331-2112), **Budget** (377-7405, 800-472-3325), **Dollar** (377-7231, 800-800-4000), **Hertz** (377-8684, 800-654-3001) and **National** (325-3716, 800-328-4567). Most also have offices downtown Nassau and at major hotels. Local agencies, with somewhat lower rates, include **Kemco Imports/Car Rentals & Sales** (323-2178), **Teglo Car Rentals** (362-4361) and **Wallace's U-Drive It Cars** (393-0650).

CAR RENTALS

New Providence Island is not well suited to bicycle touring because of heavy traffic and narrow roadways. A motor scooter, though, can double the fun of a road trip to the far side of the island. For rentals, call **Ursa Investment**. ~ 326-8329.

MOTOR SCOOTERS

▼▼▼▼▼▼▼▼▼▼▼▼▼▼▼▼▼▼▼▼▼▼▼▼▼

Addresses & Phone Numbers

Ambulance—919 or 322-2221

Bahamasair—Nassau International Airport; 377-5505

Bahamian Ministry of Tourism—Bay Street, 322-7500; Prince George Wharf Information Centre, 326-9781

Books—Island Book Shop, Bay Street, 322-1011

British High Commission—Bitco Building, East and Shirley streets; 325-7471

Canadian Embassy—Out Island Traders Building, East Bay Street; 393-2123

Directory Assistance—916

Fire Department—919

Hospital—Doctors Hospital, 322-8411; Princess Margaret Hospital, 322-2861

Library—Nassau Public Library, Bank Lane; 322-4907

Nassau Chamber of Commerce—322-2145

People-to-People Programme—326-5371

Pharmacy—Lowes Pharmacy, East Bay Shopping Center; 393-4813

Photo Supply—John Bull, East Bay Street; 322-3328

Police Department—919 or 322-4444

Post Office—Parliament Street at East Hill Street; 322-3025

United States Embassy—Mosmar Building, Queen Street; 322-1183

Weather—377-7178

FIVE

Grand Bahama

The fourth largest island in The Bahamas, Grand Bahama is located just 75 miles off the coast of Florida. Its population is a fraction of Nassau's. Charmless downtown Freeport is far from the cruise ship docks, and the cute tourist shopping district at Port Lucaya is even farther. There are two casinos, each about half the size of the ones on Nassau's Cable Beach and Paradise Island. Yet Grand Bahama surpasses New Providence Island in at least two respects: It has three national parks and four golf courses.

Virtually all development is confined to the side of the island closest to Florida, and visitors who travel to the west side find only a handful of tiny fishing villages along a straight and level road that runs for some 60 miles through an unbroken forest of pines and palmettos.

The island was as sparsely populated as the other Pine Islands, Abaco and Andros until 1955, when American developer Wallace Groves joined forces with British industrialist Sir Charles Hayward to develop Grand Bahama as a tax-free port that would support tourism and manufacturing side-by-side. Lacking the colonial charm of Old Nassau, the island's key advantage was its proximity to Florida, making it a natural extra port of call for Nassau-bound four-day "fun cruise" ships. Also lacking Nassau's offshore banks, the plan was to offer tax advantages to international companies who built factories there.

Today, the industrial zone shares the western tip of the island with the cruise ship dock. Hotels, restaurants and shopping are found in the twin towns of Freeport, about five miles inland, and Lucaya on the south shore. The beaches close to Freeport and Lucaya are enough to keep most sunworshipers comfortably languorous for days, and snorkelers can explore beneath the surface of placid coves within walking distance of the island's main shopping zones. More adventuresome vacationers discover the empty, equally beautiful beaches that line more distant areas of the south coast; the remote north coast is the place to go for some of the most thrilling scuba adventures in The Bahamas.

▼▼▼▼▼▼▼▼▼▼

Freeport

Freeport, a strangely sprawling little city far from the beach, houses more than half of the island's 50,000 residents. Established a mere 40 years ago, it has none of Nassau's colonial charm and little of the easygoing tropical funk of the Out Islands. Yet it has grown rapidly to become a successful resort area—partly because of its glitzy casino and cruise ship–approved shopping zone, partly because of its central location, a quick bus ride or motor scooter trip from a whole array of island attractions, and partly because of a virtue that is rare in The Bahamas: affordability.

SIGHTS

The traffic circle where the island's two main roads meet is right in front of the **International Bazaar** shopping area. Built during an enthusiastic burst of tourism development during the mid-1960s, the theme-park maze of little alleyways with Mideastern, European, Asian and Latin American themes has taken on a patina of genuine, if slightly seedy, charm. ~ The Mall at West Sunrise Highway.

Next door to the Bazaar, the glitzy **Bahamas Princess Resort and Casino** is Freeport's largest resort. The Las Vegas–style complex revolves around the clatter and bells of more than 500 slot machines; it is farther from the beach than any other full-service resort in The Bahamas. ~ The Mall at West Sunrise Highway; 352-6721.

About a mile to the north, **Churchill Square** is considered the center of "downtown" Freeport. This one-story concrete block sprawl surrounds a huge parking lot, the center of which is the loading zone for minibuses that carry passengers to Lucaya, Westside and McLean's Town. There is a colorful fruit and vegetable market on the north side of the mall.

HIDDEN ►

Rand Memorial Nature Centre, located just two miles east of Freeport, is a fragment of a different world. The beautiful 100-acre park features marked walking trails through the pine woods, a profusion of wildflowers and replicas of Lucayan Indian huts. A half-mile loop trail leads to a grove of ancient subtropical forest that provides a rare glimpse of what Grand Bahama's vegetation was like before it was cleared for 18th-century plantations, and again clearcut in the 1950s for paper pulp. The woods provide habitat for raccoons and more than 40 bird species. An open meadow changes with the seasons. The grove surrounds the flamingo pond, where a flock of docile flamingos is so tame that photographers and birders can approach almost within arm's reach. There are more than 20 different species of wild orchids and more than 125 varieties of native plants in the reserve. Admission. ~ East Settlers Way; 352-5438.

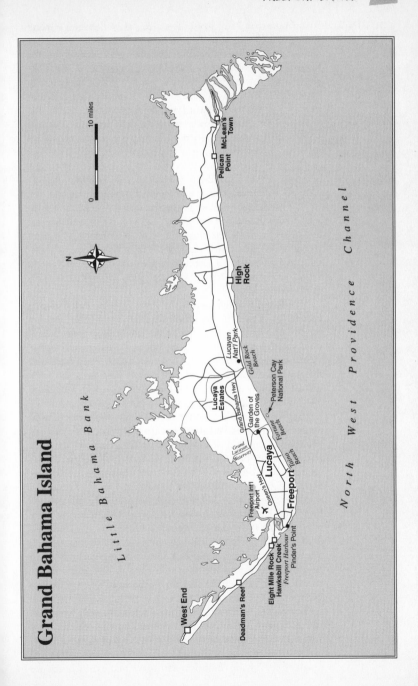

Grand Bahama Island

LODGING   Set on more than 2500 acres, the self-contained **Bahamas Princess Resort and Casino** appeals to golfers and gamblers. The resort consists of two distinct hotels under the same management; the low-rise Princess Country Club caters to golfers, while the high-rise Princess Tower draws the Vegas crows. Together, the two have more than 950 guest rooms and suites, some with kitchenettes. Besides golf, tennis, the casino and the International Bazaar, the hotel provides many activities for kids. A shuttle runs regularly to the hotel's private Bahamas Princess Beach on the south shore. ~ The Mall at West Sunrise Highway, P.O. Box 2623; 352-9661, 800-223-1818, fax 352-2542. MODERATE TO DELUXE.

Howard Hughes once took two floors at the Xanadu Beach Resort & Marina for himself.

In the heart of Freeport, yet less pretentious and certainly less pricey than the Bahamas Princess, the **Castaways Resort** is located next to the International Bazaar. This plain concrete block hotel has 130 unadorned yet clean rooms set around a flower garden. The casino is within easy walking distance, and it's a free five-minute shuttle trip to Xanadu Beach. ~ The Mall Drive, P.O. Box 2629; 352-6682, fax 352-5087. MODERATE.

The **Royal Islander**, across the street from the International Bazaar, looks more inviting from the front. Inside, the hotel has the feel of a quality motor inn, with 100 ground- and second-floor guest rooms flanking a swimming pool surrounded by plastic chaise lounges. Rooms have light wood-grain furnishings and tropical pastel accents. The shuttle runs to Xanadu Beach every half-hour during the daytime. ~ The Mall Drive, P.O. Box 2549; 351-6000, 800-327-2005, fax 351-3546. MODERATE.

Golfers in search of a housekeeping holiday will find 52 well-appointed studios and one-bedroom apartments with kitchens and balconies at the **Lakeview Manor Club**. This country club–style resort is located on the fifth hole of the Ruby Golf Course. Guests get reduced greens fees. ~ Cadwallader Jones Drive, P.O. Box 2699; 352-9789, fax 352-2283. MODERATE.

On the opposite end of the beach from the Bahamas Princess Resort, the highrise **Xanadu Beach Resort and Marina** is just a few minutes from the center of Freeport. This resort has 175 pastel-hued rooms and suites overlooking the beach and swimming pool. The place has a casual family feel. Snorkeling is good in the small bay, and local entrepreneurs are on hand to rent you a motor scooter or snorkel and fins. ~ Sunken Treasure Drive, P.O. Box 2438; 352-6782, fax 352-5799. MODERATE.

Boaters will find a nautical atmosphere at **Running Mon Marina & Resort**. Originally developed as a marina, the property added 32 guest rooms in the early 1990s. All of the simply furnished rooms in the shocking pink hotel overlook the marina and canals of the lagoon. Both Xanadu Beach and Tyne's Beach are five minutes away. ~ 208 Kelly Court, P.O. Box 2663; 352-6834, fax 352-6835. MODERATE.

Families will find 42 clean, colorful rooms—some with kitchenettes—plus a friendly staff, a garden swimming pool, a single tennis court and organized kids' activities at the **Sun Club Resort**. There's a frequent shuttle to the beach, five minutes away. This is the best budget bet in the Freeport area. ~ Settlers Way, P.O. Box 1808; 352-3462, 800-327-0787, fax 352-6835. BUDGET TO MODERATE.

The most affordable place on the island is the **Bahama Grand Hotel**. Though anything but grand, its 50 basic rooms are clean and have balconies or decks. The location is near everything you need in Freeport. ~ West Sunrise Highway, P.O. Box 2318; 352-6025, fax 352-6022. BUDGET.

DINING

Located at the Bahamas Princess Resort and Casino, the **Rib Room** is a British-style dining salon with a hunting decor and red meat—a rarity on Bahamian menus. The restaurant takes special pride in its prime rib, and also features other cuts of beef as well as local seafood. Other restaurant options in the resort include the Continental cuisine of the **Crown Room**, secluded just off the casino floor, and the Bahamian-style **Guanahani's Restaurant**, specializing in lobster, and located in the Princess Country Club. ~ West Sunrise Highway; 352-6721. DELUXE.

In keeping with the spirit of the neighboring International Bazaar, the **Pub on the Mall** is actually three different restaurants housed in one building. You can choose casual British pub grub, more elaborate Continental cuisine or Italian pasta and pizza. ~ The Mall Drive at Sunrise Highway; 352-5110. MODERATE.

Located within the International Bazaar are nearly a dozen theme restaurants—German, Japanese, French, Japanese. For the genuine Bahamian "ting," head directly to **Becky's Restaurant**. ◄ HIDDEN
Becky Tucker serves ample portions of Bahamian staples like lobster, fish and conch. The homey little restaurant opens early, providing the opportunity to sample a traditional Bahamian breakfast such as corned beef and grits or tuna and grits. ~ International Bazaar; 352-8717. MODERATE.

Geneva's, one of several of the native restaurants in the Freeport area run by Geneva Monroe and her two sons, is as local ◄ HIDDEN
as they come. Seafood is the specialty, with creative conch and grouper dishes coming out of the kitchen. ~ The Mall Drive; 352-5085. MODERATE.

Across from the International Bazaar, **Captain Kenny's Seafood Restaurant** has the feel of a nautical theme park, with lobster traps and treasure maps attracting your attention when you walk in. Your attention will quickly turn to the smell of the good cooking that is the real theme here. Try the grouper fingers or any of the other fresh seafood entrées. ~ West Sunrise Highway; 351-4759. MODERATE.

The one not-to-be-missed Freeport dining experience is five miles west of town, near the SeaEscape cruise ship dock, at **Pier One**. The restaurant is in a big wooden house that stands on stilts over the water. Catering to the cruise ship trade, it does most of its business at lunchtime, but dinner is the time to go. After dark, floodlights shine into the clear water below, attracting dozens of large sharks in from the reef where they circle below the restaurant's observation deck, waiting for the kitchen staff to throw out some fish, which touches off a ferocious feeding frenzy. Appropriately enough, the house specialty is shark. ~ Freeport Harbour; 352-6674. DELUXE.

SHOPPING The **International Bazaar** is nothing short of bizarre. Right in the heart of Freeport, as you walk through the huge Japanese-style Tori Gate of welcome you are in another world (or at least country). The Bazaar covers more than 10 acres and 25 different nationalities. From Tokyo to Paris, this is a shopping spree that could only happen in the duty-free Bahamas. There are occasional bargains to be found here, but it's the exotic wares, not the savings, that keep visitors shopping 'til they drop.

You'll find the standard jewelry, perfume, clothing and souvenir shops here, but there are also a few gems hidden amidst the glitz. Art collectors will enjoy the Bahamian and international work at the **Flovin Gallery & Craft**. ~ 352-7564. You'll find more of the same at the **Garden Gallery**. ~ 352-9755. Antique collectors will find imported British items at **The Old Curiosity Shop**. ~ 352-8008. **The Bahamas Coin and Stamp Ltd.** is also a colorful stop whether you're a collector or not. ~ 352-8989.

HIDDEN ► **Fragrance of the Bahamas—The Perfume Factory**, located in a pink replica of a Loyalist house, is for sightseeing as much as for shopping. The guided tour takes you through the process of producing perfumes. You can even mix your own personalized fragrance. ~ International Bazaar; 352-9391.

Though the **Straw Market** adjoining the International Bazaar lacks both the scale and the selection of Nassau's version, it's still fun to shop and bargain here.

NIGHTLIFE The **Bahamas Princess Casino** is cranked up every night. In addition to the standard table games, slot machines and video poker computers, the casino has a Sports Book where you can watch the action on big-screen TVs. Las Vegas–style shows are staged in the **Casino Royale Showroom**. ~ West Sunrise Highway; 352-6721.

For a reasonably authentic though tourist-oriented Bahamian cultural show, complete with steel drums, fire dancing and the limbo, make reservations at the **Yellow Bird Show Club** in the

Castaways Resort. Closed Sunday. Cover. ~ International Bazaar; 373-7368.

The **Regency Theatre** often presents productions by the Grand Bahama Players ~ 373-2299 and the Freeport Players' Guild ~ 352-5533. Call for current performance schedules.

XANADU BEACH 🏊 🏖 ⛵ 🚤 🏄 🛶 This beach is fre-   **BEACHES**
quented by many of the guests in Freeport-area hotels, so it can get a little crowded at times. You'll find most kinds of water-sports equipment for rent here. Operators can help with banana boating, parasailing, waterskiing or windsurfing. The action is at both ends of this mile-long beach. (The west end is also known as Bahamas Princess Beach because the big inland resort has its beach club there.) It's quietest toward the middle of the beach. ~ It's less than a mile south of Freeport's tourist zone; take The Mall South as far as it goes, then turn right on Santa Maria Avenue and (following the Xanadu signs) left on Dundee Bay Drive to the high-rise Xanadu resort at the east end of the beach.

The beachfront community of Lucaya is Freeport's more   ▼▼▼▼▼▼▼▼▼
tourist-oriented sister community. This resort area strives   **Lucaya**
for the feel of a small-scale Cable Beach or Paradise Island. Though the town's suburbs sprawl along miles of beach and spill inland to surround two country club golf courses, most of the ac-tion takes place in Port Lucaya, where you'll find the island's best shopping district and a world-class scuba diving center.

The 52-acre Lucayan hotel strip was in transition at press time, with several existing properties being reconstructed and consolidated into a single 1600-room resort, the second-largest in The Bahamas, scheduled to be completed in December 2000.

Port Lucaya Marketplace, a pedestrians-only waterfront mall   **SIGHTS**
featuring almost a hundred shops and two dozen restaurants. It centers around Count Basie Square, named after the Big Band–era musician who was born and raised on Grand Bahama. The band-stand on the square provides nightly entertainment for patrons of the several open-air bars and lounges that surround it. The Waterwalk, a boardwalk that runs from the marketplace along-side the Ball Channel Bay Marina to UNEXSO, makes for a ro-mantic evening stroll. ~ Sea Horse Road.

Among the unique places that make Port Lucaya Market-place as interesting to sightseers as to shoppers is **Ye Olde Bottle House**. Besides souvenirs, the shop has a museum of antique bot-tles and historical displays on the art of bottle-making. Admis-sion. ~ Port Lucaya Marketplace; 373-2000.

The **Lucayan Beach Casino** compared favorably to the Bahamas Princess in Freeport even before it closed in 1998 for a major renovation and expansion as part of the new Lucayan Resort project. The casino is scheduled to reopen in December 1999. ~ Royal Palm Way; 373-7777.

The **Underwater Explorer's Society** (UNEXSO), the premier scuba diving facility in the Caribbean, is located next to the marketplace and across the street from the casino. There's little of interest for nondivers to see through the chain link fence that surrounds the big building and boatyard, but if you've always had a yen to try a scuba experience, this is the place. UNEXSO's biggest claim to fame is that it is one of only two dive operations in the world where you can dive with free-swimming dolphins in the open ocean. ~ Royal Palm Way; 373-1244.

HIDDEN ▶   On the outskirts of Lucaya, **Hydroflora Gardens** contains more than 150 varieties of Bahamian plants, as well as exhibits about Bahamian "bush medicine." The garden was created as a demonstration of hydroponics, the science of growing plants with their roots in a liquid mineral solution instead of soil. Lush surroundings and soft music make for an ambience that seems less scientific than sensuous. Admission. ~ Sunrise Highway and East Beach, adjacent to Sunrise Medical Center; 352-6052.

LODGING   The following Lucaya accommodations are on the beach, along a road called Royal Palm Way, and are within a short or moderate walk of the casino and Port Lucaya.

The Grand Bahama's newest resort, **The Lucayan**, combines the largest existing hotels in Lucaya while adding a high-rise tower that will double the resort's capacity. As this book went to press, only the 550-room former Grand Bahama Beach Hotel had been reopened, while the rest of the amenities, including a full-service spa, casino and 2000-seat convention center, will open by December 2000. When finished, the 372-acre resort will feature 36 holes of golf, grass and clay tennis courts, volleyball and watersports opportunities, along with 14 restaurants and lounges, three elaborate swimming pool areas and the longest beach on Grand Bahama. The Kids' Camp *is* open, and offers daily activities for children under 12 years of age. There is also a babysitting service available. ~ Royal Palm Way; 373-7777, fax 373-6916; www.thelucayan.com. ULTRA-DELUXE.

The **Silver Sands Hotel** is actually a condominium development that rents out many of its approximately 100 units for their individual owners. All are uniquely decorated studio and one-bedroom apartments with kitchens and balconies, about 100 yards from the beach. ~ Royal Palm Way, P.O. Box 2385; 373-5700, fax 373-1039. MODERATE.

A bit less expensive yet, **Coral Beach** features ten one-bedroom apartments with lots of space, kitchens and lovely garden-view

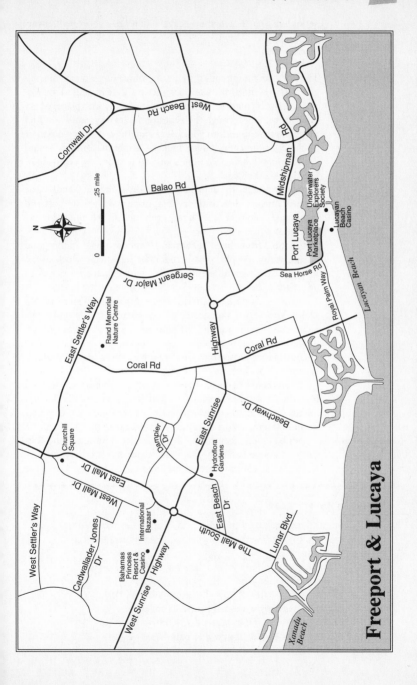

Freeport & Lucaya

verandahs. The beach and Lucaya action are a short walk away. ~ Royal Palm Way, P.O. Box 2468; 373-2468, fax 373-5140. MODERATE.

DINING

The **Lucayan's** numerous restaurants, which range from a nostalgic '50s-style diner to a Caribbean-style grill featuring island cuisine, face stiff competition from Port Lucaya Marketplace, where you can wander through the pedestrian alleyways until you find the menu that appeals to you. Check out any of the two dozen or so choices representing Greek, Italian, Caribbean, Chinese, Texan, Turkish and Bahamian cuisine along with a random sampling of U.S. fast-food chains.

For example, the **Pub at Port Lucaya**, facing Count Basie Square, offers a view of the harbor, imported beer on draft and maritime versions of English pub grub such as fish and chips and fisherman's pie. ~ Port Lucaya; 373-8450. MODERATE.

Upstairs from the pub, **Fatman's Nephew** offers equally good harbor views. People come here for the fresh fish, which comes in at least than ten different varieties, with conch chowder as an appetizer. ~ Port Lucaya; 373-8520. MODERATE TO DELUXE.

Around the corner from the square, facing the Waterwalk, **La Dolce Vita** serves tantalizing pastas, pizzas, salads and wine. Delicacies that are rare in The Bahamas range from veal to portobello mushrooms; adventurous visitors might find the linguini in conch sauce irresistible. There's both indoor and sidewalk café seating. ~ Port Lucaya; 373-8652. DELUXE.

Then there's **Pisces Restaurant**, which combines local seafood ingredients with an Italian flair and boasts one of the longest menus in the marketplace. It has a sea view and serves pizzas until 3:00 a.m. ~ Port Lucaya; 373-5192. MODERATE.

HIDDEN ►

Scuba divers flock to the **Brass Helmet Restaurant and Bar**. Located above UNEXSO, this is the place to eavesdrop on dive stories while consuming cold beer and conch fritters. The decor

✔ **CHECK THESE OUT**

- Wander the walking trails at **Rand Memorial Nature Center** to catch a glimpse of what Grand Bahama's vegetation was like prior to the 18th century. *page 96*
- Dine on fish and chips while enjoying the view at **Pub at Port Lucaya**, a spot of Olde England in the tropics. *page 104*
- Explore miles of underwater caves at **Lucayan National Park**, where freshwater passages wind more than six miles. *page 107*
- Set down for a spell at the **Deep Water Cay Club** and join the bonefishing anglers at this shallow water paradise. *page 108*

is all about diving, and there's a huge shark's head on the wall. There's both indoor and sidewalk café seating. ~ Port Lucaya; 373-2032. MODERATE.

Our personal favorite among the hotel restaurants on the beach is **La Phoenix**, located in the Silver Sands Hotel. The sea reigns supreme here, with unpretentious nautical decor and tasty lobster tails and seafood stew. ~ Royal Palm Way; 373-5700. MODERATE.

SHOPPING

The Port Lucaya Marketplace is situated on six acres of waterfront property near the beach.

For unusual gift items, check out **Ye Olde Bottle House**. The souvenir selection is enhanced by historical examples and displays. ~ Port Lucaya Marketplace; 373-2000.

Among the dozens of duty-free shops are a few places that feature Bahamian handcrafts. If you can't make it to the wonderful Out Island of Andros, the next best thing is to buy one of the famous batiks from **Coconuts by Androsia**. ~ Port Lucaya Marketplace; 373-8387.

You'll find one of the largest selections of Bahamian and Caribbean music on the island at **Intercity Records**. ~ Port Lucaya Marketplace; 352-8820.

NIGHTLIFE

Along with shopping and dining, Port Lucaya Marketplace offers nightly live entertainment from the bandstand in **Count Basie Square**. You can watch and listen from one of the nearby bars and restaurants or join the fun on the dance pavilion.

BEACHES

LUCAYAN BEACH You'll find practically every water sport imaginable on this busy strand, where most of Grand Bahama beach resort visitors bask. (See the "Diving" section in "Outdoor Adventures" for information on equipment rentals.) To get away from the action, you need only head west along the beach to quieter secluded sands. ~ The beach runs east from the Lucayan Beach Resort, paralleling Royal Palm Way.

▼▼▼▼▼▼▼▼▼▼▼▼▼▼▼▼

Greater Grand Bahama

Two highways run from Freeport to opposite ends of Grand Bahama Island. Both are paved, level and straight, and that's where the similarity ends. A westward trip skirts the island's industrial zone and ship harbor before reaching the first of the poor but picturesque fishing communities that were home to most of the people on the island before Freeport and Lucaya were built in the 1960s. There are other fishing villages to the east, along the south shore, but they are widely scattered along a road that goes on and on through the pine barrens, affording access to many breathtaking miles of pristine coastline with beaches and walking trails. Either route makes for a great day trip by rental car or motor scooter and can also be done by public minibus, a good way to meet some of the friendly folks who live out beyond the tourist zone.

SIGHTS   **TO THE WEST**   A 30-mile drive or minibus ride along **Queen's Highway** from Freeport to West End takes you along a narrow spit of land with a series of dilapidated fishing villages, where many of the island's longtime residents live. Among them is **Hawksbill Creek**, where there's often a picturesque fish market. The road continues through **Pinder's Point** to **Eight Mile Rock**, where many old houses line the road.

The name Grand Bahama was derived from the Spanish for "big underwater" —*gran bajamar*.

West End, on the very tip of the spit, was once a haven for bootleggers and rumrunners. In the early days of the 1960s tourist boom, the smugglers' cove was converted into a marina with a full-service resort hotel that promised to bring jobs and opportunities to the people of West End. But governmental in-fighting and a labor strike shut the hotel down before it had been open for a year. The abandoned hotel had all but vanished into an overgrowth of some of the island's lushest vegetation. Finally, in 1998, developers obtained government approval to turn the ruins of the old hotel into an ambitious $20 million luxury resort complex. The first phase, now under construction (although no opening date has been announced), will feature 47 cottage-style accommodations and a new 150-slip marina along with waterfront promenades, a swimming pool, tennis and volleyball courts and exercise facilities. In the long term, developers envision a 500-room, five-star hotel and oceanfront golf course to be completed by the year 2008. Meanwhile, the resort project is providing hundreds of jobs for West End residents whose previous options for earning a living were limited to fishing for conch or commuting an hour each way to work in Freeport factories.

TO THE EAST   Located just seven miles east of Freeport, **Garden of the Groves** is a lush 11-acre garden surrounding a large reflecting pool and shady fern gully. Designed and built by Wallace and Georgette Groves, the garden has a profusion of tropical flowers from around the world, as well as a fair share of birds, including a flock of flamingos. The landscaping includes a stone chapel, a replica of the first church on the island. Admission. ~ Midshipman Road and Magellan Drive; 352-4045.

Just before reaching the garden, the road crosses the **Grand Lucayan Waterway**, a manmade canal that separates the developed western part of the island from the larger, all but uninhabited eastern part. Built in the 1960s as part of a grand real estate scheme, the $30 million canal provided water frontage for hundreds of subdivision lots on which no homes were ever built. Miles of empty, unpaved roads meander through the imaginary suburbs, most of them ending in cul-de-sacs along the canal.

Peterson Cay National Park, the only island off Grand Bahama's leeward (south) shore, is made up of a mangrove-shrouded one-and-a-half-acre bird sanctuary and its surrounding reef. It's only accessible by boat, and the number of visitors is restricted; ask at any hotel about guided tours. The slender, pristine beach is ideal for beachcombing and birdwatching, and the waters just offshore are picture-perfect for snorkeling and diving. The cay lies offshore from **Barbary Beach**, one of Grand Bahama's prettiest and least-visited beaches, near Garden of the Groves.

Thirteen miles east of the waterway, just off the main road, is the fascinating 40-acre **Lucayan National Park**. Hiking trails and wooden paths lead throughout the park, a tangle of hardwood hammock dripping with strangler figs and blazing with orchids. Locals say this fragment of primeval forest was spared from the clearcutting that transformed the rest of the island because of a superstitious belief that the cave mouths found here lead to sea monsters' lairs. Recent scuba explorations have revealed that they actually lead into the longest known underwater cave system in the world. Divers have explored the freshwater passages of this underground river for six miles; experienced cave divers can apply to the Bahamian National Trust for permission to make their own expeditions into the cave. Across the highway from the main part of the park is secluded **Gold Rock Beach**, one of the most beautiful and pristine strands on the island. ~ Grand Bahama Highway; 352-5438.

◄ HIDDEN

The rest of the quiet drive out to the eastern end of the island is occasionally broken by small villages, but not much else. After passing an abandoned U.S. Air Force missile tracking station, you will come to **High Rock**, the administrative and commercial center for the east side of the island, with its scattering of stores and tiny roadside restaurants.

Pelican Point boasts the widest beach and biggest sand dunes on the island. The road finally reaches **McLean's Town**, where there's another virtually undiscovered beach near the eastern tip of Grand Bahama.

One of the best lodging options outside busy Lucaya and Freeport, **Club Fortuna Beach** caters mainly to wealthy Europeans. It sits on a nice beach on the quieter southeastern shore of Grand Bahama. The self-contained resort is a bit like a Club Med—especially the Club Meds on Eleuthera and San Salvador, where even though you're isolated, you don't miss anything. All meals

LODGING

and just about everything else except cocktails are included in the price. Club Fortuna was built in 1993, so its 200 rooms are modern, with balconies offering views of the ocean or gardens. ~ 1 Dubloon Road, P.O. Box 2398; 373-4000, fax 373-5555.

HIDDEN ►   Bonefishing enthusiasts will find the **Deep Water Cay Club** is shallow-water paradise. Located just off the east end of Grand Bahama, this small lodge features more than 250 square miles of fertile bonefishing flats. Catches average four to six pounds and the club record is a whopping 13$\frac{1}{2}$ pounds. Guests are housed in ten small cottage rooms that look to the west beach and pretty sunsets. You can fish with experienced guides, go scuba diving or simply lie by the pool or on the beach. There's a good Bahamian restaurant in the lodge. Though you can reach the club by flying to Freeport, they also operate their own charter flights from West Palm Beach to their private airstrip. ~ 1100 Lee Wagener Boulevard, Suite 352, Fort Lauderdale, FL 33315; 305-359-0488, fax 305-359-9488; www.deepwatercay.com. ULTRA-DELUXE.

DINING   Located far out at Deadman's Reef on the way to West End, the **Buccaneer Club** is a Bavarian beer garden right in the middle of The Bahamas. The German beer and food—not to mention the German hosts—make for a unique outing from Freeport or Lucaya. The beach and sunsets here are superb. ~ Deadman's Reef; 349-3794. MODERATE.

HIDDEN ►   For a cool drink or a Bahamian snack on the way to West End, eat with the locals at **Henry's Place** in Eight Mile Rock. In this no-frills diner, folks from around the long, ramshackle fishing village prop their elbows on the squeaky clean formica table tops as they gossip the afternoon away, dig into a heap of sizzling cracked conch or just wait for the bus. Tourists are rarely seen here, and the food is authentic. ~ Queen's Highway; 348-2241. BUDGET.

Way out in West End, **The Star Hotel Restaurant & Lounge** is a classic Grand Bahama outpost. Originally the first hotel on the island, this 24-hour restaurant and bar welcomes guests with friendly conversation and solid Bahamian and American fare. ~ Bayshore Road, West End; 346-6207. MODERATE.

Toward the eastern part of the island, **The Stoned Crab** on pretty Taino Beach between Lucaya and Garden of the Groves, has some of the best seafood on the island. You can eat inside or out on a beach patio. The service is superb and your fellow diners will be well-to-do islanders and visiting connoisseurs. This splurge spot can only be reached by taxi, and that's just a small part of the expense. ~ Taino Beach; 373-1442. DELUXE.

NIGHTLIFE   The Star Hotel Restaurant & Lounge in West End is open 24 hours a day, and you can find a game of pool, a cold Kalik and

local conversation there at any time of the day or night. ~
Bayshore Road, West End; 346-6207.

TAINO BEACH, CHURCHILL BEACH AND FORTUNE BEACH   **BEACHES**
East of Lucaya, these beaches string to-
gether like a strand of pearls, easily accessible yet never crowded.
The farther east you head, the less civilization you'll find. ~ Take
Midshipman Road east from Port Lucaya Marketplace. To reach
Taino Beach, turn right on West Beach Road; to reach Churchill
and Fortune beaches, turn right on Churchill Drive.

BARBARY BEACH Situated just east of the Grand
Lucayan Waterway, this is the most secluded beach in the
Freeport/Lucaya area—and perhaps the most beautiful. Beachcombers know Barbary Beach for its great variety of seashells. In
May and June, fields near the beach bloom in a spectacular display of white spider lilies. Peterson Cay, a one-and-a-half-acre island that has been set aside as a national park, lies less than a
mile offshore. ~ To get there, take East Sunrise Highway for eight
miles east of Freeport and, just after crossing the Grand Bahama
Waterway, turn right at the first roundabout and follow the road
to the beach.

GOLD ROCK BEACH Situated far east in the Lu-
cayan National Park, this is one of the best beaches on the island.
Your short hike in will be rewarded with a secluded, casuarina-
fringed stretch of golden sand that rarely sees visitors on weekdays. It is, however, popular with locals on weekends. They'll be
happy to let you join them. ~ It's located 20 miles east of Freeport, across East Sunrise Highway from the Lucayan National
Park parking area.

Grand Bahama features good boating facilities
from one end to the other—motorized boats are **Outdoor Adventures**
more widely used than sailing craft. Most of the
north shore, with its pristine cays, hidden coves and coral reef   **BOATING**
dive sites, can only be reached by boat, either by rounding the
east or west tip of the island or by cruising right through the middle of it on the Grand Lucayan Waterway.

FREEPORT **Running Mon Marina**, located east of the Xanadu
Beach Resort, has slips for 66 boats up to 80 feet in length and
a boat repair facility with lifting capability. ~ 208 Kelly Court;
352-6833.

LUCAYA The **Lucayan Marina Village**, the largest and most
modern marina on the island, has 125 slips for boats up to 200
feet long and is open for fueling 24 hours a day. ~ Midshipman
Road; 373-7616. A smaller, less busy facility, the **Bell Channel
Club & Marina** has 18 slips for boats up to 50 feet long; they

are for owners of the adjacent condominiums but are rented to the public when not in use. ~ Jolly Roger Drive; 373-2673.

Didn't bring your own boat? No problem. Several boat tours operate out of Port Lucaya. For instance, the *Mermaid Kitty* offers 90-minute glass-bottom boat trips. ~ 373-5880. And the *Bahama Mama* provides catamaran excursions. ~ 373-7863.

KAYAKING The calm and shallow waters of many parts of Grand Bahama's north side are especially good for sea kayaking. **Erika Moultrie** runs five-hour tours through several small creeks and shallow seas. ~ North Shore; 373-2485.

FISHING Grand Bahama has become one of The Bahamas' most popular deep-sea fishing areas. Sportfishing is best for king mackerel from January to April, for white marlin from April to June, for blue marlin, blue tuna and dolphin from April to July and for wahoo from November to April.

FREEPORT Several members of the Grand Bahama Charter Fishing Operators Association offer half-day and full-day operate fishing charters from the **Running Mon Marina**. ~ 208 Kelly Court; 352-6833.

LUCAYA **Reef Tours**, one of several outfitters, operates deep-sea fishing trips daily. ~ Port Lucaya; 373-5880.

GREATER GRAND BAHAMA Along with the various operators and opportunities out of Lucaya and Freeport, anglers in search of a great bonefishing vacation need look no further than **Deep Water Cay Club** off the east coast of Grand Bahama. ~ 1100 Lee Wagener Boulevard, Suite 352, Fort Lauderdale, FL 33315; 305-359-0488, fax 305-359-9488.

Serious anglers may also want to contact **World Wide Sportsman**. They offer bonefishing packages at Deep Water Cay Club, as well as other spots around The Bahamas (and the world). ~ P.O. Box 787, Islamorada, FL 33036; 305-664-4615, 800-327-2880, fax 305-664-3692.

GOLF In the 1960s, when developers started developing strategies to transform the rather bland island of Grand Bahama into an international tourist destination, the first thing they did was to design great golf courses. Today, the island has more and better courses than anyplace else in The Bahamas.

FREEPORT The Bahamas Princess Resort and Casino operates two golf courses near their property. The **Princess Emerald Course** was designed by Dick Wilson and offers a number of water hazards and sand traps. The **Princess Ruby Course** was designed by Joe Lee. ~ West Sunrise Highway; 352-6721.

Shark
Bait

On Grand Bahama, it's easy to become shark bait for the day. Shark diving is not as uncommon or uncommonly dangerous as it may sound. The **Underwater Explorers Society** (UNEXSO) was one of the first dive outfitters in the world to offer swim-with-the-sharks excursions.

The dive, called Shark Junction, has become one of the world's most talked-about scuba experiences. UNEXSO currently runs three trips to the site each week, advance reservations required. Participants start with a classroom orientation—a detailed divemaster briefing, a video from previous shark dives and a waiver that says you won't hold them responsible if you are eaten by a shark!

The boat ride out to Shark Junction is filled with heart-thumping anticipation. As you enter the water, a quick glance to the bottom reveals several sharks already circling, as if they had reservations at their favorite restaurant.

Once underwater, divers assemble in the sand in about 45 feet of water, kneeling with their backs to a big oil drum, so that sharks can't "sneak" up behind them. As the group looks on, a guide begins to feed the reef fish in the area while other UNEXSO divers provide safety for the feeder and the group. Soon, sharks begin circling the area and darting in to snatch herrings from the feeder's hand.

The sharks swarm around the feeder and divers, as everyone does their best to keep hands from shaking and bodies from quaking. People spend most of the time trying to remain as still as possible and wishing they were wearing a steel-plated wetsuit.

The sharks definitely look hungry, mean, powerful, fast and menacing. Looks can be deceiving, though. UNEXSO divers know each of the biggest sharks by name, and even know which ones will let themselves be touched. The dive lasts about 30 minutes and is (statistically, at least) quite safe. Many divers discover that the sharks grow even bigger as they tell the story later back home.

LUCAYA   The **Lucayan Country Club**'s existing 18-hole course is one of the prettiest golf courses in The Bahamas. Running through the woods and many water hazards, this course and the club-house have a real Florida country club feel to them. The **Lucayan** will open a second course at the country club in December 2000. Called the **Reef Club** course, the new par-72 championship course designed by the Robert Trent Jones II Group will feature water hazards on 13 of its 18 holes, along with spectacular sea views from the front nine. ~ Lucaya; 373-1066.

GREATER GRAND BAHAMA   The **Fortune Hills Golf & Country Club** boasts nine holes designed by Dick Wilson and nine more by Joe Lee. This inland course set among scenic rolling hills has the longest total yardage of any course on the island and some of the largest greens in The Bahamas. ~ East Sunrise Highway; 373-4500.

DIVING   Some of the top dives on Grand Bahama include **Hydro Lab, Pillar Castle,** and one of UNEXSO's pet projects, **Theo's Wreck.** Hydro Lab is an abandoned underwater experiment site that contains a recompression chamber and other objects that have created an artificial reef haven for fish and coral. Pillar Castle, as its name suggests, has so much pillar coral that it looks like a cas-tle. Theo's Wreck is an old 280-foot freighter that allows divers to go right to the edge of the 1000-foot-deep Grand Bahama Ledge.

FREEPORT   Though overshadowed by UNEXSO, divers staying at or near Xanadu Beach ought to consider the **Xanadu Under-sea Adventures,** located at Xanadu Beach Resort and Marina. This much smaller operation has a great location and daily sched-

DOLPHINS—UP CLOSE IN THE WILD

UNEXSO's popular Dolphin Experience offers a unique opportunity to interact with dolphins. The program at Grand Bahama's Sanctuary Bay takes place in the world's largest dolphin facility, with a nine-and-a-half-acre natural seawater bay. A variety of educational programs that don't require special water skills are offered. Participants take a boat to the bay and then sit on a dock as dolphins swim nearby. An experienced trainer discusses dolphins and the on-site research, including interac-tion between dolphins in the lagoon and wild dolphins in the open ocean. Then participants get to be up close and personal with the dolphins—one of the most profoundly "touching" experiences known to humans. Many people enjoy the Dolphin Experience so much that they sign up to become an assistant trainer for a day.

uled dives in the mornings and afternoons. ~ Sunken Treasure Drive; 352-3811, 800-327-8150.

LUCAYA UNEXSO is, quite simply, one of the top dive operators in the world. Divers flock from around the world to participate in a wide variety of dives, while thousands of non-divers come every year to get certified by the best in some of the best Bahamian waters. If you're a non-diver, don't miss the Dolphin Experience. If you're a diver, the **Dolphin Dive** and the **Shark Junction Dive** are both Grand Bahama highlights. At a depth of 40 feet, the Dolphin Dive lets scuba enthusiasts interact with trained Atlantic bottlenose dolphins along an offshore coral reef. Shark Junction lets divers settle on the sandy bottom at a depth of 50 feet to witness the dive staff perform their daily shark feeding rituals. The sharks are so accustomed to this easy meal that they begin to gather even before the humans hit the water. In a safely controlled environment, divers get the unique experience of observing the sharks at very close range. ~ Port Lucaya; 373-1250, 305-351-9889, 800-922-3483.

Remote beaches on the north shore have good snorkeling, but boats can also take you to good sites. Along with UNEXSO, some other contacts for snorkeling include **Bahamas Sea Adventures** ~ 373-3923; **Paradise Watersports** ~ 352-3887; and **Pat & Diane Snorkeling** ~ 373-8681.

The Lucayan resort will open a complete day-and-night tennis facility with both clay and grass courts in December 2000. ~ 373-7777.

TENNIS

For a unique Grand Bahama experience, contact **Pinetree Stables** about rides through the woods and along the beach. Most scheduled rides last 90 minutes, but they are flexible and also offer instruction. ~ North Beachway Drive; 373-3600.

RIDING STABLES

It's easy to fly to Grand Bahama's **Freeport International Airport**, the second busiest airport in The Bahamas. Bahamasair, Delta and Gulfstream International provide frequent service between Freeport and the Florida cities of Miami, Fort Lauderdale, West Palm Beach and Orlando. Bahamasair also has regular flights between Freeport and Nassau. Air Canada has flights from Toronto and Montreal several times a week. Unlike the Nassau airport, Freeport International is conveniently located—just a short taxi trip from the center of town.

▼▼▼▼▼▼▼▼▼▼
Transportation

AIR

Among the major air charter companies serving Freeport, one standout is Trans-Caribbean Air. The company offers flights aboard their five-seater Piper Aztec from Fort Lauderdale International Airport or Miami's Opa Locka Airport to Grand Bahama.

The price is the same for one to five people, making charters an attractive option for families or small groups.

The airport departure tax is higher on Grand Bahama than on other islands of The Bahamas. Remember, you will have to pay $18 per person when leaving The Bahamas from Freeport International Airport.

BOAT

Freeport's cruise ship docks are located on the western tip of the island, about five miles from Freeport. Ship passengers are shuttled in to the Freeport and Lucaya tourist zones on buses or vans. Most cruise ships, such as those operated by **Carnival**, **Contessa**, **Majestic**, and **Tropicana** lines, only put in at Grand Bahama for the day, and passengers must return to the ship without an opportunity to explore much of the island. Two companies—**Palm Beach Cruise Line** and the Fort Lauderdale–based **SeaEscape**—specialize in day cruises to Grand Bahama. You can elect to stay longer on the island and make the return trip on a later day.

The **mailboat** *Marcella III* makes weekly 12-hour trips to Grand Bahama from Nassau, leaving on Wednesday afternoons and returning on Friday evenings. Contact the dockmaster at Potter's Cay Dock in Nassau for the current schedule, which is subject to weather conditions. ~ 393-1064.

TAXIS

Taxis are readily available throughout the Freeport and Lucaya tourist zones, and after 7:00 p.m. they are the only way to get from one area to another. If none happens to be around, you can call 352-6666, 352-1701 or 352-5700 for a pickup. Prices are controlled by the government, and taxis are metered.

BUSES

Small buses run regularly between Port Lucaya and the big parking lot at Churchill Square in downtown Freeport, about a mile north of the International Bazaar. From there, other buses run several times daily to West End and to eastern villages along the road to McLean's Town. Rates are inexpensive.

A free public shuttle bus carries visitors back and forth between Xanadu Beach and the Royal Islander Hotel parking lot across the street from the International Bazaar every half-hour until 4:30 p.m.

CAR RENTALS

Freeport International Airport is serviced by the following car rental agencies: **Avis** (352-7666, 800-331-2112), **Dollar Rent-a-Car** (352-9308, 800-800-4000) and **Hertz** (352-9277, 800-654-3001). Local agencies include **Star Rent-A-Car** (352-5953) and **Courtesy Rental** (352-5212). Call to check for prices, locations and services.

Because of a peculiarity in the Hawksbill Creek Agreement, which provides autonomy for the industrial and tourism developers of the western third of the island, some rental cars technically cannot be taken east of the canal. Although no police officer will stop you for doing so, it could cause insurance problems in the unlikely case of an accident on the little-traveled eastern roadway. Ask your car rental agent for details on any current restrictions that may apply to you.

MOTOR SCOOTER & BIKE RENTALS

Motor scooters, ideal for day trips to remote parts of the island, are rented by many roadside entrepreneurs in the hotel zones. You'll find a good selection of scooters at the **Xanadu Marina and Beach Resort**. ~ 352-6782.

Though distances are sizeable on Grand Bahama, the terrain is level enough to make it suitable for exploring by bicycle. For rentals, contact the **Flamingo Beach Resort** ~ 373-1333 or the **Princess Tower** in the Bahamas Princess Resort and Casino ~ 352-9661.

▼▼▼▼▼▼▼▼▼▼▼▼▼▼▼▼▼▼▼▼
Addresses & Phone Numbers

Air-Sea Rescue—352-2628

Ambulance—919 or 352-2689

Bahamasair—Freeport International Airport; 222-4262

Fire Department—352-8888

Grand Bahama Tourism Board—International Bazaar; 352-8044

Hospital—Rand Memorial Hospital, East Atlantic Drive; 352-6735

Library—Sir Charles Hayward Library, The Mall, Freeport; 352-7048

People-to-People Programme—352-8044

Pharmacy—LMR Prescription Drugs, Mini Mall, West Mall at Explorers Way, Freeport; 352-7327

Police Department—919 or 352-8352

Post Office—Explorers Way, Freeport; 352-9371

Weather—915

SIX

The Abacos

Often called "the top of The Bahamas," the Abacos are the farthest north of the Bahamian chain, lying 20 miles from the east tip of Grand Bahama and 200 miles off the coast of Florida. The main land mass, consisting of Great Abaco and Little Abaco, stretches for about 125 miles from north to south, with a single main road and a bridge that connects the two islands. Including a number of small offshore cays, with a total population of 13,000, the Abacos encompass about 650 square miles. Although on the map Great Abaco appears to be wide, the entire west coast is spongy, barren salt flats pocked with blue holes, much of it submerged at high tide. All development is along the more hospitable eastern shore and its sheltering chain of cays.

The Abacos' distinctive character derives from their Loyalist heritage. Pro-British colonists left the United States in the first year after the American Revolution to establish plantations on the pristine islands of The Bahamas. Many moved to Nassau; others, drawn to virgin land for the taking in the Out Islands, went to the uninhabited Abacos. There 600 refugees from New York founded Carleton, the first Loyalist settlement in the islands on Great Abaco near the present-day resort of Treasure Cay.

They envisioned their town as the nucleus of a new cotton empire, and for a few years their dream came true. Abaco's economy boomed and the population grew to more than 2000, but the cotton fields failed within a few years because of pests and soil depletion. Most of the settlers moved away, leaving a population of 400 on the island by the end of the 19th century—200 white planters and 200 black slaves. The fifty-fifty ratio has held steady to this day; the Abacos have five times more white residents per capita than The Bahamas as a whole.

In the 1800s, the Abacos took on an almost New England character as fishing, wooden boat building and "wrecking"—salvaging damaged ships while they were sinking—became the mainstays of the local economy. It took nearly a century for the boatbuilding industry to strip the island of its hardwoods, and today only two firms carry on the tradition. Still, the Loyalist heritage of the Abacos remains strong. Many island residents, commonly called Conky Joes, vehemently opposed Bahamian independence and even tried to secede from The Bahamas and form their own British colony. Descendants of the original settlers even went to England to solicit the support of Queen Elizabeth II, but their efforts were rebuffed.

With excellent boating, fishing and scuba diving, the Abacos rank high among the tourist destinations in the Out Islands. The historic Loyalist settlements that survive here offer a fascinating time-travel experience and a striking contrast to both Nassau and Grand Bahama. With the coolest weather in The Bahamas, the Abacos have a completely different tourist season than the rest of the islands. April through mid-August is the peak season, and winter is the low season.

Marsh Harbour

Centrally located on the land mass formed by Great Abaco and Little Abaco, Marsh Harbor is the third largest town in The Bahamas, though its population—7000, including the "suburbs" of Murphey Town and Dundas Town—is a small fraction of Nassau's or Freeport/Lucaya's. From Marsh Harbor, it's easy to explore all of Great Abaco and Little Abaco and to reach the major offshore cays.

SIGHTS

Everything in Marsh Harbour is within walking distance of the busy harbor and marina area. "Everything" includes a department store, a hardware store, two banks and three supermarkets, as well as neighborhoods where New England–style wood frame houses mix haphazardly with newer concrete block structures around a harbor lined with boat docks, casuarinas and scattered palm trees. The main roads—**Bay Street** and **Queen Elizabeth Drive**—have most of the stores, outfitters and other businesses. The intersection of these streets boasts one of only two traffic lights in the Out Islands. (The other light is 110 miles away on Eleuthera.)

Sitting atop a small hill overlooking town is the closest thing on the island to a tourist sight—the bright yellow castle-like **Dr. Evans Cottman House**. The late Dr. Cottman, an American biology teacher, moved to the Abacos in the 1940s from Indiana. His memoir, *Out Island Doctor*, is a Bahamian classic available in Nassau bookstores and Marsh Harbour shops and details his experience "treating" Bahamians in the Out Islands. His second book, *My Castle in the Air*, relates his experience building the big yellow castle. Dr. Cottman's daughter Gayle runs a café and gift shop on the ground floor of the castle and lives upstairs. Closed Saturday and Sunday. ~ 367-2315.

The **Ministry of Tourism Office**, located on the highway near the stoplight in Marsh Harbour, distributes the wonderfully informative publication *Abaco Life*, and can help with just about any reasonable request. ~ Queen Elizabeth Drive; 367-3067.

LODGING

With one of the most developed tourist infrastructures in the Out Islands, the Abacos feature a wide range of lodging choices. Marsh Harbour has a number of quality hotels, most notable is **Abaco Beach Resort & Boat Harbour**. This 52-room hostelry is a subtropical oasis for watersports enthusiasts, with a marina on one side of the property and a manmade beach on the other. It is probably the most resortlike hotel in the Abacos. You can also rent one of six two-bedroom villas with kitchens. There are phones and televisions in the modern and clean rooms, and balconies offer views of the Sea of Abaco. The focus of the resort is its 160-slip marina, one of the best in The Bahamas; it attracts yacht people from around the world. The restaurant and bar are popular with both guests and nonguests. ~ P.O. Box 511, Marsh Harbour; 367-2158, 800-468-4799, fax 367-2819; www.abaco-bahamas. com. MODERATE TO DELUXE.

Abaco Towns by the Sea, a Marsh Harbour complex surrounded by plenty of space, has more than 60 large two-bedroom timeshare units with modern kitchens for rent. Many of the apartments overlook the Sea of Abaco and small beaches. Marsh Harbour is just outside your door. ~ P.O. Box 486, Marsh Harbour; 367-2227, 800-322-7757, fax 322-7757. MODERATE.

Across the street and up a block, the **Conch Inn Resort & Marina** (The Moorings) caters to sailors looking for a bed and bath, scuba enthusiasts diving with Dive Abaco and island wanderers on a budget. The nine hotel-style rooms overlook the marina. The restaurant and bar is a popular Marsh Harbour hangout. ~ P.O. Box 20469, Marsh Harbour; 367-4000, fax 367-4004. MODERATE.

Across from the Conch Inn, the **Lofty Fig Villas** are a good option for small groups and families. The six one-bedroom villas have sleep sofas, kitchens and balconies. A swimming pool is set amidst a pretty garden. The setting is peaceful and the price is right. By the end of your stay, you'll feel like a member of the Dawes family, Canadians who have owned and operated the inn since 1971. ~ P.O. Box 20437, Marsh Harbour; 367-2681, fax 367-2681. BUDGET TO MODERATE.

DINING

The waterfront setting at sunset, the smiling staff, the funtime bar and the food make **Mangoes** in Marsh Harbour a visitor's favorite. Specialties are conch chowder and fresh fish dishes prepared in simple, often creative ways. The seafood plate typically offers fresh fish, cracked conch and shrimp. The desserts, such as key lime pie, are superb. ~ Bay Street; 367-2366. MODERATE TO DELUXE.

Across the street, **Wally's** is located in a two-story pink building with inside and outside dining. Guests sit in large wicker

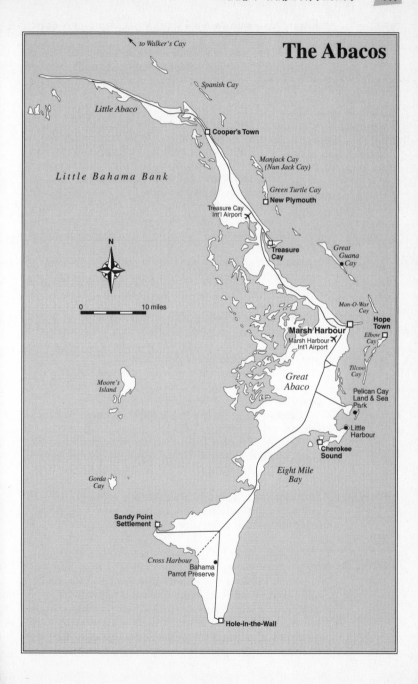

The Abacos

to Walker's Cay

Spanish Cay

Little Abaco

Cooper's Town

*Manjack Cay
(Nun Jack Cay)*

Little Bahama Bank

Green Turtle Cay

New Plymouth

Treasure Cay
Int'l Airport

N

Treasure
Cay

*Great
Guana
Cay*

0   10 miles

*Man-O-War
Cay*

Hope
Town

Marsh Harbour

*Elbow
Cay*

Marsh Harbour
Int'l Airport

*Tilcoo
Cay*

*Moore's
Island*

*Great
Abaco*

Pelican Cay
Land & Sea
Park

Little
Harbour

Cherokee
Sound

*Eight Mile
Bay*

*Gorda
Cay*

Sandy Point
Settlement

Cross Harbour

Bahama
Parrot Preserve

Hole-in-the-Wall

chairs to enjoy native seafood at lunch and dinner. ~ Bay Street; 367-2074. MODERATE.

The **Bistro Mezzomar** at the Conch Inn Resort & Marina caters to the boating set, with good seafood—snapper, grouper and conch—served in a nautical setting. The "Conch Killer," a rum drink, is a house specialty. ~ Bay Street, Conch Inn Resort & Marina; 367-2319. MODERATE.

> Leonard Thompson's book about his life in and out of the Out Islands, *I Wanted Wings*, is a perennial favorite in The Bahamas.

Across the harbor lies **The Jib Room**, with a downstairs restaurant and an upstairs bar that's popular with locals. Steak, ribs, conch *souse* and seafood are the specialties at this casual establishment. Boaters say the restaurant's rooftop creates a yellow glow at night that acts like a beacon light. ~ 367-2700. MODERATE.

If you have a hankering for pizza with a Bahamian twist, stop by or call **Sharkees Island Pizza**. The freshly made spicy chicken or conch pizzas at this wonderful little restaurant make it a local favorite. There are also a wide variety of sandwiches. You can eat your pizza there, carry it out or have them deliver it. ~ Bay Street; 367-3535. BUDGET.

SHOPPING   The Abacos are refreshingly free from duty-free shopping. Marsh Harbour has stores for most every need, including groceries and souvenirs. Most shops, along with a small straw market, are situated along the waterfront on Bay Street.

Cultural Illusions offers a wide line of unique Bahamian creations, including quilts, dolls, food items, straw work, candy, books and music. ~ Bay Street; 367-4648.

The place to go for groceries is **Bahamas Family Market**. ~ Queen Elizabeth Drive; 367-3714.

Marsh Harbour has several bakeries with tantalizing fresh-baked breads and desserts. Follow your nose from the grocery market to **Lovely's Bakery**. ~ Queen Elizabeth Drive; 367-2710.

NIGHTLIFE   Most of the nightlife centers around the bars at Marsh Harbour's various inns and marinas. The proprietors share schedules, offering live music at different places on different nights.

Great Abaco   The Abacos lend themselves more to boating than car travel. Most of Great Abaco and all of Little Abaco are far less developed than the cays that lie off the main islands' eastern shore. From Marsh Harbour, the island's only paved highway runs about 50 miles to the southern tip of Great Abaco and an equal distance in the other direction almost to the northern tip of Little Abaco. Both routes lead through sparse forests of Caribbean pine, occasionally passing farms, fishing villages and small resorts. The highlight of the trip to the north is Treasure Cay's exquisite beach; the trip south leads to the lush woodlands of Abaco National Park.

SOUTH OF MARSH HARBOUR Twenty miles south of town, the little village of **Cherokee Sound** has about 150 friendly residents. Past the southern outskirts of the village, at **Nettie's Different of Abaco**, owner Nettie Symonette maintains a small museum displaying dolls made by her daughter, folk artist Lorna Miller, along with other folk art objects, beachcombing finds and a bush medicine exhibit. ~ Casuarina Point; 366-2150, fax 327-8152.

SIGHTS

Near Cherokee Sound sits **Little Harbour**, once the home of celebrated Abacoan artists Randolph and Margot Johnson. Randolph, now deceased, cast bronze sculptures, while his wife Margot worked with porcelain figures and glazed metals. Margot now lives in Florida. Their son, Pete, lives in the former gallery and studio and sells his own jewelry as well as his parents' artworks. Those who make it out here find an adjoining bar and a festive atmosphere. There's also a **lighthouse** on the peninsula. You catch a ferry to this little bit of paradise from Marsh Harbour. Make arrangements in advance to visit the studio. ~ Little Harbour; 367-2720.

Off the coast, the **Pelican Cays Land and Sea Park** features undersea caves and seemingly endless coral reefs. It's located eight miles north of Great Abaco's Cherokee Sound. Many divers and snorkelers enjoy exploring this park, most of whose 2100 protected acres are underwater. ~ 393-1317.

◄ HIDDEN

Visitors rarely venture farther south to the fork in the road. The righthand road leads to a secluded beach at the little fishing village of **Sandy Point Settlement**, and the lefthand road to a lonely lighthouse at **Hole-in-the-Wall**.

A third, middle road runs out to the shore of pristine Cross Harbour through the 20,500-acre **Bahama Parrot Preserve**, the only major natural habitat for the endangered Bahamian parrot. Set aside in 1994 by the Bahamas National Trust, the park also provides refuge for many other bird species. Walking trails meander through one of the last remaining hardwood hammocks on the island. There's no visitor's center yet, but parking areas and trailheads are easy to spot and nature lovers are welcome. ~ 393-1317.

◄ HIDDEN

NORTH OF MARSH HARBOUR The Sherben A. Booth Highway glides smoothly through pretty pine forests north of Marsh Harbour to **Treasure Cay**. Though it was once an island, the "cay" is now connected to the mainland. No trace remains of Carleton, the original Loyalist settlement on Great Abaco.

Treasure Cay's beautiful beach has a resort community, marina, hotel and private homes. The first such tourist development in The Bahamas, Treasure Cay was the brainchild of Leonard Thompson, an Exumas native who still lives in Marsh Harbour.

With little to see north of Treasure Cay, few visitors head toward isolated **Little Abaco**, which is joined to the main island by a bridge. Those who go there soon discover why others don't. Yachtie vacation hideaways and conch fishermen's shacks dot the rocky coast, and the most exciting thing to do there is to turn around and drive back toward civilization.

LODGING

HIDDEN ▶

For something completely different from the resorts of Marsh Harbour, head about 20 miles south of town to **Nettie's Different of Abaco**. The adventurous will appreciate this genuine Out Island inn, owned and operated by Nettie Symonette, who retired after 40 years managing Nassau resorts to develop this ecolodge reflecting her love of nature and her Bahamian heritage. Nettie is known for her bush teas—five fingers, love vine, madeira, strong bark, stiff cock and many others. The eight rooms with pleasant screened-in porches at the main lodge are simple, as is the lifestyle of the surrounding community. The inn is a base for ecotours and bonefishing. There is another complex of motel-like rooms secluded toward the rear of the property between an eight-mile white-sand beach and pretty Tarpon Lake, where walking trails through one of the Abacos' most beautiful stands of hardwood forest and along the lakeshore offer great opportunities to see Bahamian parrots, flamingos and many other bird species. All meals—excellent Bahamian cooking—are included in the room rate, and the restaurant serves nonguests with advance notice. ~ P.O. Box 20092, Casuarina Point; 366-2150, fax 327-8152. MODERATE TO DELUXE.

The Treasure Cay resort community offers several lodging choices. **Treasure Cay Hotel Resort & Marina** has hotel rooms overlooking the marina as well as villas spread throughout the sprawling property. You can choose a standard hotel room, a suite or a two-bedroom villa, all with sea views on the outstanding half-mile beach. Many guests rent golf carts to get around the area. ~ P.O. Box 22183, Treasure Cay; 365-8535, fax 365-8847. Or contact 2301 South Federal Highway, Fort Lauderdale, FL 33316; 954-325-7711, 800-327-1584, fax 954-525-1699; www.treasurecay.com. MODERATE TO DELUXE.

Many other complexes on this great beach rent facilities. You can rent condominiums from the **Banyan Beach Club**. Set on the beach away from most of the other developments, these two-bedroom-plus-loft and three-bedroom condos are modern and nicely furnished. They're close to everything Treasure Cay has to offer, yet are quiet and secluded. ~ Treasure Cay; 365-8111. Or contact 2720 Biarritz Drive, Palm Beach Gardens, FL 33410; 561-625-3060, 888-625-3060, fax 561-625-5301; www.banyanbeach.com. MODERATE TO DELUXE.

Located about two miles north of Marsh Harbour in Dundas Town, **Mother Merle's Fishnet** is as traditional as any native restaurant on Great Abaco, serving tasty fish and chicken dishes in a simple candlelit atmosphere. ~ Dundas Town; 367-2770. MODERATE TO DELUXE.

DINING

◄ HIDDEN

Twenty-two miles south of Marsh Harbour at Casuarina Point, **Nettie's Different of Abaco** owner Nettie Symonette fixes tantalizing two-course native meals for her guests and anyone else who happens to be out exploring the southern end of Great Abaco. Call ahead; Nettie only cooks when she knows guests are coming. ~ Casuarina Point; 366-2150. MODERATE.

◄ HIDDEN

In Treasure Cay, **Spinnaker** offers good seafood and Continental dining with a view of the marina. The two friendly bars that overlook the water are almost always jumping with yachties, guests and locals. ~ Treasure Cay; 367-2570. DELUXE.

OCEAN BEACH 🏃 🐚 🦀 🚣 Travel-poster idyllic, this wide, sparkling three-and-a-half-mile stretch of creamy sand at Treasure Cay arcs gracefully around a shallow turquoise bay. The eastern end bustles with beach activity. Hike westward for solitude. ~ To get there, take the main highway 20 miles north of Marsh Harbour and make a right turn onto the road to Treasure Cay Hotel.

BEACHES

SANDY POINT 🐚 🎣 You'll find no beach chairs and little shade, but plenty of beached fishing boats, ropes and nets, on the beach at this untouristy little fishing village, whose primary virtue is that it's about as far from the madding crowd as you can get. ~ Follow the main highway south for about 40 miles to a marked fork in the road. Bear right and drive another eight miles to the village and beach.

Starting with Elbow Cay near Marsh Harbour, a series of cays extends northward along the east coast of the island group like a string of pearls. Reached by commuter ferry from Marsh Harbor, the cays are the Abacos' heart and historic soul.

▼▼▼▼▼▼▼▼▼

The Cays

Elbow Cay was one of the first places British Loyalists settled when they fled the newly independent United States in the 1780s. The Elbow Cay village of **Hope Town**, which was the largest settlement in the Abacos well into the 20th century but has declined to less than 300 inhabitants, feels more akin to Cape Cod than The Bahamas. The picturesque clapboard cottages with their white picket fences are easily seen on foot; the town doesn't allow cars. The tiny main road along the waterfront dons the elaborate name of Queen's Highway.

SIGHTS

HIDDEN ▶

A small road runs parallel to Queen's Highway just above town. On this upper road you'll find the **Wyannie Malone Museum and Garden**, which is usually open for a few hours in the morning. The phenomenal Mrs. Malone, a South Carolinian, founded Hope Town, which now has lots of Malones. The museum has exhibits recalling the cay's history from the 1780s to modern times. Donation. ~ Hope Town, Elbow Cay; no phone.

Outside Hope Town, the biggest attraction is the **Elbow Cay Lighthouse**. During its construction in 1863, this red-and-white tower was opposed by some locals because it would reduce the chances of shipwrecks, a source of livelihood for many residents. The kerosene-powered light is still hand-cranked by two islanders. Climb it for the view from the top, overlooking a pretty palm-fringed stretch of sand called **Tahiti Beach**.

Man-O-War Cay, while similar to Elbow Cay in its Loyalist heritage, is much less developed and best visited as a daytrip. The friendly though subdued islanders, most of whom carry the name Albury, have a reputation for being some of the finest boat-builders in the world. Though the demand for handcrafted wooden boats has diminished, you can still see local craftsmen plying their trade in the harbor's boatyard. **Albury's Sail Shop** shows how the islanders have adopted sailmaking to clothing. Nearby, **Edwin's Boat Yard** provides a chance to watch the process of sail-making and repair.

Seven-mile-long **Great Guana Cay** is the longest cay in the eastern chain. A sign in the island's small village proclaims, "It's Better in The Bahamas, but it's Gooder in Guana." As on other cays, you'll find New England–like Loyalist cottages. You'll also find one of the finest beaches in the Abacos, stretching the entire length of the island. Great Guana is difficult to visit on a daytrip; most visitors stay on the cay or anchor their boats there.

Green Turtle Cay is a real gem. The village of **New Plymouth** is where most of the island's 400 or so residents live in colorful clapboard houses.

HIDDEN ▶

The **Albert Lowe Museum** is one of the best museums in the Out Islands. A tour of this wonderfully restored former Loyalist home includes the stone kitchen, upstairs bedrooms and an incredible array of island photographs and artifacts as well as interesting paintings by Alton Lowe, son of boatbuilder Albert Lowe, who established the museum. Several of the younger Lowe's paintings have been reproduced on Bahamian postage stamps. More of his work, along with that of other local painters, can be seen in the museum's basement. Admission. ~ Parliament Street, Green Turtle Cay; 365-4094.

HIDDEN ▶

The unique layout of the **Memorial Sculpture Garden**, in the pattern of the British flag, provides a tranquil setting for plaques and statues honoring prominent island residents. ~ Across from the New Plymouth Club & Inn; Green Turtle Cay.

Twelve miles to the northwest, **Spanish Cay** is not a practical daytrip destination. Once a private island belonging to a Texas oil tycoon, in the 1980s the three-mile-long cay was subdivided into homesites for the rich and famous. The center of activity is the 70-slip marina. For guests at the island's only inn, life revolves around boating, diving and dining.

Even farther north, **Walker's Cay** is at the top of "the top of the islands." Visitors reach this private, single-resort island by small plane or boat from Florida, and most visitors come for the world-renowned fishing. At **Agualife**, you can arrange a tour of a commercial tropical fish operation. Most of the people who work on Walker's Cay live just across the water on Grand Cay.

> Keep in mind that Man-O-War Cay's population is quite religious. They are likely to be shocked by near-nudity or drunken rowdiness.

Overlooking the village and water, **Hope Town Harbour Lodge** is a convenient in-town property. Guest rooms with tropical motif overlook the harbor, and small cottages have views of the ocean on the other side of the cay. There are two restaurants and a full-service marina with watersports equipment for rent. ~ Hope Town, Elbow Cay; 366-0095, 800-316-7844, fax 809-366-0286; www.hopetownlodge.com. MODERATE.

LODGING

About one and one-half miles south of Hope Town, the **Abaco Inn** has 12 cabins nearly hidden among lush tropical palms, seagrapes and silver buttonwoods on a quiet hillside. All have modern amenities, patio hammocks and views of the Atlantic Ocean or the Sea of Abaco. Guests and nonguests congregate after dark at the inn's lively bar. ~ Hope Town, Elbow Cay; 366-0133, 800-468-8799, fax 366-0113; www.abacoinn.com. DELUXE.

Another mile or so south of town, the **Sea Spray Villas & Marina**'s six one- and two-bedroom villas overlooking the water are perfect for housekeeping holidays. The marina offers every outing imaginable. The owners, natives of Man-O-War Cay, pay personal attention to every guest and can help with activity arrangements. While there is no dining room, the owners can prepare an authentic Bahamian meal for you to enjoy in your villa. ~ Elbow Cay; 366-0065, 800-688-4756, fax 366-0383; www.seasprayresort.com. MODERATE.

Across the harbor, **Hope Town Hideaways** rents five large two-bedroom housekeeping units that are ideal for families or a small group traveling together. The cabins offer modern amenities, including direct-dial phones, VHF radios and fully equipped kitchens. There are also a 12-slip marina and a deck pool. Though the property can be reached by land, it's easier to ride across the

◄ HIDDEN

harbor in one of the boats provided for guests' use. Hope Town Hideaways also acts as rental agent for a dozen individual beach houses around the village. ~ Hope Town, Elbow Cay; 366-0224, fax 366-0434; www.hopetown.com. MODERATE TO DELUXE.

Next door, the **Club Soleil Resort** enjoys one of the most peaceful settings imaginable. The six guest rooms are clean and conventional; but then you'll spend most of your time by the pool or in the water, using the watersports equipment for rent at the marina. ~ Hope Town, Elbow Cay; 366-0003, 800-468-8799, fax 366-0254; www.oii.net/clubsoleil.html. MODERATE.

Man-O-War Cay's top lodging option, **Schooner's Landing Resort**, is a good choice for a housekeeping holiday, with four two-bedroom duplex townhouse apartments on a hillside overlooking the beach. All have kitchens. You can stock up on food before arriving or arrange for the management to call in your grocery order. Water sports are available. ~ Man-O-War Cay; 365-6072, 800-688-4652, fax 365-6285. DELUXE.

Set on Great Guana Cay's seven-mile beach, **Guana Beach Resort & Marina** is a true hideaway. The 15 rooms and suites feature kitchens and tropical furnishings. Though boating is the main pursuit, the marina can provide most watersports equipment. Many guests spend their time just lounging on some of the finest beaches in The Bahamas. ~ P.O. Box 530218, Great Guana Cay; 365-5133, or P.O. Box 530128, Miami, FL 33153, 800-227-3366; www.guanabeach.com. MODERATE TO DELUXE.

The **Green Turtle Club** has the feel of a ritzy Florida yacht club. Situated on a beautiful beach with a view of a yacht-filled harbor, this exclusive club gives priority to members and rents unoccupied units to nonmember visitors. Accommodations are in more than 30 guest rooms and suites. The ambience is genteel and the service is impeccable. It's a few miles' taxi ride into New

✔ **CHECK THESE OUT**

- Spot an endangered Bahamian parrot at the 20,500 acre **Bahama Parrot Reserve.** *page 121*
- Settle into one of Nettie Symonette's simple rooms at **Nettie's Different of Abaco** for a true Bahamian experience. *page 122*
- Hit a fishing grand slam at **Walker's Cay Hotel and Marina**, where you might catch a blue marlin, white marlin and sailfish all in the same day. *page 127*
- Eat like a Loyalist at the **Wrecking Tree Restaurant & Bar**, where you can enjoy native cooking under the shade of a casuarina tree. *page 129*

Plymouth. ~ Green Turtle Cay; 365-4271, 800-688-4752, fax 365-4272; www.greenturtleclub.com. DELUXE.

The more subdued **Bluff House Beach Hotel**, a heavily wooded, peaceful property set on a hill overlooking a pretty beach, has standard hotel rooms as well as elegant suites and villas. The secluded hillside guest units are particularly popular. Ferries leave from a small marina for the five-minute trip to New Plymouth. The complex also has tennis courts and a full range of water sports and activities. ~ Green Turtle Cay; 365-4247, fax 365-4248; www.bluffhouse.com. MODERATE.

The **New Plymouth Inn** provides a chance to stay in the midst   ◄ HIDDEN
of island history. Scuba-diving innkeeper Wally Davies has turned this old New Plymouth house into one of the most interesting bed and breakfasts in The Bahamas. There are nine simple, clean guest rooms, all with private bathrooms. The grounds offer a peaceful garden, a small pool and hammocks. ~ New Plymouth, Green Turtle Cay; 365-4161, fax 365-4138. MODERATE.

One of Green Turtle Cay's best options for groups and families, **Coco Bay Cottages** offers four private guest units at the northern end of the island, where only 600 feet separates the Atlantic Ocean from the Sea of Abaco. With beaches on each side, one of the four modern cottages faces the Atlantic, one faces the Sea of Abaco and the other two have views of both shores. Each has two bedrooms and a full kitchen. ~ Green Turtle Cay; 365-4464, 800-752-0166, fax 365-4390; www.oii.net/cocobay. MODERATE.

Linton's Beach and Harbour Cottages has just two cottages overlooking a secluded 3500-foot beach. One cottage sits slightly behind a dune in a palmetto grove and the other sits atop a crest. Each has two bedrooms and full kitchen facilities. The location offers a quiet island experience within walking distance of New Plymouth. ~ New Plymouth, Green Turtle Cay, 365-4003. DELUXE.

The only lodging on Spanish Cay, the **Spanish Cay Inn & Marina** has several pricey rental options, including a total of 14 one-, two- and three-bedroom garden suites as well as four large houses. Most of the suites and all of the houses have kitchens. The inn—and the island—are for those who are interested in getting away from it all while staying in the lap of luxury. Along with boating from the private marina, activities include diving, relaxing on quiet beaches and dining at two restaurants. Most visitors arrive on Spanish Cay in their own boats or by air charter; boat shuttle service is available from Treasure Cay. ~ Spanish Cay; 365-0083, 888-722-6474, fax 365-0466. ULTRA-DELUXE.

On Walker's Cay, the sailing set stays at **Walker's Cay Hotel and Marina**, the island's only accommodation. The hotel features more than 60 varied rooms and several villas. All have ocean views from their balconies. Groups and families can rent Harbour House, a three-bedroom/three-bath house with an extended patio. The food at the hotel dining room blends nouvelle with more traditional Continental cuisine. The Lobster Trap is where boaters head for a drink. Visitors without boats arrive by the hotel's air charter service. ~ Walker's Cay; 359-1400, 800-432-2092, fax 305-359-1400. MODERATE TO DELUXE.

The Abacos have many condominium units, villas or houses for rent by the week or month. Contact **Abaco Vacation Rentals** ~ Marsh Harbour; 508-874-5995, 800-633-9197; **Patrick Bethel Real Estate** ~ Marsh Harbour; 367-2806; or PGF **Management & Rentals** ~ Treasure Cay; 367-2570.

DINING

Elbow Cay has an unusually large number of good restaurants relative to its size. Dining out is one of the big events of a stay here, and daytrippers find plenty of lunch choices.

At **Harbour's Edge** in the village, you'll find casual lunches and dinners served in a picturesque old clapboard house that juts out over the water. Menu choices range from conch and grouper platters to imported beef steaks. ~ Hope Town, Elbow Cay; 366-0087. MODERATE.

Set on a pier at the resort's marina with a view across the harbor, the restaurant at **Club Soleil** offers an exceptional seafood platter as well as fresh catch-of-the-day and lamb dishes for lunch and dinner. Diners who are not guests of the resort must call for reservations in advance. ~ Hope Town, Elbow Cay; 366-0003. MODERATE.

The most talked-about restaurant on Elbow Cay is at the **Abaco Inn**, where the Continental cuisine with a Bahamian twist helps explain why dining in the Abacos is reputed to be the finest in The Bahamas. Start with the conch chowder, followed by expertly prepared seafood or beef. The view of the sea lives up to the food and ambience. ~ Hope Town, Elbow Cay; 366-0133. MODERATE.

HIDDEN ►

In the middle of the island, **Rudy's Place** is a favorite of Elbow Cay veterans in the know. Chef/owner Rudy Moree will send a van to pick you up and take you back to your lodging in Hope Town. The fixed-price three-course dinners, which change

SINGLE-RESTAURANT ISLANDS

On islands where the population is only 100 or so, dining options tend to be limited. The only restaurant on Man-O-War Cay is the dining area at the **Schooner's Landing** resort; 365-6072. Similarly, on Great Guana Cay, visitors are limited to the restaurant at **Guana Beach Resort**, 367-3590. Service and food quality at both restaurants is up to par; prices are on the steep side. DELUXE.

nightly, feature lobster and other local seafood. ~ Center Line Road, Hope Town, Elbow Cay; 366-0062. DELUXE.

The place for an elegant candlelight dinner on Green Turtle Cay is the dining room at the **Bluff House Club & Marina**. Located in the main clubhouse, the restaurant commands a view of the small marina and the harbor beyond. Try the blackened grouper, a house specialty. Lunch is served in an informal, open-air surfside setting at the Beach Club. ~ Green Turtle Cay; 365-4247. MODERATE.

Aside from the dining rooms at Green Turtle Cay's several resorts, the island also has several local restaurants that day-trippers and those staying on the island shouldn't miss. In the cay's little village, **Laura's Kitchen** offers authentic Bahamian dishes—cracked conch, grouper fingers and fried chicken, plus freshly baked pies and ice cream—in a homelike setting. ~ New Plymouth, Green Turtle Cay; 365-4287. BUDGET.

◄ HIDDEN

Right on the water, the **Wrecking Tree Restaurant & Bar** dishes up local cuisine under the shade of a huge casuarina tree growing through the restaurant's deck. The fare is a typical array of native conch, lobster and fish dishes, prepared with love and pride. ~ New Plymouth, Green Turtle Cay; 365-4263. MODERATE.

◄ HIDDEN

Just down the street, **McIntosh Restaurant & Bakery** serves hearty meals and is known throughout the Abacos for fresh bread, pies and cakes. ~ New Plymouth, Green Turtle Cay; 365-4625. BUDGET.

On the edge of town along the main road, **Rooster's Rest Club and Dance Hall** caters to locals. The fare includes cracked conch, fried chicken and hamburgers. ~ New Plymouth, Green Turtle Cay; 365-4066. BUDGET.

There are typical tourist-oriented shops in Hope Town on Elbow Cay and in New Plymouth on Green Turtle Cay.

SHOPPING

Albury's Sail Shop on Man-O-War Cay sells clothes and other items made from sailcloth. ~ 365-6014. Also on Man-O-War Cay, **Joe's Studio** sells magnificent model ships and nautical artwork. ~ 365-6082.

The happening place on Elbow Cay is the bar at the **Abaco Inn**, where boaters congregate after dark to talk nautical and get rowdy. ~ Hope Town, Elbow Cay; 366-0133.

NIGHTLIFE

On Green Turtle Cay, check out the scene on any day or evening except Sunday at **Rooster's Rest Club and Dance Hall**. There's live music on Friday and Saturday nights. ~ New Plymouth, Green Turtle Cay; 365-4066.

At **Miss Emily's Blue Bee Bar**, Violet Smith is following in the footsteps of her mother, 89-year-old Emily Cooper, who ran the bar for decades and became an island legend by inventing specialty drinks, including the popular Bahamian cocktail, the "goombay smash." ~ New Plymouth, Green Turtle Cay; 365-4181.

BEACHES **TAHITI BEACH** Elbow Cay's beach suits the seclusion of the rest of the island. Most Hope Town and Elbow Cay visitors are boaters who do their sunbathing on a deck instead of on dry land, so you'll often find you'll have Tahiti Beach and other sandy stretches here all to yourself. ~ The beach extends along the ocean side of the cay, on the opposite side of Hope Town from the harbor.

GUANA CAY BEACH This beautiful seven-mile beach is typically uncrowded, thanks to the relative seclusion and lack of facilities on Great Guana Cay. Though open to the public, the beach is used mainly by guests at the Guana Beach Resort. ~ Located adjacent to the ferry dock and the only resort, the beach extends almost the entire length of the small island.

Outdoor Adventures

Perhaps because of their boatbuilding heritage, the Abacos are a favorite destination for private boaters, many of whom make the crossing to Walker's Cay from Palm Beach and then head over to Grand Bahama. There is a wide variety of anchorages and marinas, including those at Marsh Harbour, Treasure Cay, Cooper's Town, Elbow Cay, Green Turtle Cay, Walker's Cay and Grand Cay. Off Little Abaco and Great Abaco lie dozens of tiny cays ideal for exploration by boat.

BOATING

MARSH HARBOUR Boat rentals can be arranged at **Sunsail** ~ 305-484-5246, 800-327-2276; **Boat Harbour Marina** ~ 367-2736; **Gratitude Yachting Center** ~ 410-639-7111; **The Moorings** ~ 367-4000; **Rich's Boat Rentals** ~ 367-2742; and **Sea Horse Boat Rentals** ~ 367-2513.

GREAT ABACO In Treasure Cay, **Treasure Cay Hotel Resort & Marina** ~ 367-2750 and **C&C Boat Rentals** ~ 365-8582 offer boat rentals.

THE CAYS Day sail possibilities from Elbow Cay include the deserted Pelican Cays Land and Sea Park and Tilloo Cay. **Abaco Bahamas Charters** ~ 800-626-5690; **Hope Town Marina** ~ 366-0003; **Island Marine** ~ 366-0282; **Lighthouse Marina** ~ 366-0154; and **Sea Horse Boat Rentals** ~ 367-2513 can help with any boating arrangements.

From Green Turtle Cay, one favorite destination is deserted **Manjack Cay**; all lodgings on the island either have their own marinas or offer guest privileges at nearby marinas where boats

Home on
the Range—
Abaco Style

Of all the species of wildlife that inhabit the Abacos, the most prized is a small herd of wild horses. The origin of these beautiful animals is uncertain. Until recently, it was assumed that their ancestors came to the island with Royalist plantation owners around the end of the 18th century. However, recent DNA tests have revealed certain genes that are "rare in all breeds," suggesting the possibility that at least some of the wild horses' ancestors may be survivors of a shipwreck in early Spanish colonial times.

The few dozen wild horses that inhabit Great Abaco today depend to a large extent on human support. The Wild Horses of Abaco Fund pays for veterinary care and emergency rescue missions by soliciting donations at grocery stores and bars and by selling wild horse T-shirts. Islanders know the name of each horse, and when one becomes ill or injured, it's big news in the local papers. During times when forage is scarce, the management of Bahamas Star Farm volunteers pasturage for the horses, and the island's Boy Scouts, Girl Scouts and Cub Scouts organize camping trips year-round to observe the horses and monitor their state of health. Without these activities, it is almost certain that the horses would now be extinct.

But despite their dependency on humans, these horses are truly wild and have not been domesticated for centuries. Though not particularly shy, they are unapproachable. When a horse is in need of veterinary care, it must be tranquilized with a dart before it can be treated. The cost of the proper tranquilizer for wild horses—$300 for a single 20 ml dose—is the Wild Horses of Abaco Fund's largest expense.

The fund's coordinators hope that one day they will have tracking collars for the horses and a well-stocked mobile clinic; they admit, however, that right now they would settle for adequate supplies of tranquilizers, antibiotics and IV fluids. Meanwhile, Abacoans have petitioned the Bahamas National Trust to help protect the horses' primary grazing area from unauthorized slash-and-burn farming by setting it aside as the Abaco Wild Horse and Scouting Preserve, a move that would cost little and would promise the herd's survival and growth in the 21st century.

Donations to the Wild Horses of Abaco Fund can be made at the Marsh Harbor and Treasure Cay airports.

can be rented. Similarly, up on Spanish Cay and Walker's Cay, both of the lone lodging choices can help with any boating arrangements needed. On Man-O-War Cay, call the Man-O-War Marina. ~ 365-6008.

FISHING

The Abacos offer excellent sport fishing, including shallow-water angling for bonefish as well as deep-sea fishing for marlin, sailfish, barracuda and wahoo. Great Abaco hosts some of the world's great sportfishing tournaments, with prize purses approaching $1 million—a pittance compared to the cost of most boats that compete in these tournaments.

MARSH HARBOUR   Bonefishing is growing in popularity in the Abacos. Though the best areas are around Casuarina Point and Cherokee Sound, most guides operate out of Marsh Harbour and take you to the fishing flats by boat. **Nettie's Different of Abaco** can arrange bonefishing guides. ~ 366-2150.

GREAT ABACO   **Treasure Cay Hotel Resort & Marina** offers a wide range of fishing options, including bonefishing on nearby flats. ~ 367-2750.

THE CAYS   On Elbow Cay, contact **Day's Catch Charters** for fishing excursions. ~ 366-0059. On Man-O-War Cay, call **Man-O-War Marina**. ~ 365-6008. On Green Turtle Cay, your lodging can arrange a bonefishing trip with **Lincoln Jones** or another local guide. **Joe and Ronnie Sawyer**, a father-and-son team, offer excellent deep-sea fishing excursions, as well as other activities. ~ 365-4173.

Walker's Cay is world-renowned for its deep-sea fishing. Anglers dream of a "grand slam"—catching a blue marlin, a white marlin and a sailfish on the same day.

GOLF

The only golf you can play on the Abacos is at the **Treasure Cay Golf Club**. This attractive Dick Wilson–designed course is rarely crowded, well-maintained, fun to play and not too difficult for most duffers. ~ Treasure Cay; 367-2570.

DIVING

Though most visitors don't come to the Abacos specifically for the diving, the islands boast one of the largest barrier reefs in the world, and several dive operators can take you there. The **San Jacinto Wreck** is one of the most famous sites in the Abacos. The first ocean-going steamship built in the U.S., the *San Jacinto* sank in 1865 and has since become home to teeming marine life, including plentiful fish and at least one huge green moray eel. At a depth of just 40 feet below the surface, this is a popular night dive.

The Pillars is named for the abundant, spectacular pillar coral formations that reach to the surface from depths of 35 feet. On a night dive, you're likely to see lots of sleeping parrot fish.

The **Tarpon Dive** is named for the huge size and number of tarpon that school at about 50 feet. You're also likely to see a moray eel or two and maybe stingrays and turtles.

Sandy Cay Reef often has spotted eagle rays and large southern stingrays in the sandy patches. **Fowl Cay Reef** has many large fish, including "Gillie," the friendly grouper. **Mermaid Reef** often hides big moray eels while **Angelfish Reef** hosts its namesake in dazzling profusion, while **Elkhorn Park** features acres of elkhorn coral and several octopus. The gardens of elkhorn and brain coral around **Hope Town Reef** are among the most beautiful in the northern Bahamas. **Pelican Cays National Park** harbors sea turtles and eagle rays.

There's a shallow plane wreck at **Smugglers Rest**; be careful—porcupine fish are now at the controls. **Crawfish Shallows** offers a great place to find local lobster and sleeping nurse sharks. For those who like exploring shallow arches and caverns, try **Pirate's Cathedral**, **White Hole** and **Spiral Cavern**.

Other dives in the Abacos include **Coral Gardens**, a garden of fan coral, gorgonian coral and sponges; **Coral Canyons**, an underwater canyon at 55 feet; and **Hole In The Wall**, a huge swim-through coral head.

Because many of Abaco's reefs are quite shallow, they are ideal for snorkeling as well as scuba diving. Among the top snorkeling spots are **Pelican Cays National Park, Mermaid Reef** and **Hope Town Reef.** In addition, **The Spanish Cannons**, where an 18th-century shipwreck left cannons and ballast stones scattered along the reef, is a favorite destination for snorkeling day trips to the northern Abaco cays.

MARSH HARBOUR   Ideally situated at the Conch Inn Marina, **Dive Abaco** has one small boat and caters to small groups with personalized dive trips. The company has all-inclusive diving-and-lodging package arrangements with the Lofty Fig, Abaco Town and Conch Inn. ~ Conch Inn Marina; 367-2787, 800-247-5338.

GREAT ABACO   In Treasure Cay, **Divers Down** offers personalized diving and snorkeling trips. ~ 365-8465.

THE CAYS   On Elbow Cay, **Dave's Dive Shop** is a small operator who arranges flexible trips. ~ Hope Town, Elbow Cay; 366-0029.

On Green Turtle Cay, **Brendal's Dive Shop** offers personalized service and a wide assortment of one- and two-tank dives, as well as a unique scuba dive and picnic lunch package and good snorkeling. In fact, the diving alone is worth the trip to this resort-oriented cay. ~ Green Turtle Cay; 365-4411, 800-780-9941, fax 954-467-7544.

Though Spanish Cay is not well known as a scuba destination, the diving is actually quite good off of this and other more remote cays. Make arrangements through the **Inn at Spanish Cay**. ~ Spanish Cay; 365-0083, 407-655-0172, 800-688-4752.

Up north on Walker's Cay, contact **Walker's Cay Undersea Adventures**, which offers several off-the-beaten-reef dive options. ~ Walker's Cay; 800-327-8150.

▼▼▼▼▼▼▼▼▼▼ Transportation

AIR

The Abacos have frequent and flexible air service compared to many of the Out Islands. There are two public airports, **Marsh Harbour International Airport** and **Treasure Cay International Airport**. Treasure Cay is the closer airport for visitors bound for the resorts on Green Turtle Cay. Service and routes change often.

American Eagle, Gulfstream, Island Express and USAir Express fly in to both airports, with one or more carriers offering daily flights from Miami, Fort Lauderdale, West Palm Beach and Orlando. Major's Air Services flies between Marsh Harbour and Freeport.

Pan Am Air Bridge flies seaplanes from Fort Lauderdale to Walker's Cay. Trans-Caribbean Air offers charter flights in a five-seater Piper Aztec from Fort Lauderdale International Airport or Miami's Opa Locka Airport to Spanish Cay, Marsh Harbour and Treasure Cay. The price is the same for one to five passengers.

BOAT

No mailboats currently run on a regular schedule from Nassau to the Abacos, though independent freighters make the trip often. Inquire at the dockmaster's office on Potter's Cay Dock in Nassau to find out when the next boat may be leaving.

Boats provide ferry service to the cays. **Albury's Ferry Service**, one of the most dependable transportation operations in The Bahamas, offers comfortable passage several times a day from Marsh Harbour to Elbow Cay, Man-O-War Cay and Guana Cay. The 20- to 30-minute trips cost $10 round-trip. ~ 367-3147.

To get to Green Turtle Cay you take one of the frequent ferries that run from the dock near Treasure Cay putting in at New Plymouth and several other stops along the cay's coastline. ~ 365-4054.

TAXIS

Taxis generally meet incoming planes at Marsh Harbour and Treasure Cay, taking passengers to mainland hotels or to the docks to board a ferry for one of the outlying cays. Taxis and rental cars are the only ways to travel any distance on the mainland. The offshore cays are small enough so that taxis aren't needed.

Rather than rent a car, visitors often hire local taxi drivers to take them on tours of the island. While many of the friendly Marsh Harbour drivers offer this service, **Fabian Archer** is a particularly entertaining guide and companion for seeing remote parts of Great Abaco. ~ 367-3780.

Renting a car, even for a day, expands your ability to explore the main land mass of the Abacos. Ask at your hotel for rental car options or call **A & A Car Rental** (367-2148), **H&L Car Rentals** (367-2840), **V & R Car Rental** (367-2001) or **Reliable Car Rentals** (367-4234).

CAR RENTALS

On Elbow Cay, you can rent a gasoline-powered golf cart from **Island Cart Rentals**. ~ 366-0332.

Carts are available on Green Turtle Cay from **Cay Cart Rentals**. ~ 365-4406.

To get around town on two wheels in Marsh Harbour, contact **R&L Rent-a-Ride** at the entrance of Abaco Towns By-the-Sea. ~ Bay Street; 367-2744.

BIKE RENTALS

Knowledgeable, friendly Curtis Sands of **Sand Dollar Tours** conducts several types of tours each week in his a comfortable van, with a different tour running each day. Various trips take in several beaches, historic sights, snorkeling, golf, native dining and an excursion to Green Turtle Cay. ~ P.O. Box 20538, Marsh Harbour; 367-2189.

GUIDE SERVICES

Island Vacations offers environment-oriented tours in the Abacos. Their Different of Abaco tour includes a stay at the unique hotel of the same name and provides the opportunity to view iguanas, flamingos and medicinal plants. The tours are designed for three nights and four days and can be adjusted to fit individual schedules and interests. ~ Contact Island Vacations in the U.S. at 4327 Reflections Boulevard North, Suite 104, Sunrise, FL 33351; 305-748-1833, 800-900-4242, fax 305-748-1965 or in Nassau at P.O. Box 13002, Town Centre Mall, Nassau, Bahamas; 356-1111, fax 356-4379.

ECOTOURS

▼▼▼▼▼▼▼▼▼▼▼▼▼▼▼▼▼▼▼▼▼
Addresses & Phone Numbers

Abaco Tourist Office—Marsh Harbour; 367-3067
Air-Sea Rescue—366-0280
Bahamasair—Marsh Harbour Airport; 222-4262
Books—Abaco Office Products, Marsh Harbour; 367-2701
Medical Clinic—Great Abaco Clinic, Marsh Harbour; 367-2320
Pharmacy—Chemist Shop, Marsh Harbour; 367-2152
Police Department—Marsh Harbour; 919 or 367-2560
Post Office—Marsh Harbour; 367-2571

SEVEN

Andros

Islanders call it The Big Yard—2300 square miles of mostly roadless wilderness. Travelers go right over Andros on commercial flights between Florida and Nassau, which lies only 20 miles to the east. About 100 miles in length and up to 40 miles wide, Andros is the largest island in The Bahamas. Virtually all of the land is covered with dense hardwood and pine forest and tangled in a maze of ocean inlets, blue holes and swampy creeks. Andros has no land higher than 75 feet above sea level. The distinction between land and water blurs in the uninhabited wetlands of the western and southern shores.

Most of the island's 7000 residents live in a string of tiny villages along the eastern shoreline, where you'll find the small dive resorts, fishing camps and other lodging possibilities. The entire length of the east coast is protected by a hidden natural wonder, the Andros Barrier Reef. Reaching for 140 miles, it is the world's third-longest, surpassed only by Australia's Great Barrier Reef. It separates Andros and the western part of the Great Bahama Bank from another equally spectacular geological feature—the Tongue of the Ocean, one of the world's deepest undersea canyons. It is a sheer drop from the reef near Nicholl's Town to the sea floor at a depth of 8700 feet below sea level.

Christopher Columbus discovered Andros and gave the island its Spanish name, *Isla del Espirito Santo* (Holy Ghost Island), but never set foot on it. Henry Morgan, reputedly the most bloodthirsty of the British privateers, lurked around the unsettled shores of Andros in the 1670s.

During the Loyalist migrations of the 1780s, Andros became the new home of the entire British population of St. Andrews, or San Andreas, a small Caribbean island off the Mosquito Coast of Nicaragua. When England ceded the island to Spain they had to be relocated. The 1400 settlers brought the name of their former home with them. It is often said that the name was modified in honor of Sir Edmund Andros, a 17th-century colonial governor of New York, Massachussetts,

Maryland and Virginia and the only known historical figure named Andros. He had no known connection to The Bahamas though; more likely, the name was simply misspelled.

The island's early British settlers established cotton plantations, which failed within a few years and were abandoned. In the mid-1800s, a new generation of planters arrived to grow sisal, a large agave plant that produces rope fiber, but they did not thrive for long either. Among the other 19th-century settlers whose descendents inhabit the island today was a tribe of Seminole refugees from the Indian wars in Florida.

Prosperity came to Andros briefly at the beginning of the 20th century when sponge gathering briefly became The Bahamas' main economic activity. A shallow underwater area known as "The Mud" off Andros' southwest shore was the richest of several sponge harvesting areas in the islands. But overharvesting combined with a 1925 hurricane devastated the sponge beds, crippling the industry. In 1938, an epidemic disease killed virtually all the sponges in The Bahamas, and there has been little commercial activity on the island since. Even the loggers who clearcut other northern islands in the 1950s and '60s were thwarted by Andros' marshy, labyrinthine terrain.

Although it is referred to as a single island, Andros is actually three islands separated by bights, narrow waterways that slice from shore to shore. No bridge has been built over any of these bights. North Andros, the largest segment, has a good road along the coast and several logging roads to the interior, but sparsely populated Middle Andros and South Andros can only be reached from the northern part of the island by ferry boat or plane.

Andros boasts no fewer than four public airports, yet the island is generally ignored as a tourist destination because of a near-total lack of resort facilities. It has fewer guest rooms than any of the other major Out Islands. However, the friendly locals welcome visitors with open arms and express puzzlement that more people don't come. Many voice the prevailing belief that the Free National Movement (FLM), the political party sponsoring the present tourism boom, has shunned Andros because it is a stronghold of the opposition Progressive Liberal Party (PLP). Whatever the reason for Andros' underdevelopment, incomparable scuba diving and birdwatching make it a natural destination for the growing numbers of ecotravelers who, many believe, hold the key to future tourism growth in The Bahamas.

NORTH ANDROS   With a population of 600, **Nicholl's Town** is the largest settlement on the island. The main road has a handful of bars and restaurants and a small clinic. The town's residential area is made up of picturesque wooden houses, many of which have lovely gardens shaded by tall Caribbean and Australian pines. Nearby, the quiet residential area of Pleasant Harbour is an enclave of modern vacation homes belonging to U.S. and Canadian owners.

SIGHTS

North of town, near the airport, lies a huge water reservoir fed by a vast underground freshwater aquifer. Andros supplies almost all of the water for Nassau and New Providence Island. About five million gallons are shipped out in barges daily.

The **Queen's Highway**, a two-lane blacktop road, runs north from Nicholl's Town and then veers south. Four miles north of town, the road turns back at the little waterfront village of **Lowe Sound**, home to many of the best bonefishing guides on Andros. Vendors at roadside stands sell fresh conch and toss the shells in huge piles along the edge of the shallows behind them.

Caves in the nearby limestone formation called **Morgan's Bluff** are said to conceal the treasure trove of British privateer Henry Morgan, who lay in wait here to attack Spanish galleons. Knighted by the King of England for his exploits, Morgan gave up piracy to serve as lieutenant governor of Jamaica, and, as far as is known, never returned to Andros. The legendary treasure has never been found, though many have searched for it.

HIDDEN ►

About eight miles past the point where the highway turns south, a side road turns off to the right and runs across the island to **Red Bays**, the only settlement on the west coast of Andros. This quiet little village of 200 was settled by runaway slaves and Seminole Indians from Florida in 1821. Though the road finally reached it in 1968, the settlement remains an isolated outpost.

Following Queen's Highway south along the east coast, motorists can complete a driving tour of North Andros in half a day. The road goes inland for a few miles to **San Andros**, the oldest settlement on the island and the only one that is not on the waterfront. Instead, it is surrounded by freshwater blue holes and small lakes fringed with casuarinas.

Returning to the coast, the highway continues south, passing through the tiny village of **Staniard Creek**. Here you'll find a long, sandy palm-fringed beach that rarely sees footprints. Nearby, a sign on the highway points the way to **Forfar Field Station**, a "sea school" operated by the University of Miami at Ohio, where students, teachers and researchers conduct field studies above and below the ocean's surface. Visitors are welcome at the main lodge. The center's namesake, Archie Forfar, originally built the facility as a dive resort and then died trying to set the world deep-diving record. ~ Blanket Sound; 329-6129 or 800-962-3805.

The long and pine tree-lined road leads south about 45 minutes to **Andros Town**, home of the **Atlantic Undersea Testing and Evaluation Center** (AUTEC), a joint U.S. and British military testing operation. Proximity to the enormously deep Tongue of the Ocean makes the site ideal for underwater weapons testing. As you might guess, no tours are available. About 400 people are stationed at the center.

Technically Andros Town is not a town at all. It denotes only the military testing base and the nearby civilian airport. The area's

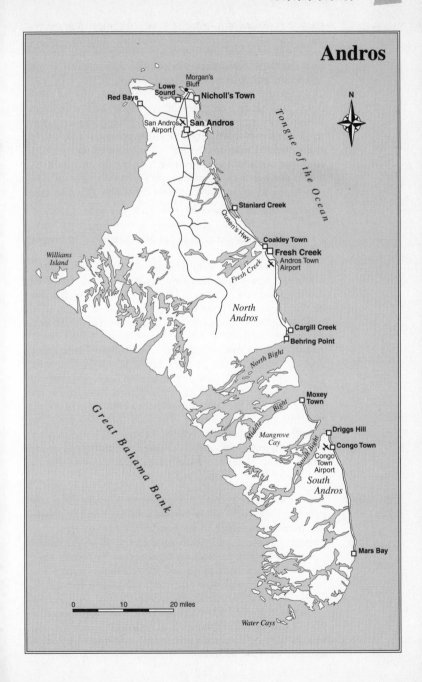

Andros

N

Morgan's Bluff
Lowe Sound
Red Bays
Nicholl's Town
San Andros Airport
San Andros

Tongue of the Ocean

Staniard Creek

Queen's Hwy

Coakley Town
Fresh Creek
Andros Town Airport

Williams Island

Fresh Creek

North Andros

Cargill Creek
Behring Point

North Bight

Moxey Town

Middle Bight

Mangrove Cay

Driggs Hill
Congo Town
Congo Town Airport

South Bight

South Andros

Great Bahama Bank

Mars Bay

0   10   20 miles

Water Cays

residential settlement is split by a small creek: the part of the village on the north bank is called **Coakley Town**; the part on the south bank is known as **Fresh Creek**; the village offers yacht marinas and the **Androsia Batik Works**, a factory where visitors can take a tour and purchase the colorful fabrics.

Palm-lined beaches and forested shorelines border the coast from **Cargill Creek**, a quiet, friendly community known for bonefishing, to the end of the road at **Behring Point**. The road ends on the bank of **North Bight**. Between this waterway and **Middle Bight**, some 12 miles to the south, lie uninhabited mangrove islands that invite fishing and birdwatching but defy human habitation. The only way to continue south is by boat or plane. The only route back to the north part of the island is the way you came.

CENTRAL & SOUTH ANDROS   Though it may be hard to imagine, Central and South Andros are even less developed than North Andros. The communities there can only be reached by boat or plane.

On Central Andros, a cluster of islands in a shallow wetland, the only settlement is on **Mangrove Cay**, a sizeable cay with more coconut palms than mangroves. There are a few small, simple inns on the five-mile-long coast road. Phones are almost unheard-of on Central Andros, and life hasn't changed much in the last century or so. Mangrove Cay is as difficult to reach from North Andros as from Nassau. Free ferries link **Moxey Town**, a tiny dockside village on the northern tip of Mangrove Cay, with **Driggs Hill**, the northernmost settlement on South Andros.

A few miles south of Driggs Hill is **Congo Town**, by far the largest settlement on South Andros, with a population of several hundred and its own airport. The road continues down the coastline across a series of one-lane bridges and through other fishing villages before suddenly ending at **Mars Bay**. Taxis are the only mode of public transportation, and few visitors venture all the way to the end of the road.

LODGING   **NORTH ANDROS**   Located in the heart of Nicholl's Town, the hostel-style **Green Windows Inn** is a solid local budget choice. The friendly owners live on the premises and run the liquor store next door. There are 12 simple guest rooms, all on the second floor. Two of them have private baths and sitting rooms, while the other ten share bathrooms and showers down the hall. The beach is a short walk down the road. ~ Nicholl's Town; 329-2194, fax 329-2016. BUDGET.

A stay at the **Conch Sound Resort Inn**, about a mile south of Nicholl's Town, is like living with an Androsian family. The innkeepers have six hotel-style rooms and six cottages with small kitchens. All have television. The family-owned and -operated inn is in the center of the village of Conch Sound. It's a short walk to the local beach. ~ Conch Sound; 329-2060. MODERATE.

On the way to Fresh Creek and Andros Town, the **Small Hope Bay Lodge** put Andros on the map as a scuba-diving mecca. Considered one of the top dive resorts in the world, the lodge was founded in 1960 by the late diver Dick Birch, who built 20 beach-front cottages out of coral rock and Andros pine. Each cottage has either a king-size bed or two double beds. Four are two-bedroom cottages for families or groups who don't mind sharing a bathroom. Bountiful family-style meals are included. Diving is still the big draw here, but the family-run resort continues to develop other outdoor activities—deep-sea fishing, bonefishing, snorkeling, hiking, biking and birding—as well as massage are being offered. Air service is provided daily from Fort Lauderdale. ~ Fresh Creek, 368-2014, fax 368-2015; or P.O. Box 21667, Fort Lauderdale, FL 33335-1667, 800-223-6961; www.smallhope.com. MODERATE. ◀ HIDDEN

Three miles south of Small Hope Bay Lodge, **Coakley House** is also owned and operated by the Birch family. This beautiful pink-and-white waterfront house has an abundance of doors and windows to take full advantage of the water views and sea breezes. There are two large master bedrooms, each with its own bathroom, and a third bedroom and bath toward the back of the house. Amenities include a large dining room, a complete kitchen, laundry facilities, a patio, a boat dock and a private swimming beach. Families and groups who rent the house can choose a "bare rental," cooking their own meals or dining out, or go for the "all-inclusive" rate, which includes home-cooked meals. Guests at Coakley House can participate in all activities at Small Hope Bay Lodge. ~ Fresh Creek, 368-2014, fax 368-2015; or P.O. Box 21667, Fort Lauderdale, FL 33335-1667, 800-223-6961. MODERATE. ◀ HIDDEN

✦✦

✔ CHECK THESE OUT

- Shop 'til you drop at **Androsia Batik Works**, where you can take a tour or buy something colorful to take home. *pages 140, 144*
- Dive into Andros life by staying at **Small Hope Bay Lodge**, where you can end a day of snorkeling or bonefishing with a relaxing massage. *page 141*
- Dine on ample servings of fresh seafood at **Big Josh Seafood Restaurant and Lounge**, a local eatery run by Malvese Bootle. *page 143*
- Explore life underwater and be bedazzled by the world's third-largest **barrier reef**. *page 146*

In the Andros Town area, check out the good-value rooms at **Chickcharnie's Hotel**, named for the three-toed, feathered elves that, according to local legend, inhabit the forests of Andros. The hotel sits right on Fresh Creek and offers eight basic rooms with private baths and another eleven that share bathrooms down the hall. ~ Fresh Creek; 368-4752, fax 368-2374. MODERATE.

Ask a local about the legendary chickcharnies, which some say still inhabit the island. These three-toed elves are descendants of the native Arawaks that once inhabited this island.

Across Fish Creek, the **Lighthouse Yacht Club & Marina** offers some of most luxurious rooms and facilities on the island. This resort has the feel of a small yacht club, with a marina as its focal point. The 20 guest rooms are decorated with colonial touches, and all have televisions, refrigerators and patios or balconies. Boating, fishing and basking by the pool or on the quiet beach nearby are the main pursuits. There are also two clay tennis courts. The namesake 19th-century lighthouse is nearby. ~ Andros Town; 368-2305, 800-335-1019, fax 835-2300. DELUXE.

Near the south end of the Queen's Highway, **Cargill Creek Fishing Lodge** is an ideal base for bonefishing. The lodge accommodates up to 30 guests in four single rooms, seven double rooms and three two-bedroom villas, all overlooking the sea or the swimming pool. There's a daily fishing excursion schedule, and unguided fishing is just outside your door. ~ Cargill Creek; 368-5129, fax 368-5046. DELUXE.

Also located in the Cargill Creek area, **Andros Island Bonefish Club** is another bonefishing beacon. Owner and head guide Rupert Leadon offers nine basic rooms, each with two beds, in five small buildings. Big breakfasts and Bahamian dinners are served at the lodge; anglers usually fix their own "Super Sandwich" to take with them for lunch on the water. ~ Cargill Creek, or P.O. Box 787, Islamorada, FL 33036; 305-664-4615, 800-327-2880. MODERATE.

The third and most recent addition to the fishing scene in the Cargill Creek area is **Tranquility Hill Bonefishing Lodge**. Each of the seven modern rooms in this hotel-style lodge has a view of the water. There are also three second-floor suites, ideal for families and small groups. The lodge has a small bar and an excellent dining room that features Bahamian cuisine. Anglers leave right from the lodge's private dock. ~ Behring Point; 368-4132, fax 368-4132. MODERATE.

At the very end of the Queen's Highway in Behring Point, **Nottages Cottages** is a clean, quiet little place across the road from the water. There are ten simple hotel rooms and one small separate cottage in a garden setting. ~ Behring Point; 368-4293. MODERATE.

CENTRAL & SOUTH ANDROS There are several small guest-houses on Mangrove Cay. They are quite basic, often with shared bathrooms and few, if any, phones. Among the best of the lot, **Elliot & Pat's Mangrove Cay Inn** offers ten simple guest rooms, all with private baths. Meals are served at this bed-and-breakfast-style inn. Nearby are nine miles of unspoiled beach. ~ Mangrove Cay; 369-0069, 800-688-4752. BUDGET.

◄ *HIDDEN*

On South Andros, **Emerald Palms By-the-Sea** is an unlikely surprise. Perfect for vacationers who want to get away from it all—and we mean *all* of it—the resort sits on a five-mile beach with hundreds of palm trees lining the sand. The 20 guest rooms have four-poster beds, mambasa netting and the sound of the sea outside the window. Many rooms have VCRs, cable television and refrigerators. A marina is nearby, and many watersports are covered in the all-inclusive price. ~ Driggs Hill; 369-2661, 800-835-1018, fax 369-2667. MODERATE.

◄ *HIDDEN*

Grassy Cays Camp, located at the southernmost point of Andros, has very basic shared cottages that can accommodate 14 guests, with freshly caught seafood providing the fare while you're there. Large schools of bonefish at this remote location keep rugged anglers returning often. To book a stay here, contact Cargill Creek Lodge on North Andros. ~ Mars Bay; 368-5129, fax 368-5046. DELUXE.

NORTH ANDROS Locals fill **Day Shell Restaurant and Bar** in Nicholl's Town for all three meals. Seafood is the fare of choice, and in the evening the place is a hub of North Andros social life. ~ Nicholl's Town; 329-2183. BUDGET.

DINING

◄ *HIDDEN*

Near Nicholl's Town, **Big Josh Seafood Restaurant and Lounge** is a Bahamian haven for many locals, who are enticed by food from the kitchen of Malvese Bootle, the widow of a well-known fishing guide. She serves fresh-caught fish nightly. ~ Lowe Sound; 329-7517. BUDGET.

◄ *HIDDEN*

Most of the fishing and diving resorts on Andros serve meals and commonly include them in the rates. One of the best places on the island to eat is the dining room at **Small Hope Bay Lodge**, where bountiful breakfast and lunch buffets are served daily. A selection of fish and meat dinner entrées accompany the all-you-can-eat salad bar. The dining room is in a clubhouselike setting overlooking the beach. Lodge guests are on the all-inclusive plan, and nonguests are welcome to stop by for a meal. ~ Fresh Creek; 368-2014. MODERATE.

CENTRAL & SOUTH ANDROS A scattering of local conch stands and hole-in-the-wall cafés serve big Bahamian lunches in Congo Town and elsewhere along the main road. None stay open past midafternoon, and the only dinner option is likely to be the hotel or guesthouse where you're staying. Good bets for lunch are **Ezrena's Eatery** ~ Driggs Hill, 369-2586; and **L & M Restaurant & Bar** ~ Congo Town; 369-2655.

SHOPPING

For the most part, shopping on Andros is limited to small general stores in the larger villages, selling basic food items and other necessities. Vendors operate tiny open-air curio stands at many of the tourist lodges. In Lowe Sound, bonefishing guide **Arthur Russell** carves beautiful ship models and uses Androsia batik for their sails. ~ 329-7372.

Craftswomen in Red Bays are known for their excellent straw work. Visitors to the town can call **Gertrude Gibson** or simply ask around. ~ 329-2369.

Though people don't come to Andros to shop, many leave with bags full of bright bright fabrics patterned with shells, birds, fish, flowers and many other motifs, in bright colors including guava, pink, sea green and aquatide, from **Androsia Batik Works**. The screen-waxed, colorfully hand-dyed cloth is sold by the yard—no two yards alike—or as shirts, dresses and sarongs. Stop by the turquoise-painted outlet store for a wide array of firsts, seconds, old designs and one-of-a-kind samples. The factory and store are open weekdays and Saturday mornings. Androsia also operates boutiques on all major islands of The Bahamas. ~ Fresh Creek; no phone.

NIGHTLIFE

Evening entertainment is centered around the hotels and resorts. In Nicholl's Town, there is often "rake 'n' scrape" music at **Dayshell's Night Club** ~ 329-2183, or live Bahamian music at **Rumours** ~ 329-2398. Or head for **Small Hope Bay Lodge** ~ 368-2014, or just ask around. **Henny's Late Night Spot** in the Conch Sound Resort Inn also features live island music from time to time. ~ 329-2529. In Fresh Creek, there's sometimes live music at **Donnie's Sweet Sugar Lounge**. ~ 368-2080.

BEACHES

EASTERN SHORE BEACHES 🏖️ 🏄 🚤 ⚓ Although visitors don't come to Andros for the beaches, there are quiet stretches of sand at Nicholl's Town, Small Hope Bay, Staniard Creek and Drigg's Hill. Lodging facilities on or near these beaches offer swimming, snorkeling, boating and fishing opportunities.

▼▼▼▼▼▼▼▼▼▼▼▼▼▼▼
Outdoor Adventures

Aside from diving and fishing excursions, pleasure boating is limited because the mucky western shore is virtually impossible for most boaters. Boat outings with or without a guide can be arranged at **Lighthouse Yacht Club & Marina** ~ 368-5099 and the marina at **Chickcharnie's Hotel** ~ 368-2025, which sit across Fresh Creek from one another.

BOATING

Hand Batiked
in
The Bahamas

One of the most popular souvenirs of The Bahamas is a batik product from the island of Andros. Androsia, a batik fabric and garment manufacturing facility located on North Andros in Fresh Creek, has been producing colorful fabrics for more than 20 years using the beauty of the environment of Andros and The Bahamas for inspiration in their print designs and brilliant colors.

Androsia Batik Works started in 1973 as a cottage industry designed to create meaningful employment for locals, and to create a high-quality product that would highlight the beauty of The Bahamas through its design and color.

All Androsia fabrics are hand-batiked, and no two yards are alike. After being printed with a design in wax, the natural-fiber fabric is dyed. When the wax is melted away in 190-degree water, the beautiful white design remains against the vividly colored background. The wax removal process preshrinks the finished fabric, which is then dried under the Bahamian sunshine.

Androsia products are sold in Nassau, Freeport and all of the inhabited Out Islands. The Queen of England received a beautiful piece of Androsia silk during one visit and, more recently, a quilt of colorful Androsia fabrics.

FISHING　　Andros just may offer the best bonefishing in The Bahamas, which is to say, the best in the world. Most the entire island is surrounded by bonefishing flats. Sometimes schools of the silver fighting fish can be found right outside your front door, practically begging to be caught (and released). Though some folks say bonefishing is better in the winter, there is no bonefishing "season." Summertime means better rates and fewer fellow anglers.

Summer is land crab season. The crabs are caught while crawling to the beach to lay eggs, then boiled with spices and served with steamed dough.

Many lodges specialize in bonefishing and either offer packages or make arrangements with particular guides. To arrange a trip on your own, contact Andros Bonefishing Guides Association members **Andy Smith** ~ 368-4261, **Simon Bain** ~ 368-5060 or **Arthur Russell, Sr.** ~ 329-7372.

World Wide Sportsman arranges bonefishing package trips that include a stay at the Andros Island Bonefish Club. ~ P.O. Box 787, Islamorada, FL 33036; 305-664-4615, 800-327-2880, fax 305-664-3692.

DIVING　　The third largest **barrier reef** in the world provides boundless opportunities for wall diving and marine life viewing. Among the most popular dives are **Hanging Gardens Wall, Giant's Staircase** and **Over the Wall**.

Scattered across Andros are more than 100 large and small blue holes, or deep freshwater springs. **Benjamin's Blue Hole**, discovered by Dr. George Benjamin in 1967, contains stalagmites and stalactites at more than 1200 feet below the surface. **Uncle Charley's Blue Hole** and **Ocean Blue Hole**, both first explored by Jacques Cousteau, offer two more mysterious dive experiences.

The Andros Barrier Reef has claimed its share of wrecks, among them the **Marion Crane**, a U.S. Navy construction crane that sank when the barge on which it was mounted capsized, and the **Lady Moore**, a mailboat that sank just 15 minutes offshore in 1990.

Good snorkeling sites include **Central Park**, where three major stands of elkhorn coral are found in less than 15 feet of water; **Solarium**, an area where lobsters and stingrays abound; **The Compressor**, an old air compressor turned into a living reef for snorkelers; **North Beach**, shoals with lots of fish and lobsters; and **Davis Creek**, a mangrove tidal flat.

Small Hope Bay Lodge is is one of the best dive resorts in the world. It has four dive boats, three scheduled dive trips daily, a wide range of instructional programs and specialty dives. ~ Fresh Creek, 368-2014; or P.O. Box 21667, Fort Lauderdale, FL 33335-1667, 800-223-6961.

There are three major airports on the island—**San Andros**, **Andros Town** and **Congo Town**. Bahamasair flies from Nassau to all three airports, with daily service to San Andros and Andros Town and less frequent flights to Congo Town.

AIR

Trans-Caribbean Air, one of several charter services that fly to Andros, offers charter flights in a five-seater Piper Aztec from Fort Lauderdale or Miami's Opa Locka Airport to San Andros, Andros Town, Bain or Congo Town. Other charter services include Lynx Air and Congo Air.

Andros can be reached by one of the easiest **mailboat** trips in The Bahamas. The M/V *Lisa J. II* leaves Potter's Cay Dock in Nassau on Wednesday afternoon for the five-hour trip to Nicholl's Town, Mastic Point and Morgan's Bluff, and does not return to Nassau until six days later. The *Lady D* leaves Tuesday around noon for Fresh Creek and other North/Central Andros destinations, returning to Nassau on Saturday mornings and the *Captain Moxey* departs on the seven-hour trip to Kemp's Bay and other South Andros ports late Monday night, returning on Wednesday evening. The schedules are changeable according to weather conditions.

BOAT

Passenger ferries connect North, Central and South Andros; they do not carry motor vehicles.

Andros is a huge island with little public transportation. Visitors usually stick with the taxi driver that met them at the airport to take them elsewhere as needed. You can call a cab at 328-2579, but you may be in for a long wait.

TAXIS

You can rent a vehicle at the Andros Town airport through AMKLCO **Car Rental** (368-2056) and **Berth Rent-A-Car** (368-2102), or at the Congo Town airport through **Executive Car Rental** (329-2081) or **Tropical Car Rental** (329-2515). In Kemp's Bay, **Rahming's Rental** (369-1608) has vehicles for rent.

CAR RENTALS

Concessioners at Small Hope Bay Lodge rent motor scooters and bikes, either of which is ideal for short trips around the island. ~ 368-2014.

SCOOTER & BIKE RENTALS

Island Vacations offers two tours on Andros. **The Small Hope Bay Water Experience** includes snorkeling, a "learn-to dive" course and reef trips for certified divers, as well as biking, hiking, massage, an island tour and a visit to the Androsia Batik Works. Participants stay at the Small Hope Bay Resort. The name of the second tour, **Bonefishing Heaven**, says it all. Tours

ECOTOURS

are for three nights and four days. ~ Contact Island Vacations in the U.S. at 4327 Reflections Boulevard North, Suite 104, Sunrise, FL 33351, 305-748-1833, 800-900-4242, fax 305-748-1965; or in Nassau at P.O. Box 13002, Town Centre Mall, Nassau, Bahamas, 356-1111, fax 356-4379.

▼▼▼▼▼▼▼▼▼▼▼▼▼▼▼▼▼▼▼▼▼▼

Addresses & Phone Numbers

Bahamasair—San Andros Airport; 222-4262

Fire Department—919

Medical Clinics—North Andros Medical Clinic, 329-2121; Nicholl's Town Medical Clinic, 329-2171; South Andros Medical Clinic, 329-4620

Police Department—919; Nicholl's Town, 329-2353; Fresh Creek, 368-2626; Kemp's Bay, 369-4733.

EIGHT

Bimini and The Berries

Bimini was an undiscovered daydream of an island when Ernest Hemingway arrived in 1935. Close enough to the Florida coast to see the glow of Miami Beach at night, it had been settled in the Roaring Twenties to serve as a staging area for rumrunners from Nassau. But with the end of Prohibition in the United States Bimini's residents were left without an economy—a common occurrence in the history of virtually every Bahamian island.

Hemingway may not have been the first big-game fisherman on Bimini. He may not have transformed the sport of deep-sea fishing, as he would later claim. But between 1935 and 1937 he succeeded in ridding this part of the Atlantic of a prodigious number of big sharks, sailfish and marlin. He wrote books, drank, brawled and turned local saloons into legends. He was the most talked-about writer of the era, and by the time he left, Bimini was on its way to becoming the sportfishing mecca it is today.

Hemingway was not the first to discover Bimini. Juan Ponce de Leon stopped there in 1513 during his expedition in search of the Fountain of Youth but did not stay long. The Loyalists who colonized other islands of The Bahamas in the 1780s bypassed Bimini because there was too little arable land to grow a decent cotton crop. But when newly freed Bahamian slaves left Nassau to homestead empty islands a number landed in Bimini, where today their descendants account for a majority of the island's 1600 residents.

Although Bimini is usually referred to in the singular, it's actually two islands—North Bimini and South Bimini, separated by 100 yards of water—and a chain of minuscule cays stretching southward for almost 30 miles. The combined land mass of the islands and cays is only ten square miles, and Bimini would have remained completely unnoticed but for its proximity to the Florida Coast. North and South Bimini lie just 50 miles from Miami Beach, much closer to the U.S. mainland than to Nassau, just outside U.S. territorial waters, and in a perfect location for weekend getaways. It has also proven to be an ideal smugglers' base, and the island's shady past as a rumrunner's haven inspired the United States to surround it with a naval blockade as part of the War on Drugs. Residents claim that the U.S. Drug Enforcement Administration is Bimini's largest employer.

Sportfishing still reigns supreme, and the clientele is more elite than in Hemingway's day. Modern sportfishing boats are likely to have global location systems, sonar capable of tracking a single large fish from miles away, and state-of-the-art fighting chairs with multiple rods and reels—and to cost $100,000 or more per foot of length.

In the 1990s a new kind of tourist has been visiting Bimini in growing numbers. The supposed discovery of the 11,500-year-old ruins of Atlantis off the coast of North Bimini has drawn myriad scuba divers to see for themselves, and more recent finds such as a possible ruined city in deeper water 25 miles offshore and strange Indian mounds best viewed by infrared photography from 10,000 feet in the sky above South Bimini tantalize the imaginations of New Agers. Although these phenomena offer nothing much for the casual sightseer to view, people flock to the island simply to experience what may (or may not) be vibrations left over from the dawn of human civilization.

Bimini's tourism profile will soon change again with the development of the $350 million Bimini Bay Hotel, Marina and Casino at the north end of North Bimini. The resort will include single-family homes, condominiums, a 500-room American-style hotel, a 250-room all-inclusive facility, a 200-room ecotourism resort designed for Atlantis believers, an 18-hole golf course and a 300-slip marina. No completion schedule has yet been announced, but the employment generated by the resort's construction has already begun to draw hundreds of workers from other Bahamian islands.

The Berry Islands lie 20 miles east of Bimini, 20 miles north of Andros and 35 miles northwest of Nassau. Unlike Bimini, they are always referred to in the plural, and the reason is obvious. The Berries consist of more than 30 tiny islands, including the most prominent, Chub Cay and Great Harbour Cay, as well as others with names like Whale Cay, Sandy Cay, Bond's Cay, Cistern Cay, Devil's Cay, Crab Cay, Cockroach Cay, Goat Cay and Frozen Cay. Altogether, the islands make up of less then 15 square miles of land area. Many are privately owned and some serve as exotic stopovers for cruise ships. Besides very limited tourism, most of the 750 or so islanders make their living from the sea.

SIGHTS   **BIMINI**   Most Bimini residents live in **Alice Town**, on the southern end of North Bimini, connected to South Bimini by a ferry that runs 100 yards across a sea channel. A paved road called the **Queen's Highway** runs north along Porgy Bay to Bailey Town, where it joins another one called **King's Highway** and continues to the island's northern tip—a total distance of three miles. Along the way, the narrow island's width is typically only about 100 yards, with beaches on the exposed western shore and marina facilities on the sheltered eastern side.

For many, Alice Town is Bimini. Though most sightseeing and activities take place in this northern outpost, there are things

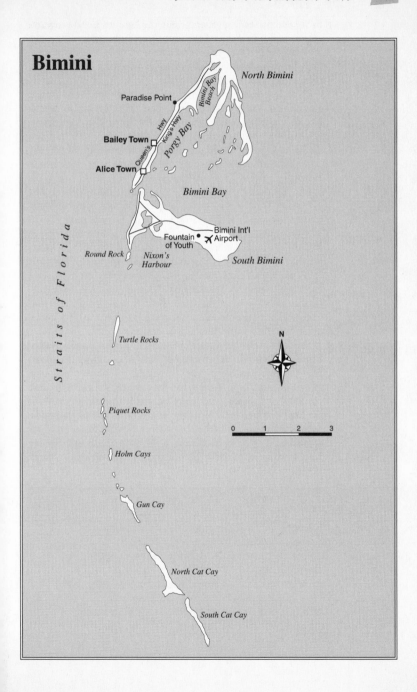

Bimini

North Bimini

Paradise Point

Bimini Bay Beach

Hwy
King's Hwy

Bailey Town

Queen's

Porgy Bay

Alice Town

Bimini Bay

Bimini Int'l
Airport

Fountain
of Youth

South Bimini

Round Rock

Nixon's
Harbour

S t r a i t s   o f   F l o r i d a

N

Turtle Rocks

Piquet Rocks

0   1   2   3

Holm Cays

Gun Cay

North Cat Cay

South Cat Cay

to see and places to go elsewhere in the Biminis. Local historian, author and poet **Ashley Saunders**, who can be reached through the Ministry of Tourism, offers a unique walking tour of the town and can provide insights on topics as diverse as folk medicine, fishing, vegetation and genealogy.

Not that you really need a guide to find your way around Alice Town, which consists of two narrow streets and an attractive beach. Most businesses are located along King's Highway. Alice Town residents are so friendly that visitors soon fall into the habit of greeting everyone they pass on the street. After a day of walking around town you'll feel as if you have said hello to everyone in Alice Town—at least once.

At the south end of town, the gutted remains of a three-story, 100-room hotel overlooks the seaplane airport. Now an overgrown ruin, the **Bimini Bay Rod and Gun Club** was built in 1919 as a Prohibition-era getaway; it was destroyed by a hurricane in 1926. The grand winding staircase remains, along with the once-lavish ballroom, tennis court and huge pool with faded tilework.

A **white arch** along the King's Highway proclaims the Biminis as "The Gateway to The Bahamas." Nearby, a small straw market lines both sides of the street. Besides straw goods and souvenirs, some of the friendly vendors sell loaves of the fresh homemade bread for which Bimini is famous.

Located in All My Children Hotel, the **Bimini Fishing Hall of Fame** pays tribute to those who have made Bimini fishing famous. Ever since S. Kip Farrington, Jr. caught the island's first blue marlin back in 1933, fishing has been the backbone of Bimini's economy and the base for many legendary anglers. Members of the Hall of Fame include Farrington, Ernest Hemingway, Mike Lerner, Bimini promoter and developer Neville Stuart and fishing guides Eric Sawyer, Manny Rolle, Bob Smith and Sammy Ellis. The displays include historic pictures and articles. ~ King's Highway; 347-3334.

✔ CHECK THESE OUT

- Follow in the footsteps of Ernest Hemingway at the museum—or the bar—at the **Compleat Angler Hotel**. *page 153*
- Rent the Marlin Cottage at **Bimini's Blue Water Resort**, the setting for Hemingway's last novel. *page 156*
- Feast on wahoo or grouper at **Capt. Bob's Restaurant**, where Captain Bob himself often brings in the daily catch. *page 159*
- Wall dive at **Chub Cay Wall**, where you're apt to spot a large marlin or shark at the drop-off for the Tongue of the Ocean. *page 164*

Farther along the King's Highway, the **Compleat Angler Hotel** has a museum devoted entirely to Ernest Hemingway's time on Bimini. The collection is in the same room where Hemingway often wrote while he was in town, completing his novel *To Have and Have Not* here. On display are dozens of black-and-white photographs documenting Hemingway's fishing exploits, along with a photo of Cuban fisherman Angelmo Hernandez, who was the model for Hemingway's hero in *The Old Man and the Sea*. ~ King's Highway; 347-3122.

Running parallel with King's Highway, Queen's Highway lacks even the limited commercialism of the lower street. It *does* have a peaceful beach that you're likely to have all to yourself.

Toward the north end of town stand several picturesque stone churches overlooking the sea.

King's Highway leads out of Alice Town and runs along the waterfront through the small, nondescript villages of **Bailey Town** and **Porgy Bay**. The road turns to dirt and leads through shady Australian pines out to a dead-end at **Paradise Point**, site of the underwater **Bimini Road**. Believers claim that this formation is a remnant of the lost civilization of Atlantis, which some say sank into the ocean 11,500 years ago after providing the inspiration for other ancient civilizations such as the Egyptians and the Maya. Many scientists ridicule the notion and assert that the huge, strange 1900-foot-long reverse-J-shaped arrangement of square stone blocks formed naturally as erosion undercut a thin layer of limestone, perhaps augmented by ballast that Spanish colonial ships may have dumped in preparation to load cargos of Mexican treasure in colonial times. The trouble is, as more and more strange stone artifacts are found in the area, skeptics' attempts to explain them away are coming to seem weirder than Atlantis believers' theories. Today, many visitors come to Bimini to see for themselves, making the area a popular diving and snorkeling site. There's a lovely two-mile beach overlooking crystal-clear waters.

From Alice Town, a passenger ferry runs to even quieter **South Bimini**. The ferry deposits visitors at a small dock where a taxi can meet visitors by advance arrangement. Touring the island takes an hour or so.

The **Sapona**, a wreck partially submerged off South Bimini's southern shore, was a concrete troop ship built by Henry Ford in the early 1900s. It sank, blew onto the reef, and was used for target practice during World War II. It's now a popular diving and snorkeling site.

The **Bimini Biological Field Station** (BBFS) is the fascinating undertaking of University of Miami professor and biologist Dr. Samuel H. Gruber. Its mission encompasses both education and research, with most of the focus on sharks, especially lemon sharks. Along with courses at secondary and university levels, there are Earthwatch trips and many other possibilities for short- or extended-research and volunteer stays. Visitors are welcome, though it is best to call Dr. Gruber's Miami office in advance. ~ 305-274-0628.

Though it hasn't yet been developed as an official tourist spot, young guides flock to show visitors the way to the rock-lined, spring-fed well near the airstrip. Local legend holds that Ponce de Leon discovered the spring in 1513 and recognized it as the **Fountain of Youth**, and a small sign identifies it as such. Some New Age and metaphysics-minded visitors believe that the well dates back to the days of lost Atlantis and possesses unique healing powers.

Out in the harbor, between North and South Bimini, bone-fishing fanatics can be seen stalking the gray ghosts. Waterways meander peacefully among the mangrove cays across the harbor, where only occasional sea kayakers venture. Down one of the narrower waterways, local guides can take you to the quiet spot known as the **Healing Hole**, where just a foot under the murky surface an underground spring releases crystal-clear water that is claimed to have curative properties. Like the Fountain of Youth, the Healing Hole is claimed to be one of the Atlantean healing wells referred to in Edgar Cayce's prophecies. Mineral analysis of its water has found high concentrations of sulphur and magnesium, along with lithium, a powerful mood stabilizer commonly used today in the treatment of mental disturbances.

THE BERRY ISLANDS   A strand of tiny cays, the Berries barely break the water's surface, marking the edge of the vast underwater canyon known as the Tongue of the Ocean. Although the modicum of dry land that makes up the islands' interior is blanketed with low scrub and palmetto, most of their land area is a coastal fantasy of virginal white-sand beaches and flat rock points that shelter shallow, pale blue coves of breathtaking clarity. Many of the 30 islands are privately owned and off-limits to visitors, and others are only accessible by private boat. Two destinations in the Berries can be reached by air, the only mode of public transportation available—except for cruise ships that anchor for the day at one remote cay.

Great Harbour Cay is the main destination in the Berries, thanks to the marina and fishing activity at Great Harbour Cay Yacht Club & Marina. The island's main town, **Bullock's Harbour**, is the largest settlement in the Berries—about 500 people. The sleepy little village may some day attain the stature of Alice Town on North Bimini, but that will take decades, and anglers and boaters who make the cay their base think that's just fine.

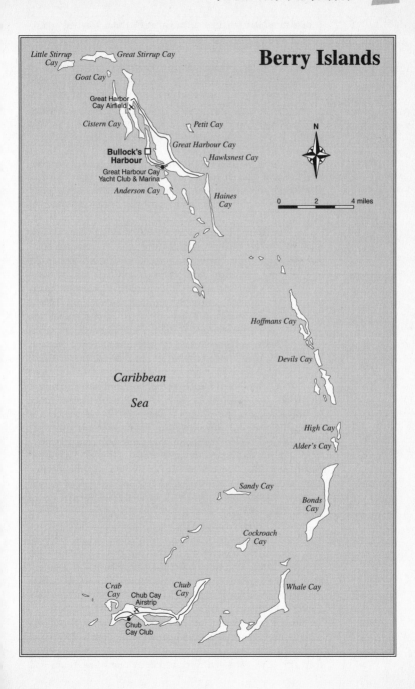

Berry Islands

Little Stirrup Cay

Great Stirrup Cay

Goat Cay

Great Harbor Cay Airfield

Cistern Cay

Petit Cay

Great Harbour Cay

Bullock's Harbour

Hawksnest Cay

Great Harbour Cay Yacht Club & Marina

Anderson Cay

Haines Cay

N

0   2   4 miles

Hoffmans Cay

Devils Cay

Caribbean

Sea

High Cay

Alder's Cay

Sandy Cay

Bonds Cay

Cockroach Cay

Crab Cay

Chub Cay

Whale Cay

Chub Cay Airstrip

Chub Cay Club

Unlike most Bahamian islands, Great Harbour Cay has rolling hills. It also boasts a virtually empty beach that stretches for almost eight miles.

Chub Cay, too, is dominated by a resort and marina. The self-contained Chub Cay Inn, once the private getaway of a small group of rich Texans, is now open to one-time visitors and dedicated members. Except for the inn and the lagoon marina, there's little else to see on Chub Cay—or in the Berries, for that matter. It is this seclusion that appeals to Berry Islands buffs.

LODGING   **BIMINI**   Most accommodation options in the Biminis are relatively simple, though you'll find more amenities than on other Out Islands. If you will be in the Biminis during one of the many summer weekend fishing tournaments, make reservations well in advance.

In Alice Town, the big resort is the **Bimini Big Game Fishing Club & Hotel**. Owned by the Bacardi International rum company, it is one of the best hotels in the Out Islands. There are 35 standard hotel rooms on two floors, 12 first-floor cottages and four third-floor penthouse apartments. Each simply furnished room has two beds, a television and a balcony or patio overlooking the pool, the marina or the harbor. Cottages and penthouse apartments have refrigerators and food preparation areas, though cooking is not allowed. There's ample storage space for fishing and diving gear near each front door. The Bimini Big Game Fishing Club has played host to anglers and celebrities for more than 50 years. A wide range of fishing and diving packages is available through the club. ~ King's Highway, P.O. Box 609, Alice Town; 347-3391, 800-737-1007, fax 347-3392; www.bimini-big-game-club.com. DELUXE.

> On any given day in the Biminis, a world record may be broken for either big game or bonefishing.

A similar resort experience can be found at **Bimini's Blue Water Resort**. Stretching from east to west across the island, the complex has a pool and marina on the harbor side and a variety of accommodations on the ocean side. The main hotel building has ten standard hotel rooms and two suites, all with balconies overlooking the water. The three-bedroom Marlin Cottage, an ideal choice for families or small groups, has a huge living room and plenty of balcony space overlooking the water. The cottage was once the home of Mike Lerner, who often had Ernest Hemingway as a houseguest; it is a key setting in the author's farewell novel, *Islands in the Stream*. ~ King's Highway, P.O. Box 601, Alice Town; 347-3166, 800-688-4752, fax 347-3293. MODERATE TO DELUXE.

Situated on the water, the three-story **Sea Crest Hotel** and Marina has 12 rooms and suites with rattan furnishings and balconies overlooking the marina. Along with standard one-bedroom units, they also have two- and three-bedroom suites for groups and families. And Alice Town is right outside the small lobby. ~ King's Highway, P.O. Box 654, Alice Town; 347-3071. MODERATE.

No relation to the soap opera, **All My Children Hotel** is a great place for kids as well as adults. The older section and new three-story annex together have 50 rooms, ranging from standard hotel rooms to family-style suites with kitchenettes. The guest rooms have modern furnishings and are so clean they sparkle. The hotel is situated on Alice Town's hill, and rooms have views of either the harbor or the open sea. ~ King's Highway, Alice Town; 347-3334. MODERATE.

The **Compleat Angler Hotel** is located above the famous bar ◄ HIDDEN
where Hemingway used to hang out. There are six simple rooms on the second floor and six more on the third, with balconies overlooking King's Highway. Pine woodwork and layers of varnish throughout give this legendary hotel the feel of an old ship. But be aware, these are very plain rooms, and the crowd and music can be loud late into the night. That's what makes this place so historic. Hemingway stayed in Room 1 on the second floor while working on his novel *To Have or Have Not*. ~ King's Highway, P.O. Box 601, Alice Town; 347-3122, fax 347-3293. BUDGET.

Just north of "downtown" Alice Town, **Dun's Bayfront Apartments** make for an inexpensive housekeeping holiday. Situated on King's Highway, overlooking the harbor across the street, are five simply furnished one-bedroom and efficiency apartments, all with full kitchens, living room areas and televisions. The rooms open onto a shared balcony overlooking the water. This is a great place to get into local life away from the tourist hubbub of Alice Town. The beach is just a short walk over the hill to the other side of the island. ~ King's Highway; 347-2093. MODERATE.

A bit farther north, **King Brown's Apartments** has three ultramodern second-floor apartments overlooking the harbor. All are similar in layout, with the best furnishings of any lodging on the island. Each apartment has a huge living room, a large kitchen, a master bedroom overlooking the water and a second bedroom overlooking King's Highway. This is a housekeeping stay in the lap of luxury. Owner Larry Brown also operates the general store next door and lives nearby. ~ King's Highway, P.O. Box 610, Alice Town; 347-2305. DELUXE.

Those seeking even more peace and quiet will find it at **Ellis' Cottages**. Clarence Ellis' three simply furnished cottages, each named for one of Columbus' ships, are ideal for small families. The largest, "Santa Maria," has a huge master bedroom, a smaller bedroom, a large living room and two bathrooms—one with a whirlpool tub. It overlooks the boat docks, as does the one-bedroom "Nina"; the "Pinta" is similar to the "Nina," without the water view. All three cottages have full kitchens and pull-out sofa beds.

This is one of the best housekeeping facilities in the Biminis. ~
P.O. Box 611, Porgy Bay; 347-2258. MODERATE TO DELUXE.

HIDDEN ▶ Located at the far northern end of North Bimini, **Bimini Bay
Guest House** provides a completely different type of stay from
that found in and around Alice Town. This secluded outpost has
six houses on its sprawling property, along with 18 well-maintained and clean hotel rooms and apartments in the innlike "Art
Deco" guesthouse. The beach is outstanding and stretches for
more than two secluded miles. ~ Bimini Bay; 347-2171. MODER-
ATE TO DELUXE.

HIDDEN ▶ On South Bimini, the secluded **Bimini Beach Club** was once
known only by divers; now word is out about this convenient
getaway for those interested in quietly communing with nature
in simple surroundings. The two-story hotel facility has 40 updated rooms with shared balconies overlooking the water. There's
also a swimming pool, and two dive operators are based right
outside the door at the full-service marina. Diving and fishing
packages are a surprisingly good value at this friendly property.
~ South Bimini; 347-3115. MODERATE.

THE BERRY ISLANDS Tropical Diversion Town Houses, Villas
& Marina once boasted Douglas Fairbanks, Jr. as chairman of
the board and hosted Hollywood celebrities on getaways to this
then-private paradise. The accommodations are two-bedroom
two-story townhouses overlooking the marina and docks, each
with a fully equipped kitchen. There are also several Mediterranean-style beach villas that can house two to six people. The
resort has a country club feel quite unlike most Out Island facilities. ~ Great Harbour Cay; 367-8838, fax 367-8115. Or 3512
North Ocean Drive, Hollywood, FL 33019; 954-921-9084, 800-
343-7256, fax 954-921-1044. DELUXE.

The **Chub Cay Club**, a quiet place that caters to anglers, boaters and scuba divers, has the only guest rooms on Chub Cay. A
900-foot surge-proof channel leads to their protected marina.
Once there you'll find a choice of standard hotel rooms or villas
with one to three bedrooms that overlook one of two freshwater swimming pools. The rooms all have modern furnishings.
The villas come with sitting rooms and kitchens. ~ Chub Cay;
325-1490, fax 325-5199. Or P.O. Box 661067, Miami Springs,
FL 33266; 305-445-7830, 800-662-8555. DELUXE.

DINING **BIMINI** Fisherman's Wharf at the Bimini Big Game Fishing
Club & Hotel is one of the finer dining establishments in the Out
Islands. Overlooking the pool, this Continental-style restaurant
specializes in seafood and meats with local and American preparation and sauces. If it's in season, the lobster is outstanding and
the fish is as fresh as you can get. Breakfast and dinner only.

Closed Tuesday. ~ Bimini Big Game Fishing Club & Hotel, King's Highway, Alice Town; 347-3391. DELUXE.

Also located at the hotel, the casual second-floor **Big Game Sports Bar** overlooks the marina. It's a popular spot for a cold drink and "pub grub" after a day on the water. The menu features a full range of seafood appetizers and entrées, and the sandwich selection is enough to tempt any hungry angler. ~ Bimini Big Game Fishing Club & Hotel, King's Highway, Alice Town; 347-3391. MODERATE.

For native cooking in Alice Town, diners head for the **Red Lion Pub**, which features friendly service and large servings of local food. The Shrimp Delight (large shrimp stuffed with conch and native fish) is one of the best dishes on the island. The barbecued ribs are also a tasty choice. Most entrées are served with peas 'n rice, corn on the cob, green beans and other side orders. There's a bar in the front and a dining room overlooking the harbor in the back, where the ribs are cooked on an ancient open brick grill. ~ King's Highway, Alice Town; 347-3259. MODERATE.   ◄ HIDDEN

On the western side of Alice Town, overlooking the sea, the **Anchorage Dining Room** is Bimini's Blue Water Resort's restaurant. The views at sunset from the large wood-paneled dining room make this location a special treat. There are many lobster, conch and seafood specials. After dining, take a stroll along quiet Queen's Highway or the beach below. ~ Queen's Highway, Alice Town; 347-3166. MODERATE.

Visitors can hang out with local anglers and eat the bounty they've caught at **Fisherman's Paradise**. The steamed grouper, various conch dishes and other seafood delicacies are the main attractions at this family-run spot overlooking the water. ~ King's Highway, Alice Town; 347-3220. MODERATE.   ◄ HIDDEN

Owned and operated by fishing captain and Hall of Fame honoree Bob Smith, **Capt. Bob's Restaurant** features hearty breakfast fare for hungry anglers heading out at the crack of dawn, and conchy lunches for those who prefer to sleep in. For breakfast, either the fish omelet or fish and eggs make a good choice, as does the famous french toast using fresh Bimini bread. Daily specials often have wahoo or grouper personally caught by Captain Bob himself. Breakfast and lunch only. Closed Tuesday. ~ King's Highway, Alice Town; 347-3260. MODERATE.

THE BERRY ISLANDS Unless your accommodations include kitchen facilities, your dining choices in the Berry Islands are limited to the restaurants at the two resorts.

With three distinct dining choices, Great Harbour Cay Yacht Club & Marina provides enough variety for even long-term visitors. **Basil's Bar and Restaurant**, at the marina overlooking the water is open for all three meals and serves local and American cuisine. Similar meals can be found at breakfast and lunch at **The Wharf**, while the more formal **Tamboo Dinner Club** features a seafood buffet and is open for dinner only and is closed Tuesday. ~ Great Harbour Cay; 367-8838. MODERATE TO DELUXE.

At the Chub Cay Club overlooking the marina, the **Harbour House Restaurant and Lounge** specializes in seafood, with lobster as the main feature. Spectacular sunset views round out a pleasant Bahamian evening. ~ Chub Cay; 325-1490. DELUXE.

SHOPPING Bimini is by no stretch of the imagination a shopping destination. King's Highway has a few small shops where you can buy T-shirts and such, and there's a small straw market. King's Highway is also the place to find the famed and fresh Bimini bread, sold at several stands and shops.

> South Florida residents have been known to fly over to Bimini just for the day to buy loaves of Bimini bread.

In Alice Town, the Bimini Big Game Fishing Club & Hotel's **Logo Shop** has a wide range of souvenir apparel as a reminder of your time in the Biminis. ~ King's Highway; 347-3391.

The all-purpose **Chic Store** has been selling a little bit of everything, from souvenirs to shampoo, since 1935. ~ 347-3184.

The perfume selection and the smiling shopkeepers make the duty-free **Perfume Bar** a fragrant and friendly shopping stop. ~ 347-3517.

NIGHTLIFE King's Highway in Alice Town, the place to be at night, can get rowdy during the summer and whenever there are fishing tournaments. Bar-hopping is as easy as walking down the street, where you may literally be weaving in the footsteps of Ernest Hemingway.

"Papa" Hemingway's legacy lives on at **The Compleat Angler Hotel**, where memorabilia of his fishing, boozing and boxing exploits are everywhere, and tourists and locals hang out. There's also a scandalous snapshot of Gary Hart and Donna Rice visiting the bar. Two bars are inside and an outside bar overlooks King's Highway. A calypso band plays on many evenings. This historic Bimini fun spot has been run by the same family since Hemingway's day. ~ King's Highway; 347-3122.

The next logical bar-hopping stop is the **End of the World Bar**, also called the Sand Bar because of its beachsand floor. Overlooking the harbor in the back, a plethora of underwear from around the world adorns the walls. Panties, bras and boxer shorts set the ambience at this friendly watering hole, said to have been the late New York congressman Adam Clayton Powell, Jr.'s favorite stop. ~ King's Highway; no phone.

Your eyes and ears will guide you to other King's Highway hangouts. Some good possibilities include the **Red Lion Pub** ~ 347-3259; the **Big Game Sports Bar** ~ 347-3391; and the **Anchorage Dining Room**, a great sunset spot. ~ 347-3166.

BEACHES

BIMINI ALICE TOWN Many people don't realize that bustling little Alice Town has a great beach scene off Queen's Highway that matches the bar scene on King's Highway. Just head up over the hill and you'll find a quiet strand occupied by a few locals and seagulls. The sun, sand, snorkeling and swimming are typically superb. Though the beach is continuous, each section has its own name—Spook Hill, Radio and Blister Beach. There are no commercial watersports operations here. ~ Located along Queen's Highway, on the west side of the two-block-wide town.

BIMINI BAY Located at the far northern end of North Bimini, this quiet two-mile public stretch is usually only used by those staying at Bimini Bay Guest House. However, adventurous visitors with a golf cart or other transportation will love the soft sand beach and crystal-clear water. No commercial water sports are available. ~ Take King's Highway north as far as it goes (about five miles). The beach is on the east side of the road.

SOUTH BIMINI Usually only visited by those with private homes or guests at Bimini Beach Club & Marina, this beach stretches for several miles along the southern side of South Bimini. Though there are no watersports operations yet, it's only a matter of time before Bimini Sands, the real estate development there, starts offering equipment rentals. ~ Take the ferry to South Bimini, then catch a cab or walk (about two miles) to the south shore. The beach extends north from the tiny settlement of Nixon's Harbor.

THE BERRY ISLANDS Most islands in the Berries have deserted cove beaches that are only accessible by boat. The beaches on the two inhabited islands look much the same as the hard-to-reach ones.

GREAT HARBOUR CAY This cay's sandy stretch runs for almost eight deserted miles. There are no watersports equipment rentals; gear and adventures can be arranged through the Great Harbour Cay Yacht Club & Marina. ~ The beach runs along the entire east shore of this long, slender island.

CHUB CAY There are several unnamed beaches within walking distance of the Chub Cay Club. You'll rarely see a soul at any of them.

▼▼▼▼▼▼▼▼▼▼▼▼▼▼

Outdoor Adventures

BIMINI Best known for fishing, Bimini is a popular boating destination as well. Boaters can dock in North Bimini, South Bimini, Gun Cay or Cat Cay.

BOATING

Boating supplies, guides and rentals can be arranged through the **Bimini Big Game Fishing Club & Hotel** ~ 347-2391; **Bimini Blue Water Marina** ~ 347-3166; **Brown's Marina** ~ 347-3227; or **Weech's Bimini Dock** ~ 347-3028. Nonmembers can dock at the marina at the **Cat Cay Yacht Club**, though only members can spend the night there. ~ 954-359-8272, fax 954-359-8273.

THE BERRY ISLANDS Most boaters come to the Berry Islands while crossing the Great Bahama Bank between Bimini and New Providence. Several of the little islands are ideal for anchorage, but most boaters head to the top-notch marinas at **Great Harbour Cay** ~ 367-8838, 800-343-7256 in the north and **Chub Cay** ~ 325-1490, 800-662-8555 farther south.

KAYAKING

Bimini Undersea Adventures rents sea kayaks, ideal for exploring the mangrove cays across the bay. ~ Alice Town; 347-3089, 800-348-4644.

FISHING

These waters are world-renowned for some of the finest big-game fishing in the world. Ernest Hemingway, Howard Hughes and Richard Nixon did their deep-sea fishing here, though not at the same time. Located in the middle of the Gulf Stream, Bimini is world-record territory for marlin, tuna and other gamefish. From spring to fall, there is a fishing tournament almost every weekend.

Hotels and marinas can help arrange boats, guides, tackle and anything else you may need. Recommended charter fishing boat operators include: **Captain Bob Smith** ~ *Miss Bonita II*, 347-2367; **Captain Jerome Stuart** ~ *Miss Bonita*, 347-2081; **Captain Alfred Sweeting** ~ *Nuttin Honey*, 347-3447; and **Captain Frank Hinzey** ~ *Nina*, 347-3072.

Bonefishing is also big business on Bimini, with "ghost fish" running year-round on the flats in the harbor area. Among the many bonefish guides for hire are **Ansil Saunders** ~ 347-2178 or 347-3098; **Cordell Rolle** ~ 347-2576; **Johnny David** ~ 347-2198; and **Jackson Ellis** ~ 347-2315.

DIVING

BIMINI The **Sapona** is probably the most famous dive in the Biminis. This 300-foot concrete ship was originally built by Henry Ford in the early 1900s as a troop carrier. It sank off the coast of South Bimini and sits partially submerged in less than 20 feet of water. Since it has been underwater so long, the coral, sponge and fish life that call it home are as abundant as they are colorful. Used for target practice during World War II, the ship has many holes for divers to swim through. This is a great site for novice divers, but veterans also enjoy returning to the *Sapona*. Other wreck dives include **Bimini Barge**, a 150-foot ocean barge located in 85 feet of water, and **Bimini Trader**, a 90-foot freighter.

Reef diving is just as good. **Shallow Rainbow Reef** has colorful coral, lots of fish and sometimes a nurse shark or two. Between North and South Bimini, **Eagle Ray Run** features spotted eagle rays in large numbers. **Cat Cay Wall** starts at 70 feet and drops straight down more than 2000 feet. Caribbean reef sharks, nurse sharks and a huge black grouper named Orsen cruise **Shark Reef**.

A mecca for growing numbers of divers with active imaginations, the **Bimini Road** was first spotted by a scientific survey plane in 1968. The formation looked to the pilot like an underwater highway paved with massive cut stone blocks. When it was revealed that, 25 years earlier, American psychic Edgar Cayce had predicted that in 1968 or 1969 Bimini would be the place where evidence of ancient Atlantis would be discovered, people started coming to explore the "ruins" for themselves. Among the metaphysically inclined, fascination with the site grows stronger by the year. Since the Bimini Road lies only 20 feet below the water's surface, it is almost as accessible to snorkelers as to scuba divers.

The oldest dive shop in the Biminis, **Bimini Undersea Adventures** offers packages in conjunction with most major hotels. Bill and Nowdla Keefe dock their dive boats just across the street from their second-floor King's Highway shop. If you have your own boat and certification card, you can get air fills for your own diving. Many South Florida divers swear that these Bimini dive packages are better than heading to the Florida Keys. ~ Alice Town; 347-3089, 800-348-4644.

♦♦

GUIDE EXTRAORDINAIRE

Bonefishing guide **Ansil Saunders** is one of the best, thanks to his experience and entertaining stories. A fishing guide in the Biminis for more than three decades, Ansil is also a fifth-generation boat builder; his ancestors were among the island's original settlers. He has guided anglers to bonefishing world records, built several beautiful boats, staged a 42-day sit-in for racial equality and even taken Martin Luther King, Jr. out to the quiet mangroves. It was there, Ansil says, that King wrote his Nobel Peace Prize acceptance speech. On that day, Ansil recited a poem he had written for King, and he will be happy to recite it to guests he takes fishing these days. ~ 347-2178 or 347-3098.

Bimini Undersea Adventures also offers **Wild Dolphin Excursions.** Wild spotted dolphins, when located, seek interaction with humans. The adventures usually last three to five hours, depending on how long it takes to locate the dolphins. The success rate in making contact is around 80 percent. Once the connection is made, the dolphins usually allow people to swim and interact with them, sometimes for as long as an hour.

At the Bimini Beach Club on South Bimini, two operators share dive packages with the resort. **Bahama Island Adventures** ~ 800-329-1337 and **Scuba Bimini** ~ 800-848-4073 offer comparably priced packages that include round-trip airfare from Fort Lauderdale to South Bimini, ground transportation to and from the resort, hotel accommodations, two dives on the day of arrival, three dives each day of your stay, one dive on the day of departure, unlimited shore diving and free breakfast and lunch.

THE BERRY ISLANDS Called the Fishbowl of The Bahamas, Chub Cay is finally getting some recognition as a scuba diving destination. The **Chub Cay Wall** offers some of the best wall diving in The Bahamas. Right on the drop-off for the **Tongue of the Ocean**, divers return to dive certain parts of the wall often, with most dives in the 80- to 120-foot range. Because this is on the edge of the deep sea, numerous fish sightings include marlin, tuna, sharks and other large marine life.

The other hot site in the Berries is **Mama Rhoda Rock**. Protected by the Bahamas National Trust, this phenomenal reef is forested with staghorn and elkhorn coral and populated by thousands of colorful fish.

At just 10 to 20 feet, the shallow Mama Rhoda Rock dive site is also by far the most popular Berry Islands snorkeling site. Most of the beaches and coves of the Berries also offer good snorkeling for those who bring their own gear.

Based at the Chub Cay Inn, **Bahama Island Adventures** offers packages at prices that have dedicated divers returning year after year. ~ 800-329-1337. (See "Bimini Diving" above.)

▼▼▼▼▼▼▼▼▼▼▼
Transportation

CAR

BIMINI The **Alice Town Airport** is served by Major's Air Services from Freeport. The **Centre Ridge Airstrip** on South Bimini lands small passenger planes operated by Bimini Island Air and Island Air from Fort Lauderdale.

Pan Am Air Bridge flies seaplanes from downtown Miami's cruise ship docks to the Alice Town waterfront. It's a great way to arrive in Bimini.

THE BERRY ISLANDS There is regularly scheduled commercial air service to the Berry Islands through Trans Island Airways, which flies to Great Harbour Cay from Nassau, and Island

Hemingway and Bimini

Bimini and Ernest "Papa" Hemingway will be forever linked in literature and life. Hemingway became interested in Bimini as a deep-sea fishing destination in the early 1930s and first visited North Bimini with his fishing boat, *Pilar*, in 1935. He found the fishing to be of world-record caliber and returned often.

Along with long days of fishing and nights of drinking at the Compleat Angler Hotel, Hemingway also engaged in boxing bouts with any local or visitor who crossed him. His fishing, drinking and boxing exploits are still legendary in Alice Town.

When he was not downing a drink, or a patron, Hemingway spent his time writing in his Compleat Angler Hotel room (Number 1), or at the hotel lounge overlooking King's Highway (now the Hemingway Museum) and at Mike Lerner's house up on Queen's Highway (now the Marlin Cottage at Bimini Blue Water Resort). He revised much of *To Have and Have Not* while there. Although critics found the novel fatally flawed, William Faulkner adapted it into the screenplay in which Humphrey Bogart and Lauren Bacall starred together for the first time. Hemingway later used his Bimini experience, together with plot fragments from *To Have and Have Not*, in his unfinished novel, *Islands in the Stream*, which was published posthumously.

You will find many Hemingway memories in pictures at the Compleat Angler Hotel, but you can also experience the islands in much the same way as Hemingway knew them. Order a cold Kalik at any one of the town bars, walk along King's Highway or wander out to the marina as the fishing boats are heading in or out. Or try your luck out in the Gulf Stream on your own "Islands In The Stream" deep-sea fishing experience. Whether or not you come back with a world-record catch, you'll have a better knowledge of why "Papa" was attracted to Bimini.

Express Airlines, which flies from Fort Lauderdale to Chub Cay's modest airstrip.

Trans-Caribbean Air offers charter flights from Fort Lauderdale or International Airport or Opa Locka Airport to Great Harbour Cay or Chub Cay. The price is the same for one to five people.

BOAT
The **mailboat** M/V *Bimini Mack* leaves Potter's Cay Dock in Nassau weekly and stops in Alice Town and Cat Cay. The sailing time is 12 hours. Contact the dockmaster at Potter's Cay for the current sailing schedule, which varies from week to week. ~ 393-1064.

TAXIS
Everything in Alice Town is within walking distance, and taxis are inexpensive ~ 357-8466. The trip between North and South Bimini is offered by **T.S.L. Water Taxi**. The company also provides taxi service and tours on South Bimini.

CART & BIKE RENTALS
Gasoline-powered golf carts are available for rent to visitors who want to explore the length and breadth of the island without walking too much. **Captain Pat's Island Golf Cart Rentals** ~ 347-3477, **Happy People Car, Scooter and Bicycle Rentals** ~ 367-8114, and **Compleat Golf Cart Rentals** ~ 347-3122 have plenty. **Bimini Undersea Adventures** has bicycle rentals. ~ 347-3089.

▼▼▼▼▼▼▼▼▼▼▼▼▼▼▼▼▼▼▼▼▼

Addresses & Phone Numbers

Medical Clinic—North Bimini Medical Clinic, 347-3210; Berry Islands Medical Clinic, 367-8400.
Police Department—919

NINE

Eleuthera, Harbour Island and Spanish Wells

Sixty miles east of Nassau, Eleuthera is one of the longest and narrowest islands in The Bahamas. It stretches more than 110 miles along the edge of the Great Bahama Bank, seldom more than a mile or two wide. The combined population of Eleuthera and the smaller islands of Harbour Island and Spanish Wells is about 11,000.

Eleuthera became the first Bahamian island to have an English-speaking settlement in 1648, when Captain William Sayle and his band of "Eleutherian Adventurers" arrived from Bermuda. Surviving religious schisms, famine and raids by Spanish pirates, the expedition charted the way for hundreds of Bermudian settlers, as well as boatloads of slaves exiled there from Bermuda. Eleuthera already boasted solid communities and a democratic government in the days when Nassau was merely a pirates' hideout.

Eleutherians have survived over the centuries through salvaging, cotton growing and shipbuilding. At one time the island's farmers grew most of the pineapples sold in the United States, but that was before Hawaii became a U.S. territory. Today, most jobs on Eleuthera are connected with tourism.

The island's physical attributes are spectacular, with miles of deserted beaches, cliffs, coves and rolling farmland between small towns and villages. Off the northern tip of Eleuthera lie two smaller, developed islands—Spanish Wells and Harbour Island. When Bahamians say "Eleuthera," they're generally referring to all three islands. Visitors, however, will find completely different experiences on each.

Known for its unusual coral-pink sands, Eleuthera's other features include lush forests, rich red soil, friendly people, brightly colored houses and tranquility. Victorian houses and art galleries, along with an 18-hole championship golf course, tennis courts, marinas, scuba diving and other watersports add to Eleuthera's draw as an Out Island vacation destination.

Eleuthera

Beginning at the northern tip of the island, in **North Eleuthera**, you'll find the local attraction, the **Boiling Hole**, a rock bank that "boils" during changing tides. Eleuthera is honeycombed with caves, both above and below water level. Visitors can easily explore **Preacher's Cave**, where the island's original settlers took refuge upon landing and, according to legend, held the first Christian religious service in The Bahamas. A pulpit was carved out of the rock. A 1992 archaeological expedition discovered 17th-century artifacts and the skeletons of early settlers in the cave's depths. Watch for the small sign near the village of The Current.

Heading south, just a few miles before you reach Gregory Town, is **Glass Window Bridge**, which connects two rock bluffs at the narrow pass between the southern and northern sections of the island. To the east is the rough Atlantic Ocean and to the west is calm Exuma Sound. Sailors named the spot because you could see through the two bluffs like a window.

Gregory Town, the next major settlement, is known for its sweet pineapples, renowned throughout the world. The farms of Eleuthera once supplied all the pineapple consumed in the United States, before Hawaii became a U.S. territory. Today, most of the local pineapple crop is used by the **Gregory Town Plantation and Distillery** to make a flavored rum liqueur called Gregory Town Special. Set on the island's western shore, the humble clapboard town is protected by the only hills on this otherwise flat island.

About eight miles south of Gregory Town, a dirt road turns off to the west and takes you to the **Hatchet Bay Caves**, a group of damp limestone caves full of stalactites and stalagmites, as well as thousands of leaf-nosed bats. The largest of the caves, easily spotted by a giant landmark fig tree in front, which locals say was planted by pirates to conceal the entrance, is known simply as The Cave. Visitors can explore it with a guide or just a flashlight. Some slopes inside are steep enough to require climbing up and down ladders.

Queen's Highway rambles its way through the best farmland in The Bahamas. There's a government-run produce stand at Hatchet Bay, one of the prettier harbors on the island. The area was formerly a large Angus cattle farm, but now much of the property is used for poultry and dairy farming.

In central Eleuthera, one of the oldest English-speaking settlements in The Bahamas is **Governor's Harbour.** It was one of the towns originally established by the Eleutherian Adventurers. Governor's Harbour used to be a very prosperous town, when 19th-century ships sent tons of fruit to the U.S. and returned laden with modern goods. Many women would travel from elsewhere in The Bahamas to buy the latest fashions in Governor's

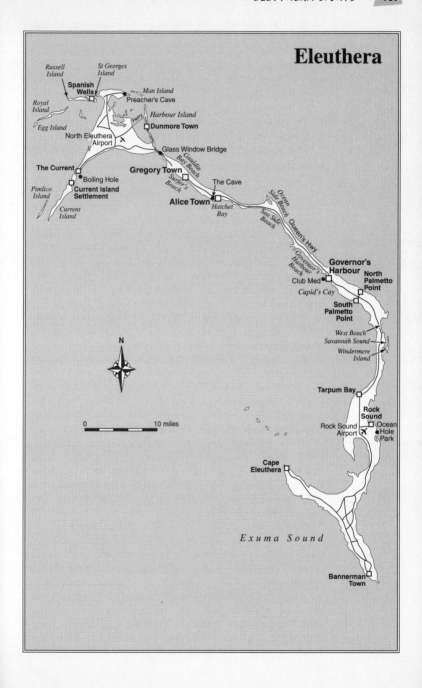

Eleuthera

Russell Island
St Georges Island
Spanish Wells
Man Island
Preacher's Cave
Royal Island
Harbour Island
Egg Island
Dunmore Town
Ferry
North Eleuthera Airport
Glass Window Bridge
The Current
Gaulding Bay Beach
Gregory Town
Boiling Hole
Surfer's Beach
Current Island Settlement
The Cave
Pimlico Island
Alice Town
Hatchet Bay
Current Island
Ocean Side Beach
Sea Side Beach
Queen's Hwy
Governor's Harbour Beach
Governor's Harbour
Club Med
North Palmetto Point
Cupid's Cay
South Palmetto Point
West Beach
Savannah Sound
Windermere Island
N
Tarpum Bay
Rock Sound
Rock Sound Airport
Ocean Hole Park
0   10 miles
Cape Eleuthera
Exuma Sound
Bannerman Town

Harbour. It still serves as a place to gather provisions for modern-day Eleutherian adventuring.

The island's second-largest community, it's still pretty sleepy, even with the nearby Club Med adding to the population. The town's Anglican Church, the pretty-in-pink government offices, the cemetery, renovated Haynes Library (built in 1897) and Cupid's Cay (supposedly the landing point for Sayle and his settlers) are the main attractions. The waterfront area, with its Victorian buildings, is especially charming at sunset.

HIDDEN ▶   Five miles south of Governor's Harbour, the quiet area of **Palmetto Point** is known to only a few locals and visitors in search of serious peace and quiet. There are several excellent local restaurants and lodging possibilities in the two villages (North Palmetto Point and South Palmetto Point), so many loyal return-visitors simply eat, sleep and relax around here.

Reached by crossing a narrow bridge on the east side of Eleuthera, **Windermere Island** is taken up by the private homes of many wealthy individuals from around the world. It once featured the Windermere Island Club, where Princess Diana was photographed pregnant and in a swimsuit, much to the chagrin of the club; it's now closed.

North of the Rock Sound Airport lies **Tarpum Bay**, a pretty little seaside town well worth a stop for picture taking, gallery gazing and shopping.

Rock Sound is now the largest town on Eleuthera, but even the main Front Street along the water is pretty quiet. A scattering of colorfully painted colonial-era houses and the small St. Luke's Lutheran Church recall the town's early days, when it grew prosperous as a haven for "wreckers," who salvaged cargos from ships that ran aground on the treacherous reefs offshore. It is said to have been common practice here to light false marker beacons, luring unwary ships onto the rocks and giving the town its original name—Wreck Sound. Today, the bayfront town is a major commercial center, where residents of southern Eleuthera come to buy groceries and catch plane flights to Miami for more serious shopping.

A little more than a mile to the east of Rock Sound, many visitors head to **Ocean Hole**, an inland saltwater lake. Called bottomless because the depth isn't known, the lake is fed by the ocean. Throw some bread into the water and watch the tropical fish gather.

A drive to **Bannerman Town**, the community farthest to the south, through quaint villages untouched by modern-day living, leads to a picturesque lighthouse. From there, a road leads north along the western shore, up a long, narrow spit of land to **Cape Eleuthera**, where the Cape Eleuthera Yacht Club has boating facilities.

LODGING

◀ HIDDEN

The Current's **Sandcastle Apartments** is actually one apartment with a bedroom and a living room with a pull-out sofa. The furnishings are simple and the surroundings rather secluded. It's across from a quiet beach. The Symonette family caters to families looking for a quiet and inexpensive getaway. There's a grocery store nearby, making it easy to use the on-premises kitchen. ~ The Current; 333-0264. BUDGET.

Gregory Town draws surfers and other adventurers with a less expensive lodging and lifestyle scene. Located right in town on Queen's Highway, **Cambridge Villas** has 20 basic hotel rooms with varying configurations, as well as four two-bedroom apartments with kitchens. This simple establishment is very clean and well-run. The owner offers shuttles to the nearby swimming beach as well as Surfer's Beach. He also has a five-passenger plane for island-hopping charters. ~ P.O. Box 1548, Gregory Town; 335-5080, 800-688-4752, fax 335-5308. BUDGET.

Monica Thompson at sweet-smelling **Thompson's Bakery** will also take in guests on a budget. She has two apartments in Gregory Town, each with two bedrooms and cooking facilities. The apartments are squeaky clean, and near a good beach and Gregory Town businesses. ~ Gregory Town; 335-5053. BUDGET.

The **Cove Eleuthera Hotel**, a beachfront resort, has 24 rooms in six buildings furnished with white rattan. Half of the rooms have sea vistas and the others offer garden views; all have balconies. The location, just outside Gregory Town, is convenient yet secluded. ~ P.O. Box 1548, Gregory Town; 335-5142, 800-552-5960, fax 335-5338. MODERATE.

The Hatchet Bay area has a perfect choice for visitors desiring a combination of seclusion with a proximity to "civilization." The **Rainbow Inn**, located just south of Hatchet Bay and Alice Town, has five hillside efficiency apartment accommoda-

◀ HIDDEN

✔ **CHECK THESE OUT**

- Live like the locals by sleeping and eating at **Laughing Bird Apartments** in Governor's Harbour, where you'll become a Bahamian in no time. *page 172*
- Slice off a piece of pineapple or conch pizza at **Mate & Jenny's Pizza Restaurant & Bar**, a popular local hangout. *page 175*
- Ferry over to Harbour Island for a walk around Cape Cod–like **Dunmore Town**, where clapboard cottages still stand some 200 years after Loyalists built them. *page 177*
- Enjoy the motto "Life's a beach" at the three-mile pink-sand beach of **Harbour Island**, one of the best in The Bahamas. *page 180*

tions, with kitchenettes, spacious porches and great views. There are also three two-bedroom villas as well as a three-bedroom villa. The Inn runs shuttles into Governor's Harbour twice a week and into a nearby town with a short stop each morning to pick up the maid. ~ P.O. Box 25053, Governor's Harbour; phone/fax 335-0294, 800-688-0047; www.rainbowinn.com. MODERATE.

Club Med Eleuthera, one of the top family-oriented choices in The Bahamas, is a bright and busy all-inclusive resort. There are 288 rooms in two- and three-story buildings. All meals, including wine and beer during lunch and dinner, are included as are most watersports and other activities. Club Med operates its own watersports marina nearby. The resort offers an incredible list of things parents and their kids can pursue together and apart. Located on a nice pinkish-sand beach, the water sports program is outstanding, though experienced divers may want to look elsewhere on the island—or head to the Club Med Columbus Isle on San Salvador. From Circus School to snorkeling, you and your kids can be as busy or as relaxed as you want to be. There are often tears at departure, as children don't want to leave. Nonguests can pay a day-visitor fee and take advantage of all resort facilities. ~ P.O. Box 80, Governor's Harbour; 332-2270, 800-258-2633; www.clubmed.com. MODERATE TO DELUXE.

One recent addition to budget offerings in Governor's Harbour is **The Buccaneer Club**. Dwight Johnson proudly and enthusiastically offers five clean, modern rooms as well as a small pool. It's a good money-saving choice in the heart of town. ~ P.O. Box 86, Governor's Harbour; 332-2000, 800-688-4752. BUDGET.

If you are going to be on Eleuthera for a week or so and plan to use Governor's Harbour as a base, check out **Laughing Bird Apartments**. These beachfront efficiencies have kitchens to help you keep your food budget to a minimum. There's a combined living, dining and sleeping area. The four units are situated in a

ELEUTHERA ECOTOURISM

Island Vacations has two tours for Eleuthera, Harbour Island and Spanish Wells. The "Eleuthera Adventure" includes a complete tour of all three islands, interspersing history and outdoor activities. The "Little Big Adventure" on Harbour Island includes a bike tour of the historic village, a "learn-to-dive" or snorkeling program, an eco-boat trip, deep-sea fishing and bonefishing. ~ Contact Island Vacations in the U.S. at 4327 Reflections Boulevard North, Suite 104, Sunrise, FL 33351; 305-748-1833, 800-900-4242, fax 305-748-1965, or in Nassau at P.O. Box 13002, Town Centre Mall, Nassau, Bahamas; 356-1111, fax 356-4379.

pretty garden setting, with hammocks and a common barbecue area. Each of the two duplexes has two units that can be combined to accommodate up to six people under one roof. ~ Haynes Avenue and Birdie Street, P.O. Box 25076, Governor's Harbour; 332-2012, fax 332-2358. BUDGET TO MODERATE.

Set amid lush tropical gardens, **Palm Tree Villas** offers one- and two-bedroom apartments equipped with full kitchen and a balcony. The villas are a short walk from downtown and the beach. ~ P.O. Box 136, Governor's Harbour; 332-2002. MODERATE.

Three miles outside town, the isolated **Wykee's World Resort** is a good family choice. There are four two-bedroom villas situated on a former estate. All offer full kitchens, screened-in porches and use of a saltwater pool. Several beaches are nearby. ~ P.O. Box 25176, Queen's Highway, Governor's Harbour; 332-2701, fax 332-2123. MODERATE.

Palmetto Shores Vacation Villas in the Palmetto Point area about five miles south of Governor's Harbour is another housekeeping possibility. These large waterfront units have one-, two- and three-bedroom layouts and wraparound balconies. There are 15 villas spread throughout the sprawling beachfront property. ~ Palmetto Point; phone/fax 332-1305. MODERATE.

For those who really want to get away from it all, **Unique Village Villas and Apartments** lives up to its name. Located about five miles south of Governor's Harbour in North Palmetto Point are ten hillside hotel rooms, two one-bedroom apartments and two two-bedroom villas. Manager Pauline Johnson lives on the property, which also has a perpetually deserted beach at the bottom of the short hill and a quiet pagoda-like lounge overlooking the water. Palmetto Point is within a healthy walking distance. ~ North Palmetto Point; 332-1830, 800-223-5310, fax 332-1838. MODERATE.

◄ HIDDEN

Windermere Island, an ultra-exclusive residential island with a long, white beach so private that international celebrities have been known to sunbathe there *au naturel,* no longer features resort-style lodging, but **Windermere Villas** and **Windermere Apartments** have one- to three-bedroom rental units. The villas and apartments, individually decorated and surrounded by lush vegetation, normally rent by the week ~ P.O. Box 25, Rock Sound; 332-2566, 800-223-6800. MODERATE TO ULTRA-DELUXE.

Tarpum Bay has plenty of budget lodgings owned and operated by local folks. Though clearly not part of the U.S.-based chain, **Hilton's Haven Motel**, just across the street from a fair beach and around the corner from the MacMillan Hughes gallery, rents ten pleasant rooms with small patios or balconies. Mary, a friendly former nurse, loves Tarpum Bay and will be happy to introduce guests to local life. ~ Tarpum Bay; 334-4231, 800-688-4752, fax 334-4020. BUDGET.

For a housekeeping holiday in quiet Tarpum Bay, **Cartwright's Ocean View Cottages** has five two- and three-bedroom cottages. All face the sea and offer alluring sunset views. Each has a full kitchen and living room area. The property is located on Bay Street, and is within walking distance of almost everything. ~ Bay Street, Tarpum Bay; 334-4215. MODERATE TO DELUXE.

In southern Eleuthera, the Rock Sound area offers two basic options for those on a budget. Located just a mile from the airport, **Edwina's Place** has nine simple and comfortable hotel-like rooms within walking distance of village shops and a decent beach. Friendly Edwina Burrows will help make your Rock Sound stay pleasant and personal. ~ P.O. Box 30, Rock Sound; 334-2094. BUDGET.

Sammy's Place is a similar in-town Rock Sound offering. Sammy Culmer and his daughter, Margarita, have four spotless upstairs guest rooms. The bright red paint and the modern furnishings in the modernized rooms make this another good local choice. ~ Albury's Lane, Rock Sound; 334-2121. BUDGET.

DINING

Restaurants on Eleuthera range from local "peas 'n rice" places to upscale resort restaurants with an international flair. Many of the lodging choices offer meal plans, which can save money on food and transportation but might give you limited flexibility in trying other eateries.

HIDDEN ▶

Rainbow Inn, north of Governor's Harbour, is one of the best restaurants on the island. Arrive early enough for a leisurely drink at the nautically themed bar. The restaurant has one of the more sophisticated menus on the island, mixing good local fare with creatively prepared Continental cuisine. Specialties include escargot, Bahamian conch or fish chowder, French onion soup and steamed fish or chicken. You'll also enjoy a lovely sea view. Dinner only. ~ P.O. Box 25053, Governor's Harbour; 335-0294, 800-688-4752. MODERATE.

Monica's Restaurant offers some of the island's best Bahamian cooking—patties, conch fritters, grouper fingers and many other tasty local treats. Closed Sunday. ~ Shirley Street, Gregory Town; 335-5053. BUDGET.

Hungry for tasty bread and pastries? **Governor's Harbour Bakery** is a favorite spot for baked goods. ~ Governor's Harbour; 332-2071.

HIDDEN ▶

North Palmetto Point is the home of **Muriel's Home Made Bread, Restaurant and Grocery**. Muriel Cooper runs an all-purpose culinary combination where visitors can buy everything from fresh-baked bread to a full meal to take home or enjoy in the simple dining room. Muriel's conch chowder is outstanding.

For dinner, call ahead to tell her you're coming and pre-order your meal. Closed Sunday. ~ North Palmetto Point, about a mile off Queen's Highway; 332-1583. BUDGET.

South Palmetto Point is the home of the popular pizza joint **Mate & Jenny's Pizza Restaurant & Bar**. Locals and a smattering of tourists head here for lunch or dinner to drink a cold Kalik beer, play a game of pool, munch on some tasty pizza and while away some time with Mate Bethel and his wife, Jenny. Pizza possibilities include conch and fresh pineapple and ham. No lunch on Sunday; closed Monday and Tuesday. ~ South Palmetto Point, just off Queen's Highway; 332-1504. MODERATE.

In Rock Sound, **Sammy's Place** is a favorite local spot. Specialties include fried chicken, seafood and *souse*, a flavorful chicken loaf commonly eaten for breakfast. Entrées come with a healthy serving of peas 'n rice and friendly smiles all around. ~ Albury's Lane, Rock Sound; 334-2121. BUDGET.

◄ HIDDEN

For seafood dining with a view, venture over to **Harbour View Restaurant**, which specializes in fresh local cuisine. Choices include of steamed fish, cracked conch and fresh lobster. The waterfront setting at sunset is hard to beat. ~ Queen's Highway, Rock Sound; 334-2278. MODERATE.

Edwina's Place, near the Rock Sound airport, is renowned for the cooking of innkeeper Edwina Burrows. To find out why try the conch fritters and any of her fresh baked fish specialties. ~ P.O. Box 30, Rock Sound; 334-2094. BUDGET.

Gregory Town is not the place to shop 'til you drop. But you can stop by the little **Island Made Gift Shop**, which carries local arts and crafts. ~ 335-5369.

SHOPPING

Governor's Harbour offers several in-town shops. Clotheshorses can browse at **Norma's Gift Shop**, which features batik clothing, much of which is handmade there. ~ Haynes Avenue, Governor's Harbour; 332-2002.

Nearby, **Brenda's Boutique** offers a wide selection of souvenirs, including jewelry made from conch shells. ~ Haynes Avenue, Governor's Harbour; 332-2089.

Prince Charles is one of Eleuthera's biggest fans, visiting Windermere Island often.

Tarpum Bay is an artist's colony of sorts. Since 1972, **Mal Flanders** has lived in Eleuthera and has painted seemingly everything and everyone. Says Flanders, "I've painted Eleuthera from one end to the other and still find something new to paint every day." An American expatriate, he is now a Bahamian citizen. His paintings are owned by the likes of Sir Lynden and Lady Pindling and His Excellency James Moultrie. Visitors are welcome at Flanders' studio/gallery, located just off Queen's Highway. ~ Tarpum Bay; 334-4187.

Just up the street from the waterfront, the **MacMillan-Hughes Gallery and Castle** is another gallery stop. Bearded Peter MacMillan-Hughes, a self-proclaimed mystic and Scotch-Irish painter and sculptor, has lived in Eleuthera since 1957. His castle-like gallery features a wide range of locally oriented sculptures and paintings. ~ Just off Queen's Highway, Tarpum Bay; 334-4091.

Also in Tarpum Bay, you'll find basic supplies and groceries at the **Tarpum Bay Shopping Centre**. ~ Queen's Highway, Tarpum Bay; 334-4022.

In Rock Sound, **Goombay Gifts** sells locally made straw pieces and shell necklaces and bracelets. ~ Front Street, Rock Sound; 334-2191.

BEACHES

HIDDEN ►

GAULDIN BAY BEACH 🏃 🏊 🚣 This secluded beach just north of Gregory Town is a local secret. You'll probably be alone with your thoughts and quiet seas and sand. ~ Head past the salt ponds and take the second dirt road by the large pasture.

SURFER'S BEACH 🏃 🏊 🏄 This renowned stretch on the Atlantic Ocean side draws surfers from around the world during the winter months, when the waves rise and curl into the kind of "pipelines" you'd expect to find in Hawaii. ~ Located just south of Gregory Town on Ocean Boulevard in Eleuthera Island Shores.

SEA SIDE BEACH 🏃 🏊 🏄 Located in the Rainbow Bay area, a few miles north of Governor's Harbour, Sea Side Beach offers very good snorkeling close to shore. But don't enter the water if the waves are big. ~ To reach the beach, travel east on Hidden Beach Drive from Queen's Highway; the dirt road dead-ends at the beach.

GOVERNOR'S HARBOUR 🏃 🏊 🚣 🎣 🏊 🚣 This beautiful pink-sand beach has Club Med located at one end, but anyone can access the beach. Most Club Med guests remain near the resort, so you're likely to have the rest of this stunning beach to yourself. There are no commercial watersports activities available, but you can buy a one-day pass at Club Med and use their facilities. ~ Heading north from Governor's Harbor on Queen's Highway, take the dirt road about 50 yards before the Club Med entrance.

OCEAN SIDE 🏃 🏊 🚣 Just south of the Governor's Harbour airport, this long, straight beach stretches for several miles. The pristine beach is so little used that the foot trail from the parking area may be choked with plant life. It offers silent beauty and solitude except when planes land and take off, which is not often. ~ Take the first dirt road on the left after the end of the runway (coming from Governor's Harbour, it's right after the first speed bump). Follow this road to the top of the hill, where you'll make a right to head down to the beach.

WEST BEACH 🏃 🏊 🚣 🐟 🚤 ⛵ Ideally situated on calm Savannah Sound, separating the mainland from Windermere Island, this beach of soft, tawny sand offers some of the island's best swimming and fishing. ~ It stretches northward around the bay from the Eleuthera side of the bridge to Windermere Island.

OCEAN HOLE PARK 🏃 At Rock Island's Ocean Hole, an inland saltwater lake officially known as Ocean Hole Park, visitors descend coral steps to feed bread to the fish, attracting bigger and more beautiful fish the longer you stay there, including huge grouper. Fed by the ocean, the hole is said to be "bottomless." ~ The park is just off the main road on the eastern outskirts of the village of Rock Sound.

▼▼▼▼▼▼▼▼▼▼

Harbour Island

Although it is tiny—just one and a half miles long—Harbour Island is rich in history and colonial charm. With its white gingerbread houses, picket fences, tropical flowers and miles of powdery pink sand, it may well be the prettiest island in The Bahamas, Settled in the 17th century by Eleutherian adventurers, its reputation spread far and wide a century later, when Lord Dunmore, the Bahamian governor who built Nassau's Fort Fincastle and Fort Charlotte, made his summer home there. He became vitally interested in the island's development and established Dunmore Town as the island's commercial hub The village soon burgeoned with Loyalist newcomers, who brought boatbuilding skills from the shipyards of New England. Within five years after it was founded, Dunmore Town was renowned for the huge sloops and schooners built there. Shipbuilding continued until the beginning of World War II. As the wooden ship era ended, Harbour Island craftsmen and their families left the island. Today tourism is the only game in town.

SIGHTS

Although it covers most of the island, **Dunmore Town** is easily explored on foot. This quaint Cape Cod–like village reminds many visitors of a miniature Bermuda, with its Georgian architecture and its fabulous beaches of coral pink sand. **Bay Street**, the main thoroughfare, is lined with New England–style homes dating back to the end of the 18th century. Surrounded by white picket fences and colorful tropical foliage, the homes are best viewed and photographed in the late-afternoon light. A short stroll through town will bring you to the **Loyalist Cottage**. Built in the 1790s, it is one of the few remaining homes of the original Loyalist settlers. Another old Loyalist house has been converted into the **Pine Sands Resort bar**.

Some of of the oldest churches in The Bahamas—**St. John's Church**, built in 1768 and **Wesley Methodist Church**, built in 1848—continue to hold Sunday services, and visitors are welcome. A fitting closure to your tour, **St. Catherine's Cemetery**, is usually filled with fresh flowers.

LODGING   Harbour Island is more expensive than the rest of Eleuthera, and you get what you pay for. One of the top choices is **Coral Sands Hotel**, owned by former Hollywood actor Brett King and his wife, Sharon, who plays full-time hostess. The Coral Sands has a loyal following of guests from all over the world, and from various walks of life. There are 33 guest rooms and several suites and villas that are popular with families, all of which are furnished in a tropical motif. Bahamian and Continental cuisine is served in the café or lounge, and is reportedly one of the reasons visitors return year after year. Or maybe it's the combination of warm hospitality, good food and access to numerous sporting activities, including tennis, fishing, boating and snorkeling. Then again it may be the lovely stretch of pink-sand beach, the hilly 14 acres or the short walking distance to town. ~ Chapel Street, P.O. Box 23, Harbour Island; 333-2320, 800-468-2799, fax 333-2368; www.coralsands.com. MODERATE.

The Pink Sands property has been officially designated as a bird sanctuary by the Audubon Society.

On the other end of the scale, **Dunmore Beach Club** is an opulent pink oasis with a quiet air of sophistication. Just 12 traditional tropical bungalows nestle in lushly landscaped grounds at the edge of a three-mile-long pink beach. Facilities include a club house, living room, library and restaurant. You can tell what kind of place it is by the request that men wear coats and ties in winter, something almost unheard-of in the Out Islands. Lodging here is on the American Plan (all meals included). ~ Colebrook Lane, P.O. Box 27122, Harbour Island; 333-2200, fax 333-2429; www.dunmorebeach.com. ULTRA-DELUXE.

Named after Harbour Island's colorful beaches and overlooking one of the prettiest sections, the **Pink Sands Hotel** is a small resort with 21 one-bedroom cottages and four two-bedroom units, each with a living room area and patio. Decor utilizes marble floors, area rugs, local artwork and oversized Adirondack furnishings with batik fabrics, all set against a mellow wash of baby pink and blue. Water sports are important here, as is the natural environment. Rates include breakfast and dinner. ~ P.O. Box 87, Harbour Island; 333-2030, 800-688-7678, fax 809-333-2060. ULTRA-DELUXE.

The **Romora Bay Club**, once a private estate, is now a luxury inn with 29 rooms and nine villas that lures romance-minded couples. The tropical guest rooms have widely ranging views and sizes, with matching prices. The watersports program (sailing, sportfishing, diving) is outstanding, with the resort located between the harbor and the beach. Meals are offered in the dining room. A private taxi and ferry service from the airport is provided. ~ Colebrook Street, P.O. Box 146, Harbour Island; 333-2325, 800-327-8286, fax 333-2500; www.romorabay.com. MODERATE TO DELUXE.

Runaway Hill Club is another small, elegant choice. The small inn was once a private home, and guests still feel as if they're staying in one. Most of the ten rooms, each uniquely furnished, face the ocean. Accommodations are situated in a main building and a villa on a hill. Join the locals for a meal in the main house. ~ Colebrook Street, P.O. Box 27031, Harbour Island; 333-2150, 800-728-9803, fax 333-2420; www.runawayhill.com. DELUXE.

A mixed bag of boaters, divers and budgeteers head for **Valentine's Yacht Club & Inn**, located at the marina. This casual place has 21 simple rooms with verandas overlooking the marina in a seafaring atmosphere. There's a small pool and dive shop. ~ Harbourfront, P.O. Box 1, Harbour Island; 333-2142, 800-323-5655, fax 333-2135. MODERATE.

Those determined to stay on Harbour Island without blowing their budgets should get in touch with Ma Ruby Percentie at **Tingum Village Hotel**. There are 12 very basic rooms, two with a shared kitchen and all quite clean and manageable. Both the beach and town are a short walk away. ~ Colebrook Lane, P.O. Box 61, Harbour Island; 333-2161. BUDGET TO MODERATE.

Most Harbour Island resort hotels offer a Modified American Plan option, with breakfast and dinner included in the room rate. Nonguests are welcome at the hotel dining rooms with advance reservations, though meal prices run high in these places— typically in the $40-a-person range. Fortunately, Dunmore Town also has some great little restaurants where prices are geared for locals.

DINING

No Harbour Island visit is complete without a stop at **Angela's Starfish Restaurant**. There may be equally good local cooking elsewhere, but few restaurants can offer the native atmosphere of this place, serving local seafood in simple surroundings. ~ Dunmore and Grant streets, Harbour Island; 333-2253. BUDGET.

◄ HIDDEN

Ruby Percentie is the exceptional hostess at **Ma Ruby's**, where conch burgers and grouper are two of her many local specialties. The decor is simple and so is the food, but you won't leave hungry. If you're only on Harbour Island for a meal or two and you're on a budget, make it Ma Ruby's or Angela's. ~ Colebrook Lane; 333-2161. BUDGET.

◄ HIDDEN

Harbour Island has enough stores to make window-shopping a pastime. At **Miss Mae Tea Room and Fine Things** you can shop for clothing, leather and jewelry, then head out on the back patio for light snacks and tea. ~ Dunmore Street; no phone.

SHOPPING

Androsia Bahamas carries bright batik clothing from Andros. ~ Dunmore Street; 333-2342.

The ferry dock area is usually a good spot to find straw goods for sale at small stands.

NIGHTLIFE Most evening entertainment possibilities in Eleuthera are found on Harbour Island. They usually consist of a local band playing familiar Bahamian and U.S. cover songs. Otherwise, you'll just find that drinking and conversation are the typical evening pursuits. Favorite spots include the historic and nautical **Picaroon Landing** ~ 333-2241, **Harbour Lounge** ~ 333-2031, **Seagrapes Night Club** ~ 333-2439 and **Vic-Hum Club** (no phone). Or try **Willie's Tavern**, the island's oldest nightspot.

BEACHES **HARBOUR ISLAND** 🧍 🏖 🛶 🤿 🏊 With three miles of pink powdery sand, Harbour Island is one of the most famous beaches in The Bahamas. You can pursue almost any watersport at one of the resorts here, but the most common pursuit is finding an ideal spot to relax on the beach. ~ Once you arrive on Harbour Island, finding the beach is easy: it extends all the way around the island, broken only by a handful of marinas.

▼▼▼▼▼▼▼▼▼▼
Spanish Wells

Spanish Wells, a New England–like gem of an island, was given its name because early Spanish explorers sank a deep freshwater well here to replenish their water supply for the long haul home across the Atlantic. Ponce de Leon stopped for water on one of his expeditions in search for the Fountain of Youth. Today, Spanish Wells is one of the wealthiest communities in The Bahamas, thanks to a thriving spiny lobster industry. It's so lucrative that many youths skip school or leave early because they can make thousands of dollars on a single fishing expedition.

The inhabitants, blonde-haired, blue-eyed descendants of early Eleutherian and Loyalist settlers, live in brightly colored clapboard houses. They speak a dialect that blends British English with Bahamian speech patterns. Many people say Spanish Wells residents aren't as friendly as most Out Islanders—there's a history of prejudice—but as more tourists visit they seem to be warming up a bit to outsiders. Still, Spanish Wells is a mainly residential community with limited sightseeing appeal and an economy that revolves around commercial fishing, not tourism.

SIGHTS It's easy to explore the town by bike or foot. What you'll find are the colorful saltbox-style houses on the eastern side of the island and an unusually large number of churches—Baptist, Methodist and the People's Church—thanks to the island's heritage. Most one-day visitors just wander around the island or use it as a base for watersports. Those who stay on Spanish Wells simply relax in the peace and sunshine, waiting for the beautiful sunsets.

The small **Spanish Wells Museum** near the dock will interest Bahamian history buffs with its collection of old photos, Loyalist memorabilia, Lucayan pottery and period costumes. There's also a small gift shop. ~ 333-4710.

Boaters and non-boaters alike will enjoy **Spanish Wells Yacht Haven**. It's small, with just three rooms and two small apartments with kitchenettes. Well-maintained, it has a swimming pool and views of the marina. ~ Harbourfront, P.O. Box 27427, Spanish Wells; 333-4255. MODERATE.

LODGING

Though they can be hard to find on Spanish Wells, renting a house is another lodging option. **Lloyd Higgs** can help you find one if you contact him well in advance. ~ Spanish Wells; 333-4101. MODERATE TO ULTRA-DELUXE.

Spanish Wells does not have many restaurants, and the island's limited lodging options typically have kitchenettes or kitchen privileges. The unpretentious restaurant at the **Spanish Wells Yacht Haven** specializes in lobster, the island's main industry. The romantic view of the yacht basin makes this a perfect sunset-watching spot. ~ Harbourfront, Spanish Wells; 333-4255. MODERATE.

DINING

The **Sea View**, on the waterfront near the Spanish Wells Yacht Haven, is a typical Bahamian fast-food place, where you can dine on grouper fingers at a small table looking out on the harbor or order a paper bag of take-out cracked conch to nibble on as you stroll around the village. ~ Harbourfront, Spanish Wells; 333-4219. BUDGET.

Roy Roberts' Ponderosa Shell Shop near the ferry dock has to be one of the best shell shops in The Bahamas. They feature collectable shells as well as folk art and gift items. ~ Spanish Wells; no phone.

SHOPPING

Straw wide-brimmed "Spanish Wells hats" can be found in many shops throughout Eleuthera. Although the hats, plaited by hand in Spanish Wells, are worn throughout The Bahamas, they aren't guaranteed to make you look like a local; in fact, they make most visitors look more like tourists than ever.

A wide variety of boating opportunities are available on all three islands. Day sailing is quite popular around the northern area of Eleuthera, Harbour Island and Spanish Wells. Longer outings to Nassau or the northern Exumas are also frequently available.

▼▼▼▼▼▼▼▼▼▼▼▼▼
Outdoor Adventures

BOATING

Most resorts and all marinas can help you arrange boat outings, from a small Sunfish to a full-fledged charter yacht. The top marinas include **Romora Bay Club** ~ 333-2325, **Spanish Wells Yacht Haven** ~ 333-4255 and **Valentine's Yacht Club** ~ 333-2142. Rentals can also be found throughout the area, including many of the hotels and independent operators such as **Ivee Boating**. ~ 333-2386.

FISHING

Bonefishing and deep-sea fishing are Eleutherian pastimes. Harbour Island serves as the best base to find outfitters. **Coral Sands Hotel** ~ 333-2350, **Romora Bay Club** ~ 333-2325 and **Valentine's Yacht Club** ~ 333-2142 can all help with arrangements. Locals say the king of the local guides is Harbour Island's "**Bonefish**" **Joe Cleare**. ~ 333-2663.

GOLF

An excellent if somewhat lonely course can be found about ten minutes south of Rock Sound. Though the resort itself is now closed, the **Cotton Bay Club** still allows visitors to play the Robert Trent Jones course. ~ Cotton Bay Club; 334-2101.

DIVING

Both Spanish Wells and Harbour Island serve as bases for exploring the **Devil's Backbone**. These razor-sharp reefs to the north have stopped many a ship, resulting in many wrecks for divers to explore. The two most popular are the 197-foot freighter **Carnarvon** and the **Train Wreck**, a shipment of Civil War–era trains that didn't quite make it to Cuba.

The four-masted *Marie J. Thompson*—at 696 tons—was the largest ship ever built in The Bahamas.

For experienced divers, the **Current Cut Dive** is spectacular, with divers traveling about a half-mile in a strong current amid a myriad of marine life, though the visibility isn't normally as good as other dive sites. **Blow Hole**, named after a rock formation that sometimes spouts water in rough conditions, is famous for the rock—not coral—that makes up the underwater landscape. A bit farther afield, a trip to **Shark Hole** almost guarantees reef shark sightings, thanks to daily feeding by dive operators.

Harbour Island is home to outstanding dive centers: **Romora Bay Club** ~ 333-2325 and **Valentine's Dive Center** ~ 333-2309. Both offer complete services, rentals and instruction. You might want to check to see where they're scheduled to dive, or if they will schedule something for you.

The large dive center at **Club Med** is open to day visitors as well as guests. ~ 332-2270. **Clearwater Dive Shop** is also in Governor's Harbour. ~ 332-2146.

Calling Tim Riley at **South Eleuthera Divers** in Rock Sound provides interesting options for divers seeking less-visited sites in the south. ~ 344-4083.

Top snorkeling sites include **Gaulding's Cay** (elkhorn and star corals, lobsters, sea anemones and bonefish), **Oleander Reef** and **Paradise Beach** (great snorkeling right off the beach at both sites), **Current Cut** (a roller coaster ride for snorkelers) and **Glass Window Bridge** (an artificial reef ideal on calm days).

TENNIS

Several resorts have courts and allow nonguests to play for a fee. They include **Club Med** ~ 322-2270, **Cotton Bay Club** ~ 334-2101, **Dunmore Beach Club** ~ 333-2200, **Pink Sands Resort** ~ 333-2030, **Romora Bay Club** ~ 333-2325 and **Winding Bay Resort** ~ 334-2020.

▼▼▼▼▼▼▼▼▼▼

Transportation

Eleuthera has three airports—**North Eleuthera Airport** near Dunmore Town, **Governor's Harbour Airport** at the center of the island and **Rock Sound Airport** in the south.

AIR

Bahamasair offers flights from Nassau to all three airports and to North Eleuthera and Governor's Harbour from Miami. American Eagle flies to Governor's Harbour from Miami. USAir Express has flights to North Eleuthera and Governor's Harbour from Fort Lauderdale. Island Express also serves Governor's Harbour from Fort Lauderdale.

BOAT

Eleuthera is also a relatively easy five-hour **mailboat trip** from Nassau, though most outbound trips arrive inconveniently late at night; passengers will want to arrange with their accommodations for a late arrival and transportation from the mailboat dock. The *Bahamas Daybreak III* makes two trips a week, leaving Nassau on Monday evening and arriving in Rock Sound late at night, returning to Nassau the following night, then leaving Thursday morning for Harbour Island and returning to Nassau on Sunday afternoon. The *Eleuthera Express* runs on a similar schedule with different destinations, leaving Nassau on Monday evening and arriving in Governor's Harbour late at night, returning to Nassau the following night, then leaving Thursday morning for Spanish Wells and returning to Nassau on Sunday afternoon. The *Briland Provider* leaves Nassau on Monday and Wednesday evenings, arriving at Harbour Island late at night and returning to Nassau on Tuesday and Thursday afternoons; it then leaves for Governor's Harbour and Rock Sound on Friday evening, arriving around midnight, and returns to Nassau on Saturday afternoon, arriving around 10 p.m. Contact the dockmaster at Potter's Cay Dock in Nassau for the current schedule, which is subject to weather conditions. ~ 393-1064.

TAXI

From the time you fly into your airport of choice or arrive by boat, you will rarely be out of sight of a taxi. If there is none waiting, the front desk at your lodging can contact one at a moment's notice. Or call independent cabbie **Tommy Pinder** ~ 332-2568 in Governor's Harbour, **Wilfred Major** ~ 334-2156 in Rock Sound, or the **Big M Taxi Service** ~ 333-2043 on Harbour Island.

CAR RENTALS

In Governor's Harbour, rental cars are available at **Highway Service Station and Rental Cars** ~ 332-2071, **Johnson's Rentals** ~ 333-2376 and **Ronnie's Rent-a-Car** ~ 332-2300. In Palmetto Point, call **Cecil Cooper** ~ 332-1575 or **Hilton's Car Rentals** ~ 335-6241. In Rock Sound, contact **Dingle Motor Service** ~ 334-2031. Though you don't need a car on Harbour Island, they are available from **Johnson's Garage** ~ 333-2376, **Ross' Garage** ~ 333-2122 and **U-Drive-It Cars** ~ 333-2122.

BIKE RENTALS

Harbour Island is fun to explore by bike, with rentals available from **Michael's Cycles** ~ 333-2384 and **Big Red** ~ 333-2045. If you are staying in Spanish Wells, Governor's Harbour, Tarpum Bay or Rock Sound for any length of time, many lodging facilities provide rentals or complimentary bikes for guests' use.

HITCHING

You'll rarely walk ten yards along any relatively busy road on Eleuthera before someone stops to see if you want a ride. Most locals will even go out of their way to get you to a restaurant or back to your hotel. In less-traveled areas, however, you can't count on being picked up by an obliging local; be prepared to walk to your destination.

▼▼▼▼▼▼▼▼▼▼▼▼▼▼▼▼▼▼▼▼

Addresses & Phone Numbers

Bahamasair—332-2648

Medical Clinic—Governor's Harbour Medical Clinic, 332-2001; Rock Sound Clinic, 334-2226; Harbour Island Medical Clinic, 333-2225

Pharmacy—Harbour Pharmacy Service, Harbour Island; 333-2174

Police Department—Governor's Harbour; 332-2111; Rock Sound, 334-2244; Harbour Island, 353-3111; Spanish Wells, 333-4030

Post Office—Governor's Harbour, 332-2060

TEN

The Exumas

The view from the air when flying south to Great Exuma, with the tiny islands stretching to the horizon, is one of the most spectacular sights in The Bahamas. It's easy to see why boating is the most popular pastime here—365 cays stretch along a 120-mile distance like a string of pearls. From busy marinas to deserted shores, boaters find the best of The Bahamas—sea, sunshine, friendly locals and seclusion—here in the Exumas. They also offer great sea kayaking, fishing and scuba diving in clear, calm waters that support a thriving marine ecosystem.

Although the northern end of the chain of tiny islands is only 35 miles from Nassau, most of the Exumas' 3700 inhabitants live at the southern end on the largest land masses, Great Exuma and Little Exuma islands, which are connected by a bridge. Great Exuma, about 45 miles long and only a few miles wide, is home to George Town, the largest community in the Exumas. To the south, equally narrow Little Exuma extends another 15 miles.

In 1829, Great Exuma was the scene of a slave revolt. The black slaves of George Town founder Sir Denys Rolle hid in the woods for a month and refused to work, setting a precedent that alarmed slave owners throughout The Bahamas. The result—44 of the slaves were sent in chains to Nassau where they received public lashings.

By the time slavery was abolished, five years later, Rolle's Exuma plantations had failed due to soil depletion. After receiving more than £4500 in government compensation for freeing his slaves, Rolle deeded all his landholdings on Exuma to his 387 former slaves, who adopted their benefactor's surname. Today, 60 percent of the people who live in the Exumas have the last name Rolle.

Most Exuma residents earn their livings from tourism, fishing or farming. Great Exuma is the onion capital of The Bahamas; other crops include tomatoes, pigeon peas, guavas, papayas and mangoes. Cotton grows wild throughout the main islands, a living testament to the islands' plantation past.

▼▼▼▼▼▼▼▼▼▼▼▼▼▼▼
Great Exuma Island

The largest community in the Exumas is George Town, on Great Exuma Island, with 1000 residents. It was founded by Loyalist Sir Denys Rolle in 1793 and named in honor of England's reigning monarch, King George III, who had granted 2300 acres on Great Exuma to Sir Denys. He and his heir, Lord John Rolle, built five major cotton plantations on the island.

SIGHTS

George Town, on Elizabeth Harbour, consists of a one-way Main Street scattered with small businesses, and another street that circles little Victoria Lake in the middle of town.

The harbor's **Government Wharf** is where you'll see mailboats loaded with Exuma-grown fruits and vegetables bound for Nassau. When the mailboat is in port the wharf bustles with frantic action. Stop by.

Just north of the big fig trees in the center of town stands the pink and white **Government Administration Building**, its Georgian style patterned after Government House in Nassau.

The government building has a view of **Stocking Island**, located just a mile off shore, where you'll find some of the area's best beachfront and watersports activities. Several mile-long palm-fringed sandy beaches draw daytrippers and overnight guests alike, and there's snorkeling and sea kayaking right off the island. Narrow, and only two miles long, Stocking Island is easy to explore. A ferry goes there twice a day from Club Peace and Plenty in George Town.

Just north of the Government Administration Building, the bright and airy **Ministry of Tourism** office can help with information and provide pamphlets, maps and contacts for anything you'd like to pursue. ~ Main Street; 336-2430.

A few steps farther north and across the street, **St. Andrew's Anglican Church** sits splendidly atop a little hill. Built in the 1840s, this little blue-and-white gem is best seen in the morning light. When it's open, the quiet church's stained glass casts a beautiful light on the pews and altar.

LODGING

In George Town, many people swear by the experience at **Club Peace and Plenty**. Located in town overlooking the harbor, this lively place is a haven for the boating and fishing set. The lobby was once a sponge warehouse, and the current owners carry on the tradition of a small Bahamian inn that was established in the 1950s. The two-story buildings, grouped around the pool and out toward the harbor, are adorned with tropical plants and furnishings. There are 35 guest rooms with balconies and views of the water, Stocking Island and a small pool. ~ P.O. Box 29055, George Town; 336-2551, 800-525-2210, fax 336-2093. MODERATE TO DELUXE.

George Town's other waterfront resort, **Regatta Point**, is on a small island reached by a short causeway. It has five good-size apartments with kitchens, porches, ceiling fans and views of the harbor. There's a small beach with water-sports activities. ~ P.O. Box 29006, George Town; 336-2206, 800-310-8125, fax 336-2046. MODERATE TO DELUXE.

The **Two Turtles Inn**, a Bahamian-style inn, offers 14 guest rooms across the street from the water in the heart of town. The traditional, tropical-motif rooms are basic and clean. Innkeeper Judith Turnquest is an island expert. ~ P.O. Box 29251, George Town; 336-2545, 800-688-4752, fax 336-2528. MODERATE.

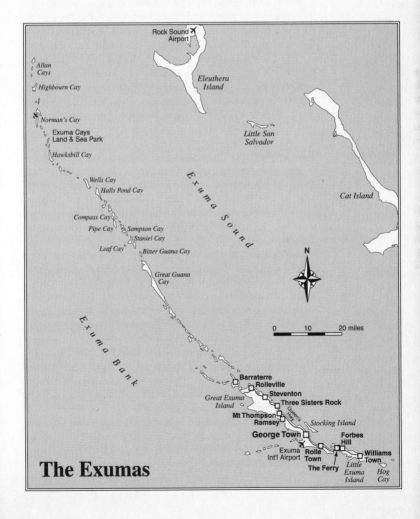

The Exumas

The most frugal of George Town visitors head for **Marshall's Guest House,** where John Marshall has ten very simple rooms and an apartment for rent. The view and amenities are limited, but the location is in the heart of George Town, and the price is hard to beat. ~ P.O. Box 27, George Town; phone/fax 336-2081. BUDGET.

HIDDEN ►

Hotel Higgins Landing was designed and constructed with care to preserve the natural beauty of Stocking Island. This inn was one of the first ecoresorts in The Bahamas. There are five cottages, each with a private setting, a spacious verandah and a gorgeous sea view. Each tile-floored unit is individually decorated with antiques. Tropical flowers bloom throughout the resort, and hummingbirds, egrets, osprey and herons visit daily. Superb snorkeling is off any of the wide palm-fringed beaches. The rate includes three extravagant meals per day. ~ P.O. Box 29146, George Town; phone/fax 336-2460; www.higginslanding.com. DELUXE.

The **Peace and Plenty Bonefish Lodge** located on the southern tip of Great Exuma is for people who are into bonefishing; others are likely to feel out of place. Modern rooms overlook the bay that leads to the bonefishing flats. ~ P.O. Box 29055, George Town; 345-5555, 800-525-2210, fax 345-5556; www.peaceand plenty.com. DELUXE.

DINING

HIDDEN ►

Eddie's Edgewater Club located on Victoria Lake is a busy restaurant. Owners Eddie and Andrea Brown cook inexpensive local food for what seems like half of George Town's residents, as well as all of the town's visitors. There's a sociable bar in the front and about ten tables in the back for dining. Curried chicken, snapper and conch are among the choices. ~ Victoria Lake, George Town; 336-2050. BUDGET.

Sam's Place, entrepreneur Sam Gray's second-story restaurant overlooking Victoria Lake, serves three meals a day, starting with hearty breakfasts for early-rising boaters and ending with dinners of fresh-caught conch, grouper and local lobster. The harbor view is the best in town, and there's a spacious indoor dining room and an outdoor deck to enjoy—when the mosquitoes aren't biting. ~ Main Street, George Town; 336-2579. BUDGET.

The small candlelit dining room at **Club Peace and Plenty** has a luxuriant water and poolside setting, with superb Bahamian and Continental fare served on white tablecloths. It's one of the better restaurants on the island and priced accordingly. ~ Main Street, George Town; 336-2551. DELUXE.

Two Turtles Inn has a casual patio restaurant and bar that serves Bahamian and American cuisine. The weekly barbecues are a hit with both locals and visiting boaters. ~ Main Street, George Town; 336-2545. MODERATE.

Women plait and sell straw work under the large fig trees in the center of George Town. This informal straw market is a far cry from the one in Nassau, and it's a fun place to shop and sit in the shade.

SHOPPING

Otherwise, gift shopping in George Town consists mainly of two adjacent shops across from Club Peace and Plenty: **Peace and Plenty Boutique** ~ 336-2551 and **The Sandpiper** ~ 336-2084. Both offer Bahamian-made arts and crafts as well as high-quality clothing and standard T-shirt selections.

Heading north out of George Town on Queen's Highway, keep a look out for a small straw stand on the left under a big tree. **Emma Glass** can often be found there there making and selling some of the finest straw work on the island. ~ Queen's Highway.

◀ **HIDDEN**

George Town closes early, and action after dark is confined to hotel bars at **Club Peace and Plenty** ~ 336-2551, **Eddie's Edgewater Club** ~ 336-2050 and **Two Turtles Inn** ~ 336-2543, which take turns presenting live entertainment on different nights of the week—typically a local band playing American tunes peppered with a few Bahamian ones.

NIGHTLIFE

STOCKING ISLAND 🏃 ⛴ 🚤 🛶 ⛵ This island has several palm-fringed sandy beaches to choose from, all within easy walking distance of the dock where the George Town ferry lands. The island is very narrow and is only a couple of miles long making it very easy to explore. The snorkeling and shelling are exceptional, and you're sure to find a beach to your liking, and likely all to yourself. ~ Located about a mile from George Town. There's a ferry from Club Peace and Plenty in George Town twice a day.

BEACHES

✔ **CHECK THESE OUT**

- Explore the Out Island village of **George Town**, a perfect place to stroll. *page 186*
- Bask in the sun at **Club Peace and Plenty**'s inn, a haven for boaters and anglers. *page 186*
- Eat and drink like a George Town resident at **Eddie's Edgewater Club**, where curried chicken, snapper and conch round out the menu. *page 188*
- Spy endangered Bahamian iguanas greeting you beachside at **Exuma Cays Land and Sea Park** during the early morning hours. *page 194*

▼▼▼▼▼▼▼▼▼▼▼▼▼▼▼
Outside George Town

Exploring the island is an adventure in itself. Queen's Highway, the only major road, runs down the middle of the island through farmland and forest, so glimpses of the sea are rare. Narrow, unpaved, unmarked roads turn off the highway in both directions at frequent intervals. Pick one and follow it, and you may find yourself on an idyllically secluded beach—or in a barnyard. Fortunately, it's hard to stay lost for very long on this long, narrow island, and locals are cheerful about giving directions.

SIGHTS

NORTH OF GEORGE TOWN   Heading up Queen's Highway you pass quickly into farm country. Just past the town of Ramsey, **Three Sisters Rocks**, a local landmark, juts out of the water 100 feet offshore.

Across the road from Three Sisters Rocks, the **Mount Thompson Packing House** is where island produce is prepared for shipping to Nassau by mailboat. The workers here welcome occasional visitors to view the heaps of pungent onions, big bananas, watermelons and bright peppers. There's no sign, but anyone can give you directions.

The road north goes through the old Steventon plantation area and into the hilly little village of **Rolleville**. The town itself is picturesque and the highlight is the **Church of God of Prophecy**, built with hand-cut rock quarried and carried by a group of Catholic nuns. The small church is still in use and is usually open to visitors.

A motoring island tour generally starts in George Town and heads north or south. To cover both ends of the island you have to backtrack through George Town.

The only other northern town of any size is **Barraterre**, a sleepy fishing village that has a dock where you can arrange a trip over to **Stocking Island** and the **Caribbean Marine Research Center** (CMRC). Since 1984, the CMRC has been one of the world's leading centers of field research and training in marine science. They conduct and support research to further the understanding of marine ecosystems. Their goal is to help save and increase important local fisheries, like mutton snapper, queen conch, spiny lobster and Nassau grouper. To visit this fascinating research facility call in advance and arrange one of their short tours, which draw many boaters but only a few tourists. The tour takes in the dive facility, test tanks and specific projects that are in progress. ~ P.O. Box 29001, George Town; 345-6039, 358-4557.

SOUTH OF GEORGE TOWN   Heading south on Queen's Highway, most people go straight to Little Exuma. Along the way you'll come to the quiet village of **Rolle Town**. The population is made up of people named Rolle who grow fruits and vegetables, just as their ancestors have done for nearly two centuries. A small sign leads the way to the old **Rolle family plot**, a set of three old tombstones dating from the 18th century, including a huge one shaped like a carriage bed. You have to dodge several grazing goats to reach the graves.

Just a mile north of George Town, **Peace and Plenty Beach Inn** is the choice for visitors who want both a beach and a nearby location. There are 16 nicely furnished rooms overlooking Bonefish Bay, all with refrigerators and televisions. This resort is an all-inclusive, with meals and most watersports activities included in the price. ~ P.O. Box 29055, George Town; 336-2250, 800-525-2210, fax 336-2253. DELUXE.

Coconut Cove Hotel sits next door to Peace and Plenty and offers similar lodging and an inn-like experience. Accommodations include seven modern rooms with terraces overlooking the ocean and two overlooking a pond and gardens. There's also the Paradise Suite, with a private oceanfront terrace and hot tub. ~ P.O. Box 29299, George Town; 336-2659, fax 336-2658. MODERATE.

About ten miles farther north, **The Palms at Three Sisters Beach Resort** is a quiet beachfront option. All 12 simple rooms have oceanfront terraces and television. There are also two cottages that each have a large bed in the living room area, as well a separate bedroom. The kitchen facilities make the cottages useful for families. Watersport activities are available. ~ P.O. Box 29215, Mount Thompson; 358-4040, 800-688-4752, fax 358-4043. BUDGET TO MODERATE.

Apartment and house rentals are available on Great Exuma and Little Exuma. Contact **Best Choice Apartments** ~ 345-5042, **Candy's Apartments** ~ 345-3569, **Rosetta Maynard** ~ 336-2953 or **Nixon's Rentals** ~ 336-2740.

Iva Bowe's **Central Highway Restaurant and Bar** on Queen's Highway is a classic island cookery. Iva's daughter, Lorraine Lloyd, prepares local dishes like grouper fingers, crawfish salad and cracked conch, served up with tasty peas 'n rice. There's a small bar in the front and ten tables in the back—the atmosphere is secondary to the food. Lunch only. Closed Sunday. ~ Queen's Highway; 345-7014. BUDGET.

In Barraterre, **Fisherman's Inn** is famed for its creative seafood preparation, showcasing lobster, snapper, grouper and conch in its large dining room adorned with nautical furnishings. For fresh seafood and a great view, this is one of the best spots in the islands. Call ahead to Norman, who can help arrange transportation to the restaurant. ~ Barraterre; 355-5016. MODERATE.

Kermit's Airport Lounge, an unofficial waiting room for the airport directly across the street, is a local institution. The food is basic, with sandwiches and burgers the main fare. More creative Bahamian dishes are often available on request. The drinks are cold and the company in this large and breezy place is more fun than you'll find at most airports. ~ Exuma International Airport; 345-0002. BUDGET.

NIGHTLIFE In Rolleville, stop for a drink at **Kermit's Hilltop Tavern**, a classic Out Island drinking establishment. Though there's no entertainment, locals gather here day and night and visitors are made to feel welcome. ~ Rolleville; 345-6006.

BEACHES **GREAT EXUMA** 🏃 🐌 🌊 The beaches in front of La Shante, Peace and Plenty Beach Inn, Coconut Cove and The Palms at Three Sisters are worth a visit even if you're not staying at one of them. Because most beach hoppers pass them by on the way to the truly extraordinary beaches on the southern end of Little Exuma, they are quiet.

▼▼▼▼▼▼▼▼▼▼▼▼▼
Little Exuma Island

From the southern tip of Great Exuma, a narrow bridge leads to Little Exuma, a thin island of about fifteen miles of scrubland, mangroves and coves. The island is hillier than Great Exuma and has a large inland salt bed. Salt mining was Little Exuma's main industry for many years, though the salt works are now closed.

SIGHTS The small village on the Little Exuma side of the bridge is called **The Ferry** because a ferry took people to and from the island before the bridge was built in the 1960s. This town is the home of **Gloria Patience**, known as the "Shark Lady" or "Barefoot Lady." From a little shop in her memorabilia-filled home she sells handmade island items, many of which utilize the thousands of shark teeth she retrieves on her frequent sea expeditions. Her book, *Gloria, the Shark Lady*, is sold around the island. Speaking of ladies and fish, nearby **Pretty Molly Bay** is named for the mermaid who is said to make her home there.

Farther south in **Williams Town**, a small sign points the way to **The Hermitage**, the only relatively intact reminder of the island's cotton plantation days. Originally built by the Kendall family in the late 1700s, it thrived for only a few years. The foundations of the main house and some old tombs are all that remain.

LODGING Either of the two choices—one chic, the other cheap—on the southern end of Little Exuma is perfect for those who really want to get away from it all.

HIDDEN ► Located down a long dirt road near the end of the island, **Cut House Villas** offers three very modern and upscale villas with every imaginable amenity, lots of space and spectacular views. Two of the villas are connected by a family room, and the third stands alone. Both have hot tubs. A beautiful, secluded beach is a short

walk away. Stays here are all-inclusive. ~ P.O. Box 29192, Little
Exuma; 345-5096, 800-583-9862, fax 203-389-8409; www.cut
housevillas.com. ULTRA-DELUXE.

Geared toward adventurous visitors, the three-room **La Shante
Beach Club and Guest House** is one of those special locally owned
guesthouses that you occasionally find in The Bahamas. The clean,
modern, basic rooms have contemporary hotel furnishings. But
then again, guests spend most of their time on the quiet cove and
beach. ~ P.O. Box 29183, Forbes Hill, Little Exuma; 345-4136.
BUDGET.

While exploring Little Exuma be sure to stop by the restaurant at
La Shante Beach Club and Guest House. Diners overlook the sea
from the large, plainly furnished restaurant, while hostess Janet
Bowe prepares Bahamian seafood dishes, cracked conch and tasty
soups and stews. ~ Forbes Hill, Little Exuma; 345-4136. BUDGET.

DINING

◄ HIDDEN

TROPIC OF CANCER BEACH 🏃 🐚 🛶 This graceful crescent
of pale sand borders the phenomenally blue-green water along
the south coast of Little Exuma. The longest beach on the island,
it is one of the prettiest in the Exuma chain, and you will probably have it all to yourself. The imaginary line that defines the
northern extent of the tropics is said to run right along this beach.
Numerous cove beaches farther along the island, past Williams
Town, are nameless, inviting and intimate—often less than 100
feet long. ~ Tropic of Cancer Beach is located at the end of an unpaved half-mile side road that turns south (to your right as you're
heading away from The Ferry) off Queen's Highway about two
miles past the old beacon tower that locals use as a landmark.

BEACHES

Starting with Stocking Island, the Exumas
chain extends all the way to Sail Rocks,
a distance of more than 90 miles. Locals
claim there's a cay for each day of the year. Many of the small
islands are uninhabited, while others have vacation homes.

▼▼▼▼▼▼▼▼▼▼▼▼▼▼▼

Other Islands and Cays

Staniel Cay, which was used as a shooting location for the James
Bond films *Thunderball* and *Never Say Never Again,* is one of only
a few islands with tourist facilities. You can reach it by boat, private plane or a scheduled flight from Fort Lauderdale. Boaters particularly like Staniel Cay because it provides a first-rate port and
marina in the middle of the Exumas chain. Bonefishing is available and good, but Staniel Cay is primarily for those who want
peace and quiet with very few distractions.

SIGHTS

Sampson Cay has a marina that also provides anchorage in
the mid-Exumas. The tiny village clusters around the marina,
and there's not much else on the island.

LODGING

On Staniel Cay, sailors and adventurous souls eat, sleep and drink at **Happy People Marina**, which has 12 hotel rooms overlooking the harbor and a small restaurant and bar. This marina hotel caters mainly to the sailing set. ~ Staniel Cay; 355-2008. BUDGET.

Staniel Cay Yacht Club rents a large cottage (four or more people), a waterfront cottage and a houseboat cottage, both that sleep two. All are simply furnished and come with small kitchens. There's little else here on this quiet island. ~ Staniel Cay; 355-2024, fax 355-2044; www.stanielcay.com. MODERATE TO DELUXE.

On Sampson Cay, the **Sampson's Cay Colony** is a fun housekeeping possibility. Rosie and Marchus Mitchell offer four apartments with small kitchenettes. Three are on the beach, with a fourth, larger one up on the hillside. The small apartments are simple and tropical in style. The little restaurant and bar are popular with boaters and guests. ~ Sampson Cay; 355-2034, fax 355-2034. BUDGET TO MODERATE.

HIDDEN ▶

Bowe Cay, situated off Great Exuma, offers an unusual deserted-island stay that daydreams are made of. Guests fly into George Town, pick up supplies and then boat over to the island. There is one building, a cabana, that offers the barest necessities for eating and sleeping: solar panels for lighting, a grill, a freezer/refrigerator and a two-way radio for emergency use. The cabana is suitable for a one- or two-person getaway, but as many as eight people can camp on the beach and use the cabana as a common area. (Bring your own camping gear.) ~ Ultimate Adventures, P.O. Box 1241, Melrose, MA 01176; 617-397-1481, 800-992-0128. MODERATE TO DELUXE.

DINING

On Staniel Cay, you can head for the **Royal Entertainer Lounge** at Happy People Marina ~ 355-2008 or the small restaurant at **Staniel Cay Yacht Club** ~ 355-2024. Both serve a mixed bag of Continental cuisine and Bahamian dishes. MODERATE.

Sampson's Cay Colony has a little local restaurant and bar. You can get a drink anytime, but advance reservations are required for the single seating dinner. ~ Sampson Cay; 355-2034, fax 355-2034. MODERATE.

BEACHES & PARKS

EXUMA CAYS LAND AND SEA PARK 🏃 🚣 ⛵ 🤿 ⛴ Protected by the Bahamas National Trust since 1958 when it became The Bahamas' first national park, this expanse of shallow banks and minuscule cays extends for 22 miles northwest of Staniel Cay, from Wax Cay Cut in the north to Conch Cut in the south. The larger islands within the park include Bell Island, Cistern Cay, Halls Pond Cay and Warderick Wells.

Along with boaters and divers, birdwatchers are drawn to the park. They come in hopes of seeing the long-tailed tropic bird, the rare red-legged thrush and many other species of birds. All plants, animals and marine life within the park are fully protected by law. The endangered Bahamian iguana, which lives on Allan's Cay and Leaf Cay, is specifically covered by the conservation regulations, with harsh penalties for killing or capturing one. Iguanas will often come to the beach to greet morning arrivals and beg for a food handout. (Please don't give them one. It diminishes their ability to digest wild food.) The park's small headquarters on the pretty little island of Warderick Wells has maps, brochures and books.

> The Exuma Cays Land and Sea Park was the first national land/water park of its kind in the world.

There are marked nature trails on Hall's Pond, Hawksbill Cay and Warderick Wells. Shroud Cay offers beautiful beaches and large expanses of mangroves. The hutia, a medium-sized rodent that is the only mammal indigenous to The Bahamas, lives on Little Wax Cay but only comes out at night.

Outdoor Adventures

BOATING

Stretching practically from New Providence down past Little Exuma, the Exumas are some of the most famous boating waters in The Bahamas. Boating destinations include Leaf Cay, Hawksbill Cay, Great Exuma, Little Exuma and just about anywhere in the Exuma Cays Land and Sea Park. **Peace and Plenty** ~ 336-2551, **Exuma Fantasea** ~336-3483 and **Rolle's Charter Fishing** ~336-2324 can help with rentals and charters. The northern end of Exuma Cays Land and Sea Park is actually closer to Nassau than to George Town, and several tour operators guide day trips to Allen Cay, Ship Channel Cay and Saddleback Cay on high-speed power boats. See the "Outdoor Adventures" section in Chapter Four for more information.

There are hundreds of excellent anchorages and several fine marinas around the Exumas. Along with George Town and other natural ports on Great Exuma and Little Exuma, Staniel Cay and Sampson Cay are favorite sailing ports of call.

KAYAKING

Sea kayaking conditions are ideal throughout the Exumas. **Exuma Cays Land and Sea Park** can only be explored by boat. If you don't have your own boat, it can be quite expensive to hire one. Contact **Happy People Marina** on Staniel Cay for boat and kayak rentals. ~ 355-2008. **Stocking Island**, just a mile across the harbor from George Town's Government Wharf, is a favorite spot for sea kayaking. The island is the ideal size for circumnavigating to explore the more secluded east shore. Several beachfront operations have kayaks for rent.

FISHING

By far the biggest game in town is bonefishing, which draws serious anglers from around the world. More than 60 miles of flats surround Great Exuma and Little Exuma, providing some of the very best bonefish habitat anywhere. The fine white sand and clear waters are tailor-made for wading or fishing from a skiff. Vast schools of three- to six-pound bonefish provide excitement and opportunity for novices, while smaller pods of larger bonefish test veterans. Wary permit can also be found, as well as the diversion of ever-present barracuda. Most fish are caught and released, left to be lured by future anglers.

The guides of the **Exuma Guides Association** are friendly, knowledgeable and willing to assist as much or as little as is required. They have all participated in the local certification program and are sensible environmentalists. ~ 336-2222.

You can also contact particular guides in advance or once you're on the island. Top names in local bonefishing include **Marvin Bethel** ~ 336-2448, **J. J. Dames** ~ 345-5049, **Bob Hyde** ~ 336-2222, **Alston Rolle** ~ 358-7052, **Wilfred Rolle** ~ 345-5106 and **Garth Thompson** ~ 345-5062.

Most hotels can make arrangements with local guides. Besides providing lodging, the innkeepers at **Peace and Plenty** will arrange all of the details for bonefishing. ~ P.O. Box 9173, George Town; 336-2551, 800-525-2210.

Though overshadowed by the bonefishing, deep-sea fishing off Great Exuma includes marlin, tuna and other billfish, as well as smaller game. **Rolle's Charter Fishing** offers an array of short and long deep-sea charters. ~ Main Street, George Town; 336-2324.

DIVING Though not as well-known as some other Bahamian diving destinations, the waters of the Exumas offer fine dives. Typical of Bahamian diving, the abundant, colorful coral life represents the full range of reef stands found in The Bahamas, including brain, elkhorn, staghorn and oscillating corals, many of them reaching almost to the surface. The tropical fish population, including large schools of grunts and yellowtail snapper along with huge groupers, is dazzling, and sea turtles and lobsters cluster under each coral stand.

Marine biologist Ed Haxby and his full-service **Exuma Fantasea** on Victoria Lake offers "ecodiving," providing specific insights into the habits of the various reef dwellers. The full-service dive center offers a wide variety of trips, rentals and instruction. Ed can take you to blue holes—inland saltwater dives fed by an underground tunnel and cave system. ~ Queen's Highway, George Town; 336-3483.

Top spots, all reached from George Town are **Angelfish Blue Hole**, where the flushing actions of the tides bring lots of nutrients to the waiting angelfish, and **Sting Ray Reef**, just on the far side of Stocking Island, an abundant tropical fish and stingray

Ways
to See
the Islands

Many of the Exumas' most tantalizing destinations lie offshore among the island group's fishing grounds and tiny cays, but for casual visitors who do not have their own boats, getting there can pose a challenge. A number of adventure tour operators offer special packages that take you to remote areas where land and sea mingle.

Island Vacations, the leading outdoor adventure packager throughout The Bahamas, offers two tours in the Exumas. Their Exuma Historic Excursion takes you to assorted historic towns, plantation ruins and natural habitats. High points include a visit to the "Shark Lady" and a boat tour of the Exuma Cays Land and Sea Park. The Exuma Cruising-Fishing Adventure, which starts and ends in New Providence, makes its way along the best boating and fishing grounds in the Exumas. ~ Contact Island Vacations in the U.S. at 4327 Reflections Boulevard North, Suite 104, Sunrise, FL 33351; 305-748-1833, 800-900-4242, fax 305-748-1965, or in Nassau at P.O. Box 13002, Town Centre Mall, Nassau, Bahamas; 356-1111, fax 356-4379.

What better way to explore the Exumas than in a group kayaking trip? Boating/camping expeditions to virtually unexplored islands north of Great Exuma are offered by several outfitters. Most trips last a week or longer, with little or no experience required for kayaking in these calm waters. One operator, Ibis Tours, also provides sails for the kayaks, letting you use the wind instead of paddle power when conditions are right. ~ Contact Vancouver-based **Ecosummer Adventures** at 800-688-8605, Boynton Beach–based **Ibis Tours** at 800-525-9411 or **Steve Curry Expeditions** at 800-937-7238.

habitat with a drop-off for wall diving. Other sites include **Crab Cay Crevasse** and **Jolly Hall**, which is also a popular snorkeling destination. North of Great Exuma, virgin diving awaits those with their own equipment, a boat and the experience to dive without a local divemaster. The tidal bluehole known as **Mystery Cave**, a challenge for scuba experts, is virtually "bottomless" in that it extends much deeper than any diver can explore. Jean Michel Cousteau once conducted dye trace tests in the cave and found that the dye surfaced four miles out to sea in 3000-foot-deep Exuma Sound.

Harbour Buoy Portside and **Harbour Buoy Starboard** are prime snorkeling sites, with lots of tropical fish and big brain corals. **Liz Lee Shoals** also showcases brain corals as well as an assortment of other formations. **Duck Cay South** and **Duck Cay East and West**, reached by boat, offer super snorkeling off these islands' deserted beaches. **Three Sisters Rocks** are teeming with schools of fish.

Off Harbour Island, choice sites include the shallow and calm **Three Fingers** for beginning snorkelers, the entire three-mile length of the **Devil's Backbone**, the small tunnels of **Tunnel Reef** and the **Potato and Onion Wreck**, a 200-foot-long freighter sitting in 15 feet of water.

▼▼▼▼▼▼▼▼▼▼▼▼
Transportation

AIR

Regularly scheduled passenger planes fly in to **Exuma International Airport** on Great Exuma. American Eagle and Gulfstream Airlines offer service from Miami. Island Express flies to the Exumas from Fort Lauderdale. Bahamasair comes from Nassau.

BOAT

Exuma has frequent **mailboat** service. The *Grand Master* normally sets out from Nassau's Potter's Cay Dock on Tuesday afternoon for the 12-hour trip to George Town, arriving in the early morning hours, and sets out on the overnight return trip Wednesday evening, arriving back in Nassau Thursday morning. The *Sea Hauler*, which goes from Nassau to southern Cat Island, continues to George Town before stopping back at Cat Island on its return trip to Nassau. This is a new service, and the schedule for the Exuma segment of the trip may vary. Check with the dockmaster at Potter's Cay Dock in Nassau, 393-1064, for current information.

TAXI

Taxis are prevalent at the airport and wherever there's a road. Once at your accommodation, the front desk can contact one for you quickly. To arrange a pickup call **Exuma Transport** (336-2101) or **Luther Rolle Taxi Service** (345-5003).

Car rental agencies include **Thompson Car Rental** (336-2442), **Club Peace and Plenty** (336-2551) and **Exuma Transport** (336-2101).

▼▼▼▼▼▼▼▼▼▼▼▼▼▼▼▼▼▼▼▼▼▼▼▼▼
Addresses & Phone Numbers

Exuma Tourist Office—George Town, 336-2430
Medical Clinic—George Town Clinic, 336-2088
Police Department—George Town; 919 or 336-2666

ELEVEN

The Southern Bahamas

Planes, boats and lodgings get smaller and smaller as you venture southeast to the outer islands of The Bahamas. Instead of an international jet or even the 20-seat Bahamasair turboprops that hop back and forth between Nassau and the other main islands covered in previous chapters of this book, in the more remote Out Islands you're likely to find yourself booked on an "airliner" that carries only four passengers. Instead of luxury ocean liners, these ports of call are visited once or twice a week by mailboats laden with livestock, construction materials, crates of canned goods and the occasional adventuresome traveler. Once you get there, you'll find no casinos, golf courses or, for that matter, air conditioners. Welcome to the *really* hidden Bahamas!

These more remote inhabited islands—Cat Island, San Salvador, Long Island, Crooked and Acklins Islands, Mayaguana and Inagua—represent The Bahamas' past and future. Though a few hardy families have been living a Robinson Crusoe–like existence out here since Columbus founded the first Bahamian colony five centuries ago, the Southern Bahamas remain all but untouched by the 20th-century tourist industry. Tropical islands an hour or so by air from Miami? Don't expect them to remain pristine far into the 21st century. Get there now, before the international resort hotel chains do.

The seven inhabited islands of the Southern Bahamas have a combined population of 9000; only Cat Island and Long Island have more than a thousand residents. The array of islands, each more remote than the last, includes one with a major luxury resort, several others that seem likely to develop more tourist facilities in the near future, and a few that are unlikely to ever attract more than a handful of adventuresome birdwatchers or dropout beach bums.

Some of the islands covered in this chapter are targets of the Bahamian government's push to develop "ecotourism"—by which they seem to mean small dive resorts in the Out Islands. It would enhance the appeal to adventure travelers if Bahamasair or the agency that contracts with mailboats would implement a schedule making it possible to island-hop through the Southern Bahamas, instead of the present system whereby you can only travel between Out Islands by first returning to Nassau and then heading out again. At present, however, there are no plans for this, and the best bet is to focus on a single island, go there and slow *way* down.

▼▼▼▼▼▼▼▼▼▼
Cat Island

Cat Island is the quintessential hidden island of The Bahamas. It has dense tropical bush jungle and an abundance of brilliant flowers, as well as caves, historic ruins, lakes, blueholes, walking trails, pristine beaches many miles long and the highest "mountain" in The Bahamas. The island is 50 miles long and averages four miles in width.

Until the 20th century, historians agreed that Cat Island—then called San Salvador—was the site of Christopher Columbus' first New World landfall. Although the landing spot and the name San Salvador were officially moved in 1926 to the former Watling's Island, 55 miles to the east, Cat Islanders have refused to relinquish their claim to the distinction.

Some historians say it's called Cat Island after a pirate named Catt who used to hide out there. Locals claim the name derives from the wild descendants of cats that the Spanish released in the 1500s to control rats around the port of Columba. By the time William Sayle and his Eleutherian Adventurers rediscovered the island more than a century later, the cats had bred in such numbers that they overran the island.

Cat Island was the site of the Spanish port of Columba, established in 1495 during Christopher Columbus' reign as governor of the New World. Columba started as a farming community, but soon became the center for shipping captured Lucaya Indians to the mines of Hispañola. When the last of the Indians had been shipped off, the town declined to an outpost where ships put in to stock up on fresh water and firewood.

With some of the richest soil in The Bahamas, Cat Island was occupied by a dozen or so Old Inhabitants families, farmers who emigrated from Bermuda in the mid-1600s. In the 1780s, Loyalists established 16 cotton plantations on the island and imported more than 400 slaves to work them. The genetically mixed descendents of Old Inhabitants and slaves make up the present-day population of 1700 residents.

After emancipation, Cat Islanders made their livings growing sisal and pineapples for export, but today remote and wild Cat Island has captured the imagination of a new generation of adventurer.

Orange Creek, the northernmost settlement on Cat Island, dates back to the year 1800, when the threat of pirates lessened and island residents abandoned their original towns on the ridgeline,

SIGHTS

moving to this site for better protection against hurricanes. The name Orange Creek comes from the light that sometimes makes the creek take on an orange glow before sunset.

King's Road runs the entire length of the island, passing through one tiny 200-year-old settlement after another. A few miles south of Orange Creek, the road reaches **Arthur's Town,** the main town on the north side of Cat Island. The town was a major commercial and government center for the southern Bahamas until the 1960s, when expanded air travel made Nassau more accessible. Ruins of homes built by early British Loyalist settlers can still be seen today.

Continuing down King's Road you'll come to the tiny settlement of **Dumfries,** which is surrounded by mangrove forest and has a large freshwater blue hole. The town was settled by Loyalists who had originally emigrated from Dumfries, Scotland, and founded the town of Dumfries, Virginia, only to abandon it and move to Cat Island in the 1780s after the United States won its independence from Great Britain. Little of Dumfries' Loyalist heritage is evident today; the town is best known as the home of several popular Bahamian recording artists.

Bennett's Harbour, the next community of any size that you come to as you proceed south on King's Road, got its start as a pirates' hideout and developed into a permanent settlement in the early 1800s, when black captives on illegal slave ships were set free on Cat Island. The settlement then obtained its income by exporting hundreds of tons of salt from evaporating ponds along the edges of the salt lake east of town.

Past Bennett's Harbour, King's Road veers inland through the woods for several miles before returning to the coast near the two contiguous villages of Cairey's and Gaiter's. **Cairey's** was settled by pineapple farmers from Eleuthera in the late 1800s, when the demand for Bahamian pineapples was growing so fast that planters had to expand to more islands. Today, the town is a center for the export of cascarilla, the highly prized aromatic bark of a wild bush native to Cat Island that is used in perfumes and as a flavoring for liqueurs such as Campari.

The small village at Industrious Hill, a few miles south of Cairey's and Gaiter's, is the site of **The Caves,** a series of large, dry caverns that have traditionally been used by island residents as shelter from hurricanes. Flashlights are necessary to explore the caves, and guide services are available in the village.

Just east of the town of **New Bight,** visitors can climb a limestone stairway to **The Hermitage,** on the summit of Mount Alvernia (elevation 207 feet). This is the highest point in The Bahamas, and there's a spectacular 360-degree view from the top. Monsignor John Hawes, known in Bahamian legend as Father

Jerome, designed St. Augustine's Monastery on New Providence Island and two landmark mission churches on Long Island, as well as other churches—first Anglican and later Catholic—throughout The Bahamas. He retired to Cat Island to spend his last days—in fact, his last 20 years—as a hermit. Jerome started by building a cramped monk's cell and a shrine for worship. As the years wore on, his construction project grew to sprawl across the

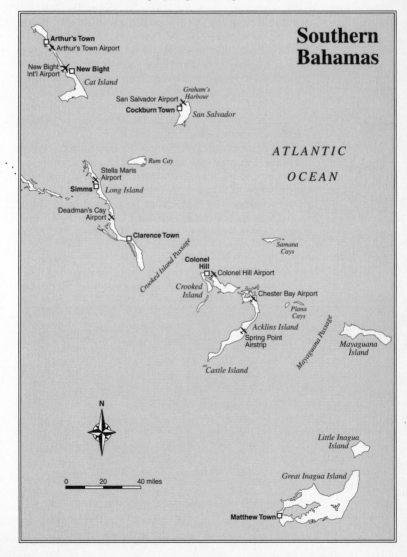

Southern Bahamas

Arthur's Town
✕ Arthur's Town Airport

New Bight ✕ ◻ **New Bight**
Int'l Airport
Cat Island

Graham's Harbour
San Salvador Airport
Cockburn Town ◻ *San Salvador*

Rum Cay

Stella Maris Airport
Simms ◻ *Long Island*

Deadman's Cay ✕ Airport

◻ **Clarence Town**

ATLANTIC

OCEAN

Samana Cays

Crooked Island Passage

Colonel Hill
◻ ✕ Colonel Hill Airport

Crooked Island
✕ Chester Bay Airport

Plana Cays

✕ Acklins Island
Spring Point Airstrip

Mayaguana Passage

Mayaguana Island

Castle Island

N

Little Inagua Island

0   20   40 miles

Great Inagua Island

Matthew Town ◻

mountaintop like a miniature castle. The complex, a scaled-down version of European monastic hermitages, features a cave with a massive stone that can be rolled to block the doorway, a reference to Christ's tomb.

One of Father Jerome's classic stone churches, **St. Francis of Assisi Catholic Church**, stands in the nearby community of **Old Bight**. This is the most traditional-feeling village on Cat Island, which is perhaps the most traditional island in The Bahamas. Abandoned stone cottages in various stages of collapse line the roadside, outnumbering occupied ones and giving the impression that New Bight and other villages are in the process of becoming ghost towns. In fact, the island's population is stable and has not declined. Residents follow the old custom of abandoning homes when their owners die, leaving them to stand as monuments to the deceased while younger generations build their own limestone-and-cement dwellings. Some cottages stand for a century or more before hurricanes crumble them to rubble.

On the south coast, **Port Howe** is the most historic town on Cat Island. Old stone ruins dot the landscape, and some are said to date back to the Spanish slave port of Columba, which was established in 1495 and thrived through the early 1500s. The present settlement was once a center for Loyalist cotton plantations. The ruins of **Deveaux House**, an 18th-century plantation manor, stand at the edge of town.

LODGING   At New Bight, **Fernandez Bay Village** has 12 stone cottages, duplexes and villas, each different, interspersed among a handful of private vacation residences on a gleaming, gracefully curved

✔ **CHECK THESE OUT**

- Climb to **The Hermitage** at the summit of 207-foot Mount Alvernia, the highest point in The Bahamas, for a view of Cat Island's limestone cliffs and remote ocean beaches. *page 202*
- Visit the **monuments**—no less than four of them on San Salvador alone—marking where Columbus is thought to have first set foot on the New World. *page 212*
- Swim among giant predators at the the **Stella Maris Shark Reef** off the coast of Long Island—and live to tell about it! *page 219*
- Become one of the few travelers to set foot on the least-known major islands in The Bahamas—**Acklins** and **Crooked Islands** and **Mayaguana**. *page 220*
- Witness the spectacle of more than 60,000 protected pink flamingos in **Inagua National Park** on Great Inagua. *page 224*

beach. The property is a 200-year-old Loyalist plantation, though the historic buildings crumbled long ago to make room for the guest accommodations, cozy clubhouse, dining room and general store. The lodgings are exceptionally spacious and beautifully furnished in tropical style, and many have full kitchens and upstairs sleeping lofts with king-size beds. Guests have free use of snorkel gear, canoes and sea kayaks, and bicycles, cars and scuba gear are available for rent. A Modified American Plan (including dinner and either breakfast or lunch) is available. Room rates and meal prices are competitive with far less luxurious accommodations at many of Nassau's big resorts. ~ New Bight; 342-3043, 800-940-1905, fax 342-3051; www.fernandezbayvillage. com. ULTRA-DELUXE.

Owned by the captain of the *Sea Hauler* mailboat, the **Bridge Inn** at New Bight has a dozen motel-style units ranging in size from one to three bedrooms. The wood-paneled rooms are comfortable by Out Island standards and come with satellite TV. The beach is a short distance away. There is a combination bar and restaurant on the premises. ~ New Bight; 342-3013, fax 342-3041. MODERATE.

The German-run **Greenwood Beach Resort** advertises mainly in Europe and consequently seems to attract a Continental crowd. Originally an old plantation, its owners planned to subdivide it into lots for vacation homes, but before such essentials as roads and utilities could be finished, the owner passed away, leaving only the central lodge and a cluster of 18 motel-style rooms, which his heirs converted into a dive resort that is both secluded and remarkably affordable by Bahamian standards. The resort is situated on a spectacular ten-mile-long beach on the wild ocean side of the island northeast of Port Howe. It has large double rooms, clean and pleasantly though not luxuriously furnished, a short walk from the beach. The resort is far from anything else, half an hour's drive from the nearest town, but there may not be much reason to go anywhere. A dining room, honor bar, library and swimming pool are on the property; guests have the complimentary use of sea kayaks and snorkeling gear, and there is a complete dive shop for scuba rentals. Dive trips to pristine reefs are offered daily, weather permitting. ~ Port Howe; phone/fax 342-3053, 877-228-7475; www.hotelgreenwoodinn.com. MODERATE.

For those so inclined, the members-only **Cutlass Bay Resort,** on the south shore of the island west of Port Howe, is one of the few "clothing-optional" resorts (in other words, a nudist camp) in The Bahamas. What you'll get are 18 rather spartan guest rooms on an all-inclusive plan. ~ Port Howe; 342-3085. For membership information, contact P.O. Box 273767, Tampa, FL 33688-3767; 813-269-0153, 800-723-5688. DELUXE.

DINING   All Cat Island lodgings have their own restaurants, and most operate on the American Plan, meals included. Other restaurants are all but nonexistent. A handful of simple, ramshackle bar-and-grill establishments can be found in scattered settlements around the island serve steamed or cracked conch, mutton souse, peas 'n rice and Kalik beer. Among them are the **Gossip Bar and Restaurant** ~ Queen's Highway, Dumfries, no phone; **Triple X Bar and Restaurant** ~ Queen's Highway, The Bluff, no phone; **Bachelor's Restaurant and Bar** ~ Queen's Highway, Knowles Village, 342-6014; and **Peter Hill Restaurant and Bar** ~ Queen's Highway, Old Bight, no phone. ALL BUDGET. All restaurants on Cat Island except those at the resort hotels are closed on Sunday.

In Orange Creek, the **Sea Spray Restaurant**, a plain, white stucco-walled place with never-in-a-hurry service, offers a full menu of Bahamian fare ranging from stewed fish and grits to conch burgers. ~ Queen's Highway, Orange Creek; 354-4116. MODERATE.

Arthur's Town had the first high school in The Bahamas outside of Nassau and was actor Sidney Poitier's boyhood home.

The **Cookie House** in Arthur's Town, though primarily a bakery, also serves a limited and changeable selection of local dishes such as conch fritters, grouper fingers and mutton souse, on an open-air terrace that offers a fine sunset view over the water. ~ Queen's Highway, Arthur's Town; 354-2027. BUDGET.

In New Bight, the dining room at the **Bridge Inn** serves inexpensive conch dishes as well as pricey American fare—pizzas cost almost $20—in a pool-hall atmosphere. ~ Queen's Highway, New Bight; 342-3013. BUDGET.

You'll find limited stocks of picnic fixings in small grocery and convenience stores located in Orange Creek, Arthur's Town, Dumfries, Bennett's Harbour, Smith Bay Settlement, New Bight, Old Bight and Port Howe. In several other small villages, residents sell fruits, vegetables and baked goods out of their homes. Inquire locally to find out who has food for sale at any given time.

NIGHTLIFE   Cat Island nightlife, such as it is, centers around Arthur's Town and New Bight, while small bars and grills in several other towns stay open late and, at unpredictable times, may feature impromptu live "rake'n'scrape" music, a Cat Island specialty employing homemade instruments such as goatskin drums, conch shell horns, comb-and-tissue-paper "harmonicas" and a bass built from a washtub, a broomstick and tissue paper. The island's various evening hangouts tend to share the same itinerant musicians on various nights.

The hot spot in Arthur's Town is the **Hard Rock Disco**, no relation to the international rock-and-roll café chain. Live bands sometimes perform on weekends, but the main entertainment consists of oldies-but-goodies on genuine vinyl. ~ Queen's Highway, Arthur's Town; no phone.

Dumfries is well known as the hometown of some of the top musicians in The Bahamas. Oddly enough, it has no established night spot, but musicians sometimes gather to jam at night in the **Gossip Bar and Restaurant**. ~ Queen's Highway, Dumfries; no phone.

In New Bight, the **Sailing Club** offers disco reggae on weekends and live rake and scrape bands on holidays. ~ Queen's Highway, New Bight; no phone. **Hazel's Seaside Bar** is the place to go to watch or play a lively game of dominoes. ~ Queen's Highway, New Bight; no phone. There's also disco music at the **Blue Bird Club** ~ Queen's Highway, New Bight; 342-3095. Locals take their domino games seriously and play intensely at the **Pass Me Not Bar**. ~ Queen's Highway, Old Bight; 342-4016. There is sometimes live music on weekends in the **Bridge Inn**. ~ Queen's Highway, New Bight; 342-3013.

FERNANDEZ BEACH 🏃 🏊 ⛵ The longest and most beautiful of the slender sugar-white beaches found along the mangrove-shrouded western shore of Cat Island, this casuarina-fringed strand curves around the shoreline of shallow, crystalline Fernandez Bay. Snorkels and sailboards are available for rent at Fernandez Bay Village. ~ The beach lies west of Queen's Highway three miles north of New Bight. Take the turnoff to Fernandez Bay Village, which is located on the beach.

FINE BAY AND SANDY POINT 🏃 🏊 ⛵ More than fifty miles of pinkish sand beaches extend along the uninhabited east side, which locals for some reason call the "North Side," of Cat Island. You can see them from the summit or Mount Alvernia, but most of them are hard to reach by land because of dense bush and lack of roads. Atlantic ocean currents litter these beaches with piles of plastic and other detritus discarded from ships on the far side of the ocean, and beachcombers sometimes find treasures among the trash. One Cat Islander has found dozens of messages in bottles along the North Side beaches. ~ An unpaved road east from the village of Smith Bay leads past farmers' slash-and-burn fields, providing access to a spectacular stretch of beach on Fine Bay. A turnoff from Queen's Highway two miles north of the road to the Hermitage on Mount Alvernia runs about four miles to a long, beautiful stretch of beach at Sandy Point.

BEACHES

▼▼▼▼▼▼▼▼▼▼▼▼▼
Outdoor Adventures

DIVING

Among Cat Island's better known snorkeling sites are **Jumping Rocks Point** with its ledges and crevices housing lobster and stone crabs; **Lump of Limestone**, just off the beach and busy with big grouper;

Greenwood Beach with huge coral heads just off the beach; and Shipwreck, a half-submerged ship alive with lobsters and sea fans.

ECOTOURS Island Vacations' **Mystery Island tour** includes historical, ecological and cultural island highlights, a trip to Mount Alvernia and Father Jerome's monastery, accommodations in a local inn, Bahamian meals and many chances to meet islanders. Though the tour is designed for three nights and four days, it can be adjusted to your time and interests. ~ Contact Island Vacations at 4327 Reflections Boulevard North, Suite 104, Sunrise, FL 33351; 305-748-1833, 800-900-4242, fax 305-748-1965, or Nassau at P.O. Box 13002, Town Centre Mall, Nassau, Bahamas; 356-1111, fax 356-4379.

▼▼▼▼▼▼▼▼▼▼
San Salvador

Christopher Columbus' first landfall in the New World was on the island known as Guanahani to the Lucayan people who greeted him and his men as they strode onto the beach. Columbus christened the island with a new, Spanish name, San Salvador. For centuries, historians believed that Columbus' San Salvador was Cat Island, but in 1925, for reasons having as much to do with politics as historical scholarship, the British colonial government of The Bahamas declared that this island, then known as Watling's Island after buccaneer George Watling, who lived there in the 18th century, was the true site where Columbus had first landed and renamed it San Salvador. Today, four separate monuments on various parts of the island commemorate Columbus' landing.

San Salvador has an informal People-to-People program.

The easternmost island in The Bahamas, San Salvador has been dubbed the "Land of Lakes" by the local tourist industry because of its 28 landlocked, brackish lakes—the largest of them 12 miles long. The island can be toured in a day, though its pristine, secluded beaches tempt visitors to linger for much longer.

Despite the opening of two upscale resorts, the 20th century has brought little change of pace to San Salvador life. With less than 700 residents, mostly in and around the small village of Cockburn Town, a visit to San Salvador usually revolves around your lodging choice and the beach in front of it. Sightseers can circle the island on Queen's Highway. The road is not always good or well-marked, so a taxi tour is a reasonable alternative to an expensive rental car.

SIGHTS **Cockburn Town**, pronounced "Co-burn" (named after the first royal governor of The Bahamas to visit the island), is easily reached by bike or foot from the island's two resort facilities,

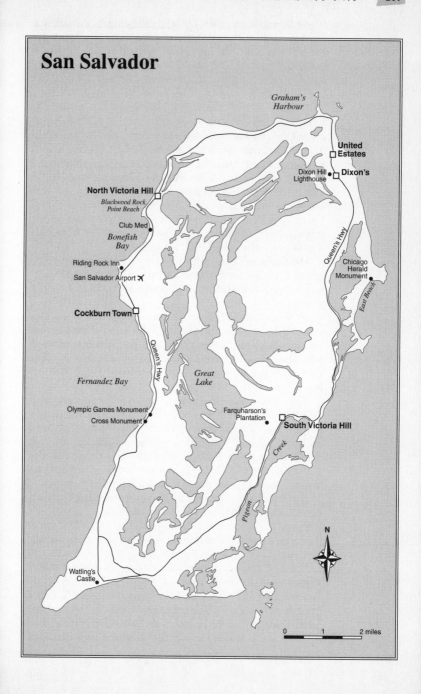

San Salvador

Graham's Harbour

United Estates

Dixon Hill Lighthouse   **Dixon's**

North Victoria Hill

Blackwood Rock Point Beach

Club Med

Bonefish Bay

Riding Rock Inn

San Salvador Airport ✈

Queen's Hwy

Chicago Herald Monument

East Beach

Cockburn Town

Queen's Hwy

Fernandez Bay

Great Lake

Olympic Games Monument

Cross Monument

Farquharson's Plantation

South Victoria Hill

Creek

Pigeon

Watling's Castle

N

0   1   2 miles

Club Med and Riding Rock Inn. Only a few blocks wide, the village has a few small shops, government offices and an attractive bar and restaurant. The big almond tree in the center of town is called the "Lazy Tree" by locals—who sometimes laze the day away under its cooling shade. After riding or walking into town, so can you.

Cockburn Town's pretty pink **Holy Savior Roman Catholic Church** was funded by the Knights of Columbus of North America and dedicated in 1992, 500 years after Columbus conducted the first Christian service in the New World. Only one K.O.C. member, Clifford Fernander, actually lives on San Salvador.

Next door, the small **San Salvador Museum**, housed in the former jail, provides a good overview of the Lucayan period in one room while Columbus' explorations are featured in the other. Upstairs there's a collection of 19th-century plantation photographs. Note that the museum is usually closed. Ask around for it to be opened, which will happen quickly.

Heading north from town on Queen's Highway, you go by Riding Rock Inn, over (no kidding) the end of the airport runway and past the entrance to Club Med before heading into open country.

In North Victoria Hill, the privately owned **New World Museum** exhibits pottery, rock art and other relics of the Lucayan Indians who once inhabited the island. The palm-fringed beach below, **Blackwood Rock Point Beach**, has great bonefishing flats. Turn around for a spectacular view of the colorful Club Med and Bonefish Bay.

Just past **Graham's Harbour**, which sits at the northern tip of the island, a short path up a rocky slope from Mile Marker #20 on the left leads to the **grave** of Father Chrysostomus Schreiner, the priest/historian who persuaded the colonial legislature to change the island's name from Watlings Island to San Salvador in 1926. Schreiner died in 1928 and was buried, according to his wishes, overlooking the placid turquoise harbor.

The **Bahamas Field Station for the Study of Archaeology, Biology, Geology and Marine Science**, on the right side of Queen's Highway, is a U.S. college consortium where students and scientists come to study The Bahamas, above and below the surface. However, it is not open to the public.

The next small settlement you will come to is called **United Estates**, or "U.E." by its residents. On your right as you come into town, is **Ed's First & Last Bar**, aka Club Ed. Here Ed Butler has amassed an astonishing collection of stray buoys that he's found washed up on the nearby shore. Just up the hill from Ed's is his brother Solomon's house, also decorated with dozens of colorful buoys.

United Estates is also the site of **Dixon Hill Lighthouse**, one of the world's few remaining manually operated lighthouses. You reach the top of this gleaming white lighthouse by climbing 80 narrow iron steps. The view from the top shows off every square inch of San Salvador's land and lakes. Built in 1856, the kerosene-powered set of prisms produces a double-blink every ten seconds. It is controlled by weights and clockworks, which are maintained by the two lighthouse keepers that live in the homes at the base of the beacon. The prisms are shaded during the day to prevent accidental fires from the sun's reflections. Stop by at sunset to see them being lit.

> When Columbus anchored in Graham's Harbour, he wrote that it could accommodate all the ships in Christendom.

East of United Estates is one of the island's many Columbus monuments—albeit a decidedly minor one. The **Chicago Herald Monument** at Crab Cay, erected in 1892, was intended to mark the spot where Columbus landed, but it's highly unlikely that he came ashore on this rocky side. You'll need a driver or local guide, a rugged car and good hiking boots to get there. Nearby **East Beach**, a pretty, deserted mile-long strand, might make the trip worth it.

A little farther along Queen's Highway is the marker for **Watling's Castle**, named after the notorious British privateer who settled into plantation life here in the 18th century. It is also known by its original name, Sandy Point Estate. Bahamian history buffs will love wandering around the ruins of this old plantation, perched almost 100 feet above Great Lake and the Atlantic Ocean. The former plantation and cattle farm has a huge stone main house and a cook house, with a giant wood-burning stove and chimney, as well as several smaller storage buildings. Across the road on an overgrown path are the slave's quarters.

Nearby, a guide can take you down a series of dirt roads to bright blue **Pigeon Creek**—actually a narrow saltwater inlet—connects several small inland lakes with the ocean. There are several nice homes here, as well as excellent bonefishing. At the north end of the "creek" is **Pigeon Creek Indian Site**, where Bahamian archaeologists have excavated portions of a village that may have been the home of the Lucayan people who welcomed Columbus to the New World. Visitors are welcome.

As Queen's Highway makes its way back to Cockburn Town, the small settlement of **South Victoria Hill** presents the ruins of **Farquharson's Plantation**, a large Loyalist farm. Established in the early 1800s by Charles Farquharson, the island's justice of the peace, the plantation's main crop was guinea corn, which was grown as food for slaves. Ironically, it rarely produced a surplus for export because most of the corn went to feed the more than 50 field hands who grew it. Today only the foundations of the great house, kitchen and a scattering of outbuildings can be found.

About three miles south of Cockburn Town, **Landfall Park** at Long Bay features four historic monuments. One Columbus monument commemorates the spot where Columbus is officially said to have landed. The pretty white cross was erected on Christmas Day in 1956 by Ruth Durlacher Wolpher, a Columbus scholar and wife of Hollywood mogul David Wolpher. Another Columbus monument nearby is a modern cross donated by Spain in 1992 to commemorate the 500th anniversary of Columbus' landing. The colors are those of the Bahamian flag—black to represent the people, yellow for the sunshine and aquamarine for the water. The third monument at the site, the **Olympic Games Memorial**, was erected in 1968 for the Olympic Games held in Mexico. The Olympic torch circled the island, ending where this monument now stands. The newest monument in the park was erected by the Japanese in recognition of Columbus' intended destination, Japan and the East Indies.

LODGING   San Salvador is one of the few Out Islands with an internationally owned resort, the **Club Med Columbus Isle**. This is one of the most luxurious Club Meds in the world. Situated on two miles of the best beach on the island, this brightly colored village opened in 1992 to rave reviews. The public rooms feature art objects from around the world. The 268 guest rooms are located in a large collection of colorful two-story buildings on the sprawling grounds, with each building containing four suites. Each suite has custom-made furnishings, a television, mini-fridge, telephone, huge sliding glass doors and a balcony or patio. The international staff of *gentils organisateurs* (GOs) help with your every need, from bike tours to a wide array of water sports, and they eat meals with guests, making for a friendly village atmosphere. Scuba divers will love this "dedicated dive village." The resort employs a large portion of the island's 700 residents and takes its environmental programs very seriously. Nonguests can pay for a day-visitor fee to take advantage of the restaurants, water sports and activities here. ~ Cockburn Town; 331-2000, 800-CLUB MED, fax 331-2458; www.clubmed.com. DELUXE.

The **Riding Rock Inn** is one of the Out Islands' pioneer resorts. Opened in the early 1960s, the inn has been an outpost for adventurous divers ever since. There are 42 basic rooms and time-share villas equipped with modern full kitchens. Hundreds of devoted divers are frequent repeat visitors. The resort sits on the water's edge in Cockburn Town, and has a small beach and pool. The dive packages are a great deal, and the island's only marina is just down the street. ~ 331-2631, 800-272-1492, fax 331-2020; www.ridingrock.com. MODERATE.

For basic accommodations contact **Clifford Fernander** who rents rooms to Club Med employees across Queen's Highway from the ocean. He sometimes has rooms available for short-term rentals; if not, he can tell you about other guest rooms and houses for rent on the island. ~ Church Street, Cockburn Town; 331-2676. BUDGET TO DELUXE.

For a truly local meal, head to Cockburn Town's **Three Ship's Restaurant**. Featuring the home-style cooking of Faith Jones, this simple establishment serves cracked conch, fresh seafood and peas 'n rice. Faith started out by cooking for townspeople at her house next door. ~ 1st Avenue, Cockburn Town; 331-2787. BUDGET TO MODERATE.

DINING

◄ HIDDEN

The cuisine at the **Club Med** is exquisite. Most diners are guests of the resort, but nonguests can buy a day pass for a fee. Dining here is especially enjoyable on the weekly "Island Night." Along with lavish gourmet buffets served in the main dining room, there are two specialty restaurants, one that features creative pizzas, and the other that offers grilled meats and Italian cuisine. ~ Cockburn Town; 331-2458. DELUXE.

Local cooking and a casual atmosphere make the **Riding Rock Inn** worth a visit for a drink and a meal even if you're not staying there—nonguests are welcome at the small dining room. Seafood specialties and Bahamian dishes are the fare. ~ Cockburn Town; 331-2631. MODERATE.

The boutique at the **Club Med** is one of the best shops to be found in The Bahamas. Along with Club Med logo clothing and other such items, they have a wide array of unique artwork from around the world. ~ 331-2000.

SHOPPING

Cockburn Town offers a few small shops, including **J's Discount Drugs** ~ 331-2750 and **Laramore's of The Bahamas** ~ 331-2025, which have basic necessities and some souvenirs.

As you can guess, nightlife on San Salvador is rather limited. Entertainment nights are shared between the various establishments, so ask around to see what's scheduled and where it is.

NIGHTLIFE

The highly recommend **Harlem Square Club** is a San Salvador landmark and a great place to meet friendly locals, with weekly local bands playing Bahamian and international music. ~ Cockburn Town; 331-2777.

The entertainment at the **Club Med** is slick and semiprofessional. The main bar has a dancehall that presents live music on many evenings, and staff members double as performers in the improv-style open-air theater. ~ Cockburn Town; 331-2458.

The Riding Rock Inn's **Driftwood Lounge** draws a crowd most evenings with its big-screen TV showing sporting events and movie videos, even though the rooms at both this resort and Club Med have their own television sets. ~ Cockburn Town; 331-2631.

BEACHES **BONEFISH BAY** 🏃 🏊 🚤 ⛵ 🚣 🌊 Club Med takes up only a small part of this pretty two-and-a-half-mile strip. Walk just beyond the Club Med and the beach is typically deserted. Of course, the Club Med features virtually every water sport imaginable to guests and those who pay the day-use fee. ~ The beach, accessible from Queen's Highway, extends northward from Riding Rock Point, about two miles north of Cockburn Town.

EAST BEACH 🏃 🏊 🎣 Almost always deserted, this mile-long stretch near the Chicago Herald Monument on Crab Cay is an ideal spot for snorkeling and beachcombing. As on other, smaller beaches on the island's remote "ocean side," however, the surf can be high and sometimes treacherous. Ask a driver to take you here in a four-wheel-drive vehicle, or you'll need to hike the last mile or so. ~ Located at the end of the sandy jeep track to Crab Cay that turns off Queen's Highway near Mile Marker 24.

▼▼▼▼▼▼▼▼▼▼▼▼
Outdoor Adventures

The Riding Rock Inn put San Salvador on the map as a great scuba diving destination and the Club Med has enhanced that reputation. The resorts have two of the finest dive operations in The Bahamas. Club Med led the way in establishing anchor buoys so dive boats won't harm the reefs. The resort is keenly concerned with raising the environmental awareness of their employees and guests. (Also, the Club Med has a multilock hyperbaric chamber on-property.)

There are literally dozens of dive sites just off the west and south coasts of San Salvador and you could easily go several weeks without visiting the same site twice. Among the sites are **Telephone Pole**, a cave with a telephone pole and lots of Nassau grouper at the entrance; **Great Cut** with its colorful coral; **Devil's Claw**—large pillar coral and swim-throughs; and **Hole in the Wall**. San Salvador still has virtually virgin diving on many reefs, and with the excellent visibility you'll probably see more marine life than you ever imagined possible.

San Salvador **snorkeling sites** include **Snapshot Reef**, where swarms of colorful fish seem to pose for pictures; **Staghorn Reef**, named for the huge staghorn corals; and the coral forest of the appropriately named **Elkhorn Gardens**.

▼▼▼▼▼▼▼▼▼▼
Long Island

For scuba diving, snorkeling, bonefishing or deep-sea fishing, Long Island is a delightful discovery. Most of the island's hardy inhabitants live much as their ancestors have for more than a century, little affected by the tidal wave of tourism that has swept across much of The Bahamas in recent

times. Except for a couple of small guesthouses that cater mainly
to visiting Out Islanders, the only tourist lodgings on the island
are at the far north end, where two internationally renowned
luxury dive resorts contrast with the frontier outpost feel of the
rest of the island. The main occupation on the
south part of the island is harvesting sea salt.
Long Island is a haven for those who *really* want
to get away from it all.

It was on Long Island
that Columbus
reportedly discov-
ered hammocks.

Columbus, who made Long Island his third stop
in the New World, named it Fernandina in honor of
King Ferdinand of Spain. Eighteenth-century plantation
owners changed the name to Long Island and later abandoned it, leaving behind the slaves whose descendants
make up the island's population of about 3500 people.

The Stella Maris Inn put Long Island on the map. There are
now two other accommodation options, and only now is Long
Island beginning to draw attention for its great beaches, seclusion, Out Island history and exceptional diving and snorkeling.
Outside the hotel areas, Long Islanders don't seem to be as accustomed to tourists as they are on other Out Islands and may
act a bit aloof at first.

Despite its name, at 75 miles in length, Long Island is not nearly
the longest island in The Bahamas, but it is strikingly slender, av-
eraging only one and a half miles in width and is just three miles
wide at its widest point. You can easily see most of the sites in a
day or less, depending on your interests. Steep cliffs cascade down
to the sea on the eastern side of the island, while multihued
beaches slope gradually into a gentle surf on the western side.
The interior consists of rolling hills clad in low jungle with many
small lakes and ponds.

SIGHTS

Twelve miles north of the Stella Maris Inn, near the north end
of the island, lies **Cape Santa Maria**, a sugar-white three-mile
beach so soft it feels like satin between your toes. At the northernmost tip, you'll find a dramatic rocky shoreline with high
cliffs, adorned with a small Columbus monument.

Located off Long Island's northern tip, **Conception Island** is
protected by the Bahamas National Trust. Visitors will find many
birds, including laughing gulls, royal terns, cormorants and fri-
gate birds, as well as an occasional green sea turtle nest. The diving off this island is extraordinary. It's a two- to four-hour boat
trip, depending on the craft and sea conditions.

On the way to Cape Santa Maria, a red house in the tiny village of **Burnt Ground** is among the oldest on the island. Also
nearby, **Adderley's Plantation** is well overgrown, but you can still
see the ruins of several buildings from an old cotton plantation
as well as a small slave cemetery.

Heading back south past the Stella Maris Inn, **Queen's Highway** leads past the small town of Millerton and into Simms, where the **government packing house** is worth a visit on mailboat days, when it's filled with produce destined for Nassau. Many of the small houses have emblems painted near their roofs to ward off evil spirits.

The next major town is **Salt Pond**, the harbor site of the Long Island Regatta, by far the island's biggest event. It's held each year on Whit Monday—the same date as Memorial Day in the United States. The town is also the headquarters for a thriving lobster boat fleet, which sustains a good part of the economy for Long Island.

The road continues south through a number of small towns, like **Gray's**, where parts of the houses from Gray's Plantation are still standing, and **Deadman's Cay**, one of the most productive farming communities in The Bahamas. Here fruits and vegetables are grown for shipment to Nassau. Up on the hill overlooking town, stands the ruins of **Dunmore Plantation**, owned by the same Lord Dunmore for which Harbour Island's Dunmore Town was named. You can see parts of the gatepost and house as well as several fireplace chimneys. Two **caves** at Deadman's Cay are best explored in the company of a competent local guide, which the innkeeper at your lodging can arrange on a day's notice or less.

The island's unofficial capital, **Clarence Town**, boasts two stone churches built by architect priest Father Jerome. On opposing hills offering fantastic views, **St. Paul's Anglican Church** is on the western side of town and **St. Peter's Catholic Church** is to the east. Sent to The Bahamas as an Anglican minister to rebuild churches damaged by a hurricane, Father Jerome later converted to Catholicism. He died in 1956 at age 80, having spent his last 20 years as a hermit on neighboring Cat Island.

LODGING   German entrepreneurs showed plenty of foresight when they designed the sprawling **Stella Maris Inn** for European visitors back in the 1950s. The 43 accommodations are varied—from single rooms and studios to cottages, apartments, bungalows and two-, three-, and four-bedroom villas, some with private swimming pools. Confirm exactly what you're getting beforehand. A vast former plantation estate, the property has its villas and bungalows interspersed among many vacation homes along the east shore of the island, while the main inn and motel-style guest rooms are set on a hilltop in the center of the island with sea views in both directions. Units typically have white rattan furnishings, sandproof tile floors and tropical pink color schemes. All have refrigerators, and the villas and bungalows have kitchenettes or full kitchens. The resort has a marina, a restaurant and pub, a general store, three freshwater swimming pools, tennis and water sports. The dive operation can arrange virtually any water-oriented pursuit for you, with superb snorkeling and fishing two of the best options. There are twice-daily shuttles to Deal's Beach and Cape Santa Maria Beach, snorkeling trips, bikes and rum punch parties. They even have a popular rental-plane program for licensed pilots. Stella Maris is also the host for many parties and other planned entertainment events. ~ 338-2050, 800-426-0466, fax 338-2052; www.stellamarisresort.com. DELUXE TO ULTRA-DELUXE.

Situated on a fabulous snow-white beach near the island's northern extremity, the upscale, Canadian-run **Cape Santa Maria Beach Resort** has it all. With most Out Island lodging, you sacrifice certain amenities—but not here. The are 12 well furnished one- and two-bedroom cottages with screened-in porches and fabulous sunset views. Watersports are right outside your door, including excellent bonefishing. An all-inclusive plan is optional. ~ Cape Santa Maria; 357-1006, 800-663-7090. ULTRA-DELUXE.

The much more modest **Thompson Bay Inn** is a simple two-story hotel-style inn offering eight basic rooms with four shared baths. It's very isolated, about 12 miles south of the Stella Maris Inn. ~ P.O. Box 30123, Main Road, Thompson Bay; 337-0099. MODERATE.

No local dining spots have really developed on Long Island. Some of the villages have little cafés or snack bars, usually open for lunch only. For the most part, visitors are limited to dining at the lodging options mentioned above. All offer excellent fare for varying tastes and budgets. The menus change frequently at all three restaurants, and the dining plans can be a very good deal.

DINING

The relatively elegant atmosphere of **Stella Maris Inn**'s main restaurant sets the stage for well-prepared, attractively presented meals. The chefs go out of their way to provide variety in deference to its mainly European clientele, meals tend to feature an assortment of German dishes and local seafood with a Continental flair. The clublike atmosphere is congenial, and mealtime talk usually centers around diving. The Stella Maris also serves German and international cuisine at their tennis club, and there's Bahamian cooking at the **Pepper Pot**, down by their marina. ~ Ocean View Drive, Stella Maris; 336-2106. DELUXE.

The **Thompson Bay Inn** offers the best Bahamian dining on the island. All types of fish are featured, with typical island side dishes. There's much more of a local feel here than you'll find at most Out Island resorts. ~ Queen's Highway, Thompson Bay; 337-0099. MODERATE.

The clubhouse dining room at the **Cape Santa Maria Beach Resort** offers even more in the way of ultracasual elegance. The menu changes according to the catch of the day and often features lobster in season. Nonguests are welcome with advance notice. ~ Cape Santa Maria; 357-1006.

SHOPPING   No duty-free perfume shops here; if you need anything and it's available on the island, you'll probably find it at the general store of the **Stella Maris Inn**. ~ 336-2020.

Down in Deadman's Cay, try **C.J.'s Convenience Store**. ~ 337-0034. In Clarence Town, there's **True Value Food & Drug Store**. ~ Dial 0 and asked to be connected. And in the small village of McKenzie's, you'll find **Knowles Supplies**. ~ 337-0566.

It may be quite awhile before you see straw markets on Long Island, but you'll find good examples of this traditional folk art for sale at Alecia **Knowles' Straw Work** near the Stella Maris ~ Simms, 338-8768; **C & M's Straw Work** ~ Scrub Hill, 338-8246; and **Lula Pratt's Straw Work** ~ O'Neals, 338-8765.

NIGHTLIFE   As with dining, you're generally limited to the big three—**Stella Maris Inn** ~ 336-2106, **Cape Santa Maria Beach Resort** ~ 337-1006 and **Thompson Bay Inn** ~ 337-0099—which alternate entertainment nights. The "cave party" at Stella Maris and dancing at Thompson Bay Inn are particularly popular.

Down in Deadman's Cay, **Ruth Watkins's Twilight Club** has a local flavor. ~ 337-1076. So does **Sierras Club** near the airport, which features dancing to recorded music on weekend nights. ~ Deadman's Cay.

BEACHES   **CAPE SANTA MARIA BEACH** 🧍 🏖 🎣 🚤 Quite simply one of the finest beaches in The Bahamas, this three-mile stretch is virtually deserted except for the few guests at Cape Santa Maria Beach Resort, which provides a wide variety of watersport options to day visitors on the beach. Nonguests can get there using the Stella Maris Inn's twice-daily shuttles to the beach from nearby towns. ~ The beach is located on the northernmost tip of the island, beginning where the highway ends.

◆◆◆◆◆◆◆◆◆◆◆◆◆◆◆◆◆◆◆◆◆

Stella Maris' famed Shark Reef was one of the world's first "shark dives" commercially available to divers.

DEAL'S BEACH 🧍 🏖 🎣 🚤 This northern beach, well maintained by the Stella Maris Inn, offers a full range of water sports on the beach. It is a great beach for families. ~ Located on the eastern side of the island adjoining the Stella Maris Inn on the north.

LOVE BEACHES 🧍 🏖 🎣 Also part of the Stella Maris property, these five connected beaches add up to more than three miles of pretty pinkish sand. You may be the only one on your particular Love Beach of choice. Lovely, shallow coral gardens are easy to reach from shore, making some of these beaches ideal for casual snorkeling. ~ Located just south of the Stella Maris Inn.

CONCEPTION ISLAND NATIONAL PARK 🏃 🏊 🚣 Off the island's north end, this pristine island has many tropical and migrating birds, as well as occasional sea turtles. It's protected by the Bahamas National Trust. There are also good beaches and terrific diving just offshore. ~ The Stella Maris Inn operates boat excursions to the island.

SOUTH END BEACHES 🏃 🏊 🚣 As you approach the south end of Long Island along Queen's Highway, you'll be drawn by the sight of a number of sandy stretches that may go weeks without a human footprint. Just pick your own piece of paradise. There are no facilities, so bring along any gear you may want. ~ These beaches are located along the eastern or "ocean" side of the island and can be reached from the road between the small villages of Roses and Ford.

▼▼▼▼▼▼▼▼▼▼▼▼▼▼▼

Outdoor Adventures

The full-service marinas at **Stella Maris Inn** ~ 336-2106 and **Cape Santa Maria Beach Resort** ~ 337-1006 offer rentals and excursions of all types. The Stella Maris' marina is by far the biggest and best in the Southern Bahamas.

BOATING

FISHING

All three resorts on the island can arrange popular bonefishing and deep-sea fishing excursions. Bonefishing flats are located offshore along the northwestern part of the island, and there's deep-sea fishing nearby.

DIVING

The success of the Stella Maris Inn attests to the great scuba diving off Long Island. The convenience, visibility and variety off the northern end of the island make it a diving treasure. The **Stella Maris Shark Reef** is one of the best-known dives in The Bahamas. Frequently seen sharks on the dive (normally 5 to 15 of them) include reef sharks, nurse sharks, bull sharks and sometimes a hammerhead. Stella Maris divemasters have long fed the sharks, who return often. Located about a half an hour from the resort, the dive takes place on a sandy bottom in about 25 feet of water. For divers, it's definitely a career highlight.

Grouper Valley is another one of Stella Maris' most popular dives. Divers are usually shuttled by van and boat, making the trip much shorter. The huge grouper and jewfish normally seen on the dive make it well worthwhile. An ideal dive for all levels is **Flamingo Reef,** with a shallow fish-packed section and a good wreck and drop-off nearby. There's also a **blue hole** and a **green hole dive** that attract Stella Maris guests.

For a special treat, the Stella Maris diving excursion to **Conception Island** is unique. The entire perimeter of the island offers virtually virgin diving on walls and huge coral formations teeming with marine life. It's a two- to four-hour boat trip, depending on the boat and sea conditions.

Long Island's many snorkeling highlights include **Coral Gardens**—beautiful valleys, caves and overhangs, with the possibility of viewing sea turtles; **Flamingo Tongue Reef** is packed with coral and fish; **Rock Pools** has a tidal pool and many rock formations; **Eagle Ray Reef** offers eagle rays and giant grouper; and **Watermelon Beach** has colorful parrotfish and lots of staghorn coral just off the beach.

▼▼▼▼▼▼▼▼▼▼▼▼▼
Acklins Island and Crooked Island

Located about 225 miles southeast of Nassau, Crooked Island and Acklins Island are Out Island frontiers that rarely receive attention from visitors. Crooked Island, on the north, forms a semicircle with Acklins Island, and is separated only by the narrow Crooked Island Passage through which Columbus sailed. Acklins Island is the slightly larger of the two, occupying 120 square miles to Crooked's 70. Crooked Island is the most "developed" of the two. Today, about 400 people live on the two islands combined.

However, two centuries ago these islands were far busier than they are today, with nearly 50 cotton plantations and more than 1000 slaves. But in 1800, blight and soil depletion wiped out the plantations and by the 1820s most people had left. Those who stayed tried their hand at salt mining, but this enterprise also failed.

Today, the descendants of these early settlers and slaves live a pastoral existence as farmers and fishermen. Tourist facilities are extremely limited on these islands, and only those desiring a genuine Out Island adventure should come. Those who do make their way to these islands are rewarded with a Bahamas experience far beyond a Nassau sightseer's wildest imaginings. Amid the brightly painted clapboard houses visitors soon slip into the slow rhythms of local life. They discover deserted beaches, scuba diving on virgin reefs and friendly people just waiting for their islands to be discovered—or hoping that they remain a secret.

SIGHTS

Now in ruins, **Marine Farms Fortress** was once a large British fort used to protect the Crooked Island Passage. The cannons still overlook the passage. The grounds are maintained by The Bahamas National Trust.

Nearby, the **Bird Rock Lighthouse** was built in 1872 and still guides sailors through the sometimes treacherous route. Your only company at Bird Rock Lighthouse will probably be the numerous ospreys.

Castle Island, south of Acklins Island, has another lonely lighthouse that was built in 1867.

Flamingos are sometimes spotted among the mangroves at **French Wells Bay** on Crooked Island. This remote shoreline also hosts many other bird species throughout the year.

Several **underground caves** on Crooked Island were once used as shelters by Lucayan Indians. Today, only bats live among the tunnels and caverns that drip with stalactites. You can arrange for a guided tour with Pittstown Point Landings. ~ 344-2507.

Located at the northwest point of Crooked Island, **Pittstown Point Landings** is a frontier secret. Most of its guests arrive by private plane at the small private airstrip. (The island's public airport is about 45 minutes away.) Twelve rooms with modern furnishings and fixtures are located in three pink buildings. Half of the rooms face the water while the others have views from their side windows. Though there's no air conditioning, sea breezes and ceiling fans keep guests cool. It's just a short walk from the water and there are beaches in both directions. The nearest settlement, tiny Landrail Point, is about two miles away. Most guests take their meals at the lodge. ~ Landrail Point, Crooked Island; 344-2507. Or in the United States: 238-A Airport Road, Statesville, NC 18677; 704-881-0585, 800-752-2322, fax 704-881-0771. MODERATE.

LODGING

◄ *HIDDEN*

A more basic choice is the **Crooked Island Beach Inn**. Situated on a quiet beach near the usually quiet airport, there are six guest rooms in a concrete building. Each room has a balcony or patio overlooking the sea. The owners will prepare meals for you on request. ~ Cabbage Hill, Crooked Island; 344-2321, fax 344-2502. BUDGET.

Crooked Island's best bet for dining out is **Ozzie's Café**, the restaurant located at Pittstown Point Landing. Floor-to-ceiling windows offer up great sunrises and sunsets that accompany tasty Continental cuisine or Bahamian fish dishes. It was built around what is said to have been the first post office in The Bahamas. ~ Landrail Point, Crooked Island; 344-2507. MODERATE.

DINING

SHELL BEACH 🏃 ⛱ 🚤 🛥 Shell Beach is one of several excellent Crooked Island beaches on the southwest side, this strand is known for shelling and snorkeling. ~ It's reached only by boat; Pittstown Point Landings runs excursions; 344-2507.

BEACHES

BATHING BEACH 🏃 ⛱ 🛥 This wonderful Crooked Island southwest beach has crystal-clear water for swimming and a deserted sandy beach for sunning. There are also inland springs nearby. ~ Reached only by boat, Pittstown Point Landings takes people there; 344-2507.

▼▼▼▼▼▼▼▼▼▼▼▼▼▼ Fishing is a way of life for most Acklins and
Outdoor Adventures
Crooked Island residents. Because of the island's small population and limited tourist trade, how-

FISHING &
BOATING
ever, there are only a few fishing boats available for charter.

Thunderbird's Boating Activities at Pittstown Point Landings offers deep-sea fishing trips, sightseeing charters and snorkeling trips. ~ 344-2507.

Shakey's Bonefishing, also associated with Pittstown Point Landings, has full- and half-day bonefishing charters. ~ 344-2507.

DIVING

Acklins and Crooked Islands are surrounded by more than 50 miles of barrier reefs, which form undersea walls dropping off as much as 3500 feet. The only scuba outfitter on the islands, **Johnny & Big Ben's Scuba Diving** at Pittstown Point Landings, offers personalized diving on a per-dive basis. ~ 344-2507.

▼▼▼▼▼▼▼▼▼▼ Tiny Mayaguana, just 24 miles long and six miles wide
Mayaguana
at its widest point, went unnoticed and all but uninhab-ited until 1961 when the Cuban missile threat prompted the U.S. Government to install a missile tracking station there. This created jobs and supported enough of a population—about 300—to include Mayaguana in public transportation schedules.

Most of the island hasn't changed much since . . . well, since it was uninhabited. Covered with hardwood coppice, fringed with palm trees, Mayaguana is so far out in the mid-dle of nowhere that there would be no point in mentioning the place except that it has gained a cultlike reputation as the closest thing in the Carib-bean region to the end of the earth. As such, Maya-guana is a perfect place to drop out in. In fact, it is one of the only places in The Bahamas where tent camping is allowed, making it a small-time mecca for island-hopping backpackers. None of the rules the Bahamian government had deemed necessary to an orderly tourist-based economy are en-forced on Mayaguana.

> All of the beaches on Mayaguana are clothing-optional.

The only thing close to a population center on the island is Pirate's Well, a village on the northwest part of the island. There are no real stores here. People simply stock up on staple foods and supplies in bulk quantities when they travel to Nassau and sell or trade them to other island residents.

In addition to untrammeled beaches, Mayaguana has coral reefs along the south side of the island and around Northwest Point that very few divers have ever explored. There are no dive operators on the island, nor are there guided tours, duty-free shops, restaurants or guesthouses. There is only an endless beach party.

Lying closer to Haiti and Cuba than Nassau, Great Inagua is still very much a Bahamian island. Situated between Cuba and the Turks and Caicos islands, Great Inagua is the southernmost island in The Bahamas and the third largest in land mass—25 by 45 miles.

Great Inagua

The first known resident of Inagua was Haitian tyrant Henri Christophe, who built a vacation palace there in 1800, and later, when his subjects revolted, used Inagua as an escape route because of its proximity to Haiti. Legend has it that he hid a cache of gold looted from the Haitian treasury somewhere on Inagua; it has never been found.

It was salt that first brought permanent settlement to this flat barren land in the mid-1800s. By the 1870s, as the salt mining industry flourished, the population boomed to more than 1000—roughly the same population as you'll find there today. The locally owned company was eventually acquired by the Morton Salt Company, which still harvests more than 12,000 acres from Great Inagua's salt ponds today. More than a quarter of the population works for the company. Some of the older salt ponds are now being used for marine life experiments.

Great Inagua has always been a haven for birds. Once found in great numbers throughout The Bahamas, flamingos almost vanished after their plumage came into vogue a century ago. By the 1950s, the national bird of The Bahamas was found only on Great Inagua. Inagua National Park was formed to protect and save these shocking pink birds as well as many other species. Birdwatchers flock to the island to see some of the 50,000 flamingos, as well as the graceful Bahamas parrot (found only here and on Abaco) and more than 200 other species. Less enjoyable flying creatures are the abundant mosquitoes; so bring plenty of repellent.

Matthew Town, the largest village on the island, is one block wide. The pink government building contains the commissioner's office, the island's post office, the small library and several other government offices. Some of the 19th-century homes reflect the riches of the early salt mining days, but this is still a true Bahamian backwater town. Situated on the western side of the island, the town's best attraction may be the glorious sunsets.

SIGHTS

The **Erickson Museum and Library** is housed in the former residence of the local manager of the Morton Salt Company. It contains exhibits on the history of the island, with special attention to the salt industry. ~ Matthew Town; 339-1863.

A picturesque lighthouse stands on **Southwest Point**, about a mile south of Matthew Town. Built in 1870, it is one of the few hand-operated kerosene lights still used in The Bahamas. From the top, on a clear day, you can sometimes see Cuba to the west.

HIDDEN ► **Inagua National Park** is the highlight of Great Inagua, and it's reason enough to come here if you're at all interested in birds, nature and Bahamas Out Island life as it once was. At more than 300 square miles, this park comprises close to 50 percent of the island's land mass. The 23-mile drive from Matthew Town to the park takes about an hour. What draws many birders are the flamingos. These pink "walking stilts" were once a delicacy and were almost hunted to extinction. However, the national park has become a sanctuary and you can see them throughout the year. The best times are during the mating season from October to February and the nesting season from February to May or June. The flightless baby flamingos are a hilarious sight right after they've hatched. Most people come to the park for the day, but serious birders stay longer. ~ Bahamas National Trust; 393-1317.

The Morton Salt Company manufactures more than a million pounds of salt a year, some of which, ironically, is used to melt icy U.S. streets in winter.

The Morton Salt Company produces more than a million pounds of salt annually around large **Lake Windsor**. You'll see the huge mounds of salt from the air and on the ground, but if you want a more upclose-and-personal view you can arrange a tour of the facility and learn about the solar salt production process. ~ Lake Windsor; 339-1300.

Located off the northern coast of Great Inagua, 50-square-mile **Little Inagua** is uninhabited and is usually only visited by boaters or daytrippers from Matthew Town. Here, as on Great Inagua, birds abound.

LODGING The most traditional "hotel" on the island is **Crystal Beach View Hotel**. Its 13 rooms make it the largest lodging option. The one-story building and grounds feature a busy lobby and lounge, simply furnished rooms, a pool and a restaurant. For a splurge, they offer a larger "honeymoon suite." ~ Gregory Street, Matthew Town; 339-1550. BUDGET TO MODERATE.

Located a half-mile south of Matthew Town, **Walkine's Guest House** provides a great Bahamian village experience. Kirk and Eleanor Walkine run this friendly little inn, which sits across from the town's beach. Five simple and clean rooms are painted a nice flamingo pink. If you want to live like a Bahamian you'll like this place. ~ Gregory Street, Matthew Town; 339-1612. BUDGET.

Owned by the Morton Salt Company, **Morton Main House** is a typical Bahamian guesthouse. There are six simple rooms, with two of them offering private baths. They, too, have a "honeymoon suite." The small restaurant here features fresh Bahamian-style seafood. ~ Kortwright Street, Matthew Town; 339-1267. BUDGET.

South of Matthew Town, right on the water, Ezzard Cartwright runs **Sunset Apartments**, a choice island housekeeping option. Each of the four modern two-bedroom apartments has a kitchen, television and a terrace. There's a small secluded beach nearby. ~ Matthew Town; 339-1362. MODERATE.

If you're interested in renting a house, contact Larry Ingraham of Great Inagua Tours about the four-bedroom **beach house** on the secluded northwest side of the island. For a family or group, it's an ideal getaway. ~ Matthew Town; 331-2458. BUDGET TO MODERATE.

At **Inagua National Park**, Bahamas National Trust property warden Henry Nixon can arrange camping facilities for visitors interested in roughing it. This does not mean tent sites, but barracks-style lodging in two large bare-wall cabins, each of which houses up to 14 people. Sheets and mattresses are provided, but a sleeping bag will be more comfortable. There are cooking facilities and two freshwater showers. ~ Matthew Town; 339-1616. BUDGET.

DINING

Along with the modest restaurants at Morton Main House and Crystal Beach View Hotel, there's the **Cozy Corner Restaurant & Bar**. This typical Bahamian restaurant specializes in locally caught seafood. Foreign currency from afar is the colorful wallpaper behind the bar. Locals come here to drink beer and shoot pool. ~ William Street, Matthew Town; 339-1440. BUDGET.

◄ HIDDEN

Topps Restaurant also features local seafood. Tasty cracked conch is a specialty. Here, too, foreign currency is the decor. ~ Matthew Street, Matthew Town; 339-1293. BUDGET.

If you're out exploring the island or visiting the Morton Salt Company plant, you may want to stop by **Traveller's Rest**, located near the plant. As with every other restaurant on the island, they serve cracked conch and other seafood dishes. ~ Lake Windsor; no phone. BUDGET.

SHOPPING

If it's for sale on the island, you'll find it in Matthew Town at **Inagua General Store** ~ Gregory Street, 339-1460 or **Ingraham's Variety Store** ~ Kortwright Street, 339-1232.

BEACHES

GREAT INAGUA BEACHES 🚶 🏊 🚣 The beach situation on Great Inagua is not great, but there are decent ones near Matthew Town and on the northern end of the island. Northwest Point's Farquharson, Beach is considered the best. ~ It's located about eight miles north of Matthew Town, a short distance beyond the old Morton Salt Dock.

▼▼▼▼▼▼▼▼▼▼▼▼▼▼
Outdoor Adventures

There are virtually no facilities on Inagua for boating, scuba diving or any of the other water sports that prevail on most other Bahamian islands. The sport of choice here is flamingo watching.

ECOTOURS

Island Vacations' **Inagua Safari** includes birdwatching, a tour of the Morton Salt Company, a visit to the lighthouse, accommodations at a local inn and local dining. Though the tour is designed for three nights and four days, it can be customized for your needs. ~ Contact Island Vacations in the U.S. at 4327 Reflections Boulevard North, Suite 104, Sunrise, FL 33351; 305-748-1833, 800-900-4242, fax 305-748-1965, or in Nassau at P.O. Box 13002, Town Centre Mall, Nassau, Bahamas; 356-1111, fax 356-4379.

▼▼▼▼▼▼▼▼▼▼▼▼
Transportation

AIR

CAT ISLAND **Arthur's Town Airport** and **New Bight International Airport** have regularly scheduled (though not daily) flights to and from Nassau on Bahamasair. In addition, Air Sunshine operates regular flights from Fort Lauderdale to New Bight on Tuesday, Wednesday, and Thursday.

SAN SALVADOR The **San Salvador Airport** is a short distance north of Cockburn Town. American Eagle offers flights from Miami. Bahamasair offers daily flights from Nassau and Miami. Club Med has its own charter flights from Nassau, Eleuthera and Miami, while Riding Rock Inn brings in guests from Fort Lauderdale.

LONG ISLAND There are two small airports on the island, one at **Stella Maris Resort** on the north and the other at **Deadman's Cay** in the center of the island. Bahamasair and Island Express have regularly scheduled flights to the island.

ACKLINS AND CROOKED ISLANDS Bahamasair flies twice a week to **Colonel Hill Airport** on Crooked Island and **Chester Bay Airport** and **Spring Point Airstrip** on Acklins Island. **Pittstown Point Landing** also offers weekly flights from Nassau to their airstrip on Crooked Island.

MAYAGUANA Bahamasair flies from Nassau to the **Mayaguana Airport** three times a week.

GREAT INAGUA Bahamasair flies to **Matthew Town Airport** from Nassau several times a week.

BOAT

CAT ISLAND The *North Cat Island Special* departs Nassau on the 14-hour trip to Arthur's Town on Tuesday afternoon, returning on Thursday. The mailboat *Sea Hauler* serves New Bight; it also leaves Nassau for the 12-hour trip on Tuesday afternoon and does not return until Sunday.

SAN SALVADOR   The *Lady Francis* serves San Salvador and Rum Cay, leaving Nassau on Tuesday evening for the 12-hour trip and returning on Friday.

LONG ISLAND   The *Mia Dean* serves Clarence Town, leaving Nassau on Tuesday evening for the 12-hour trip and returning on Thursday. The *Sherice M* goes to Salt Pond and Deadman's Cay, a 15-hour trip, leaving Nassau on Monday afternoon. It sometimes returns on Thursday and other times on Friday; ask the boat captain.

OTHER ISLANDS   The *Lady Mathilda* runs to Mayaguana, Acklins and Crooked Islands on a varying schedule; call the dockmaster at Potter's Cay Dock in Nassau (393-1064) for current departure information. There is presently no mailboat to Inagua.

CAT ISLAND   There are no taxis on Cat Island. Most lodgings furnish airport transportation. If you walk along the roadside, just about any car that passes will stop to offer you a ride; the bad news is that you may have to wait hours for one.

TAXIS

SAN SALVADOR   There are numerous independent taxi operators on the island. **Clifford Fernander** is a great guide, as is his son, Bruno. ~ 331-2676. Or call **Livingston Williams**. ~ 331-2025.

LONG ISLAND   It's best to let your lodging choice help with taxis and then keep using the driver you like. **Jerry Knowles** and **Veronica Knowles,** both based at the Stella Maris Inn, are excellent guides. ~ 336-2106.

ACKLINS ISLAND AND CROOKED ISLAND   There is taxi service from the airports, but limited phone service on the islands can make calling a cab tricky.

GREAT INAGUA   The few taxis on Great Inagua meet each flight, and you can talk to your driver about any outings you want to make. **Rocky Barbes** is a good bet. ~ 339-1284.

CAT ISLAND   Rental cars are available but very expensive— around $85 a day for an aging vehicle. Contact the **Sea Spray Hotel** ~ Orange Creek, 354-4116; or the **Shell Gas Station** ~ New Bight, 342-3011.

CAR RENTALS

SAN SALVADOR   You can arrange a rental car from **C & S Car Rentals** ~ Cockburn Town; 331-2714. You can also arrange a rental at your resort hotel's front desk; it comes from the same place.

LONG ISLAND   The **Stella Maris Inn** ~ 336-2106 and **Thompson Bay Inn** ~ 337-0099 can provide rental cars; or call **Stan's Car Rental.** ~ Miller's, 338-8987.

GREAT INAGUA   Larry Ingraham can help with a car rental during your stay. ~ Great Inagua Tours, 339-1204.

**BIKE
RENTALS**

CAT ISLAND   Guests can rent bikes for $7 a day at **Fernandez Bay Village**. ~ 342-3043.

SAN SALVADOR   Bicycles are available for rent at **Riding Rock Inn**. ~ 331-2631.

LONG ISLAND   Guests have free use of bicycles at **Stella Maris Inn**. ~ 336-2106.

GREAT INAGUA   You can rent a bike from your lodging or from Ingraham's Variety Store. ~ 339-1232.

Recommended Reading

Bahamas Handbook and Businessman's Annual. Etienne Dupuch, Jr. Publications, 1999. Updated annually, this hefty reference book combines a detailed almanac of The Bahamas with a resource guide to offshore banking.

The Bahamas Today by Neil E. Sealey. MacMillan Caribbean, 1991. This secondary school textbook reveals the Bahamian culture and economy.

Bahamian Landscapes by Neil E. Sealey. Media Publishing, 1994. The complex geology and geography of The Bahamas are the subject of this textbook, which every Bahamian high school student knows by heart.

The Conch Book: All You Ever Wanted to Know About the Queen Conch from Gestation to Gastronomy by Dee Carstarphen. Pen & Ink Press, 1982. The title says it all.

Edgar Cayce on Atlantis by Edgar Evans Cayce. Warner Books, 1968. The famed psychic's visionary accounts of ancient Atlantis, including predictions of archaeological discoveries on Bimini.

The Ephemeral Islands: A Natural History of The Bahamas by David G. Campbell. MacMillan Education, 1978. The definitive text on wildlife and flora on the islands and the Bahama Banks.

How to Be a True-True Bahamian by Patricia Glinton-Meicholas. Guanima Press, 1994. This wry inside look at Bahamian lifestyles, language and foibles is a sequel to the author's earlier book, *Talkin' Bahamian,* which is now hard to come by.

Imagining Atlantis by Richard Ellis. Alfred A. Knopf, 1998. A skeptic's view of the controversy over Atlantis and the Bimini Road.

Islands in the Stream by Ernest Hemingway. Charles Scribner & Sons, 1970. Hemingway's last novel, unfinished when he died, recounts three episodes of the life of Thomas Hudson, Hemingway's fictional alter-ego, in Bimini.

Sources of Bahamian History by Phillip Cash, Shirley Gordon and Gail Saunders. MacMillan Caribbean, 1991. This high school and college level text unveils Bahamian history through quotes from historical documents in the National Archives of The Bahamas.

The Story of The Bahamas by Paul Albury. MacMillan Caribbean, 1975. This in-depth history traces the development of the islands from the Lucayan migrations and Columbus' landing to independence.

Index

Lodging Index

LODGING SERVICES

Dining Index

HIDDEN GUIDES

Adventure travel or a relaxing vacation?—"Hidden" guidebooks are the only travel books in the business to provide detailed information on both. Aimed at environmentally aware travelers, our motto is "Adventure Travel Plus." These books combine details on unique hotels, restaurants and sightseeing with information on camping, sports and hiking for the outdoor enthusiast.

THE NEW KEY GUIDES

Based on the concept of ecotourism, The New Key Guides are dedicated to the preservation of Central America's rare and endangered species, architecture and archaeology. Filled with helpful tips, they give travelers everything they need to know about these exotic destinations.

Order Form

HIDDEN GUIDEBOOKS

____ Hidden Arizona, $14.95
____ Hidden Bahamas, $14.95
____ Hidden Baja, $14.95
____ Hidden Belize, $15.95
____ Hidden Boston and Cape Cod, $13.95
____ Hidden British Columbia, $17.95
____ Hidden Cancún & the Yucatán, $16.95
____ Hidden Carolinas, $17.95
____ Hidden Coast of California, $17.95
____ Hidden Colorado, $14.95
____ Hidden Disney World, $13.95
____ Hidden Disneyland, $13.95
____ Hidden Florida, $17.95
____ Hidden Florida Keys & Everglades, $12.95
____ Hidden Georgia, $14.95
____ Hidden Guatemala, $16.95
____ Hidden Hawaii, $17.95

____ Hidden Idaho, $13.95
____ Hidden Maui, $13.95
____ Hidden Montana, $14.95
____ Hidden New England, $17.95
____ Hidden New Mexico, $14.95
____ Hidden Oahu, $13.95
____ Hidden Oregon, $14.95
____ Hidden Pacific Northwest, $17.95
____ Hidden Rockies, $16.95
____ Hidden San Francisco & Northern California, $17.95
____ Hidden Southern California, $17.95
____ Hidden Southwest, $17.95
____ Hidden Tahiti, $17.95
____ Hidden Tennessee, $15.95
____ Hidden Washington, $14.95
____ Hidden Wyoming, $14.95

THE NEW KEY GUIDEBOOKS

____ The New Key to Costa Rica, $17.95

____ The New Key to Ecuador and the Galápagos, $17.95

Mark the book(s) you're ordering and enter the total cost here ⇨ [ ]

California residents add 8% sales tax here ⇨ [ ]

Shipping, check box for your preferred method and enter cost here ⇨ [ ]

☐ BOOK RATE   **FREE! FREE! FREE!**

☐ PRIORITY MAIL $3.20 First book, $1.00/each additional book

☐ UPS 2-DAY AIR $7.00 First book, $1.00/each additional book

Billing, enter total amount due here and check method of payment ⇨ [ ]

☐ CHECK   ☐ MONEY ORDER

☐ VISA/MASTERCARD_____EXP. DATE _____

NAME _____PHONE _____

ADDRESS_____

_____

CITY_____ STATE _____ ZIP_____

MONEY-BACK GUARANTEE ON DIRECT ORDERS PLACED THROUGH ULYSSES PRESS.

ABOUT THE AUTHORS

RICHARD HARRIS has written or co-written 21 other guidebooks including Ulysses' *Hidden Cancún and the Yucatán* and the bestselling *Hidden Southwest*. He has also served as contributing editor on guides to Mexico, New Mexico and other ports of call for John Muir Publications, Fodor's, Birnbaum and Access guides. He is a director and past-president of PEN New Mexico, as well as a director and officer of the New Mexico Book Association. When not traveling, Richard writes and lives in Santa Fe, New Mexico.

LYNN SELDON is a Southeast U.S.–based freelance travel writer and photographer whose work has appeared in *The New York Post*, *The Los Angeles Times*, *Caribbean Travel & Life*, *Golf Magazine*, *Ski Magazine*, *Travel Weekly* and more than 200 other national publications. He has penned many other travel books, including *Virgin Islands Dive Travel Guide*, *Quick Escapes Florida* and *Country Roads of West Virginia*.

ABOUT THE ILLUSTRATOR

DOUG McCARTHY has illustrated a number of Ulysses Press guides, including *Hidden British Columbia*, *Hidden Tennessee*, *Hidden Baja* and *The New Key to Ecuador and the Galápagos*. A native New Yorker, he lives in the San Francisco Bay area with his family.